RECONSTRUCTION

Other titles in the Perspectives in American Social History series

PERSPECTIVES IN
AMERICAN SOCIAL HISTORY

Reconstruction

People and Perspectives

James M. Campbell and
Rebecca J. Fraser, Editors
Peter C. Mancall, Series Editor

A B C $\bullet$ C L I O

Santa Barbara, California · Denver, Colorado · Oxford, England

Library of Congress Cataloging-in-Publication Data

Reconstruction : people and perspectives / James M. Campbell
    and Rebecca Fraser, editors.
        p. cm.—(Perspectives in American social history)
    Includes bibliographical references and index.
    ISBN 978-1-59884-021-6 (hard copy : alk. paper)
    ISBN 978-1-59884-022-3 (ebook : alk. paper)
    1. Reconstruction (U.S. history, 1865-1877)-Social aspects.   2. Reconciliation-Social
aspects—United States—History.   3. United States-Social conditions—1865–1918.
4. Southern States-Social conditions—1865–1945.   5. United States-Race relations—
History—19th century.   6. Southern States—Race relations—History—19th century.
7. African Americans—Social conditions—19th century.   8. Women-United States—
Social conditions—19th century.   9. Indians of North America—Social conditions—
19th century.   I. Campbell, James M.   II. Fraser, Rebecca J., 1978–

E668.R423 2008
973.8—dc22
                                                                                    2008029995

12 11 10 09 08   1 2 3 4 5 6 7 8 9 10

Production Editor: Anna A. Moore
Production Manager: Don Schmidt
Media Editor: Jason Kniser
Media Resources Manager: Caroline Price
File Management Coordinator: Paula Gerard

ABC-CLIO, Inc.
130 Cremona Drive, P.O. Box 1911
Santa Barbara, California 93116-1911

This book is also available on the World Wide Web as an e-book. Visit www.abc-clio.com for details.

This book is printed on acid-free paper. ∞

Manufactured in the United States of America

Contents

Series Introduction

Social history is, simply put, the study of past societies. Social historians attempt to describe societies in their totality, and hence they often eschew analysis of politics and ideas. Though many social historians argue that understanding how societies functioned is impossible without some consideration of the ways in which politics worked on a daily basis or of what ideas could be found circulating at any given time, they tend to pay little attention to the formal arenas of electoral politics or intellectual currents. In the United States, social historians have been engaged in describing components of the population that had earlier often escaped formal analysis, notably women, members of ethnic or cultural minorities, or people who had fewer economic opportunities than the elite.

Social history became a vibrant discipline in the United States after it had already gained enormous influence in Western Europe. In France, social history in its modern form emerged with the rising prominence of a group of scholars associated with the journal *Annales Economie, Societé, Civilisation* (or *Annales ESC,* as it is known). In its pages and in a series of books from historians affiliated with the École des Hautes Études en Sciences Sociales in Paris, brilliant historians such as Marc Bloch, Jacques Le Goff, and Emmanuel LeRoy Ladurie described seemingly every aspect of French society. Among the masterpieces of this historical reconstruction was Fernand Braudel's monumental study, *The Mediterranean and the Mediterranean World in the Age of Philip II,* published first in French in 1946 and then in a revised edition in English in 1972. In this work, Braudel argued that the only way to understand a place in its totality was to describe its environment, its social and economic structures, and its political systems. In Britain, the emphasis of social historians has been less on posing questions of environment, per se, than on describing human communities in all their complexities. For example, social historians there have taken advantage of that nation's remarkable local archives to reconstruct the history of the family and details of its rural past. Works such as Peter Laslett's *The World We Have Lost,* first printed in 1966, and the multiauthored *Agrarian History of England and Wales,* which began to appear in print in 1967, revealed that painstaking work could reveal the lives and habits of individuals who never previously attracted the interest of biographers, demographers, or most historians.

Social history in the United States gained a large following in the second half of the 20th century, especially during the 1960s and 1970s. Its development sprang from political, technical, and intellectual impulses deeply embedded in the culture of the modern university. The politics of civil rights and social reform fueled the passions of historians who strove to tell the stories of the underclass. They benefited from the adoption by historians of statistical analysis, which allowed scholars to trace where individuals lived; how often they moved; what kinds of jobs they took; and whether their economic status declined, stagnated, or improved over time. As university history departments expanded, many who emerged from graduate schools focused their attention on groups previously ignored or marginalized. Women's history became a central concern among American historians, as did the history of African Americans, Native Americans, Latinos, and others. These historians pushed historical study in the United States farther away from the study of formal politics and intellectual trends. Though few Americanists could achieve the technical brilliance of some social historians in Europe, collectively they have been engaged in a vast act of description, with the goal of describing seemingly every facet of life from 1492 to the present.

The 16 volumes in this series together represent the continuing efforts of historians to describe American society. Most of the volumes focus on chronological periods, from the broad sweep of the colonial era to the more narrowly defined collections of essays on the eras of the Cold War, the baby boom, and the Vietnam War. The series also includes entire volumes on the epochs that defined the nation, the American Revolution and Civil War, as well as volumes dedicated to the process of westward expansion, women's rights, and African American history.

This social history series derives its strength from the talented editors of individual volumes. Each editor is an expert in his or her own field who selected and organized the contents of his or her volume. Editors solicited other experienced historians to write individual essays. Every volume contains first-rate analysis complemented by lively anecdotes designed to reveal the complex contours of specific historical moments. The many illustrations to be found in these volumes testify, too, to the recognition that any society can be understood not only by the texts that its participants produce but also by the images that they craft. Listings of primary source documents in each volume allow interested readers to pursue some specific topics in greater depth, and each volume contains a chronology to provide guidance to the flow of events over time. These tools—anecdotes, images, texts, and timelines—allow readers to gauge the inner workings of America in particular periods and yet also to glimpse connections between eras.

The chapters in these volumes testify to the abundant strengths of historical scholarship in the United States in the early years of the 21st century. Despite the occasional academic contest that flares into public notice, or the self-serving cant of politicians who want to manipulate the nation's past for partisan ends—for example, in debates over the Second Amendment to the U.S. Constitution and what it means about potential limits to the rights of gun ownership—the chapters here all reveal the vast increase in knowledge of the American past that has taken place over the previous half century. Social historians do not dominate history faculties in American colleges and universities, but no one could deny them a seat at the intellectual table. Without their efforts, intellectual, cultural, and political historians would be hard pressed to understand why certain ideas circulated when they did, why some religious movements prospered or foundered, how developments in fields such as medicine and engineering reflected larger concerns, and what shaped the world we inhabit.

Fernand Braudel and his colleagues envisioned entire laboratories of historians in which scholars working together would be able to produce *histoire totale:* total history. Historians today seek more humble goals for our collective enterprise. But as the richly textured essays in these volumes reveal, scholarly collaboration has in fact brought us much closer to that dream. These volumes do not and cannot include every aspect of American history. However, every page reveals something interesting or valuable about how American society functioned. Together, these books suggest the crucial necessity of stepping back to view the grand complexities of the past rather than pursuing narrower prospects and lesser goals.

Peter C. Mancall
Series Editor

Portrait of former slave W. L. Bost, ca. 1937. (Library of Congress)

Introduction

Like millions of other African Americans in 1865, W. L. Bost and his mother approached emancipation with a sense of caution, yet with a clear understanding of the meaning and significance of freedom. Speaking as an elderly man in the 1930s, Bost recalled that when first liberated from slavery, his mother labored for her former owner, "Marse Jonah," for a year before accepting an offer from "old man Solomon Hall" to work as his cook and for her six children to tend to his crop. For the first time in her life, Bost's mother could move about the country, choose her own employer, negotiate a wage, and decide how to dispose of the income she earned. These were remarkable opportunities for an African American woman in a society that, for more than 200 years, had been based on the principle that black people were members of an inferior race who could be bought and sold at the whim of whites. However, although slavery was abolished following the end of the Civil War, the racist ideology and culture of the Old South persisted through the postwar decades and served to check the ambitions and achievements of freedpeople. This darker side of freedom was embodied most explicitly in the actions and beliefs of the Ku Klux Klan and other white supremacist groups that served, in effect, as a paramilitary wing of the Democratic Party. From the mid-1860s, groups of white Southerners unleashed a reign of violent terror, targeting not only African Americans but also their white, Republican allies and eventually contributing to the "redemption" of the Southern states and the restoration of conservative, Democratic Party rule. For African Americans like the Bost family, the premature end of federal intervention in the states of the former Confederacy had dire implications. "[T]hem was bad times," Bost recalled, "them was bad times." The efforts of black men and women to reconstruct lives, families, and communities persisted, for the state was always a peripheral player in these processes, but they persisted against mounting odds as the great expectations that had accompanied freedom were compromised for generations to come (interview with W. L. Bost, Library of Congress 2001, 144–145).

The Civil War, Abolition, and the South

When civil war came to the United States in April 1861, few could have foreseen either the scale of the conflict that would unfold or the extraordinary changes to American life that would follow in the war's wake. The four years of bloody carnage between the Union and the Confederacy had a cataclysmic effect on the entire structure of American society. Some 650,000 people died during the war, and the total casualties numbered more than 1 million. Few American men and women from any walk of life could escape the impact of the war and all that it encompassed.

Aside from the millions of personal tragedies bound up in the devastating toll of the dead and the injured, the Civil War and its aftermath left the United States profoundly changed. The greatest changes were felt by people like the Bosts and the nearly 4 million other African Americans who, in the final years of the war, were freed from slavery by a combination of their own resistance to slaveholders' authority and the actions of abolitionists, Republican politicians, and Union troops. Few freedpeople had either property or education, and many had seen their families broken up during slavery. However, black communities were strong, and with the support of federal agencies and relief efforts, the early years of Reconstruction held great promise for African Americans despite the widespread racial violence and discrimination they faced.

The abolition of slavery deeply affected other Americans, too. White Southerners who had owned slaves feared a loss of political power, were stripped of valuable property, and had to adjust to new ways of securing laborers to work their land. Many elite white women, meanwhile, had to accustom themselves to running households without the aid of enslaved domestic servants. For nonslaveholding whites, abolition presented different challenges and uncertainties. It brought about the prospect of increased competition from African Americans for employment and land, and it meant the end of a system that had served an important ideological function in convincing even the poorest white men and women that, on account of the color of their skin, they could never be reduced to the lowest rungs of the social ladder. If these profound changes to the very basis of Southern society were not challenging enough for white Southerners, they were compounded by the hardships of endemic poverty and the physical dilapidation of cities, farms, and plantations that had been ruined by the war and neglected for the four years during which the region's young white men were engaged in the military conflict.

The fate of the hundreds of thousands of Civil War veterans from both the Union and Confederate armies who had to rebuild their civilian lives during the Reconstruction era while coping with the physical and psychological wounds of their military service was especially traumatic. At the end of the war, many veterans found that they had little to return home to, and large numbers chose to start new lives in different parts of the country. Many Union soldiers remained in the South once the war ended, and in doing so they formed part of a mass movement of Northerners, along with teachers, entrepreneurs, and politicians, who traveled south after the war in search of new lives and opportunities. Meanwhile, Confederate troops who returned home to destitution and personal ruin often chose to leave the region they had fought to defend and reconstruct their lives in the West, where they encountered Americans from all other parts of the United States, as well as African Americans from the South who perceived a better future for themselves and their families beyond the geographical confines of the defeated Confederacy. The ramifications of this expansion into western territories were widespread, but they were felt no more keenly than by Native Americans, for, as before the war, so too during Reconstruction, Southern tribes faced unique challenges as the frontier pushed ever farther westward and encroached upon their lands.

The Course of Reconstruction

From the moment that Confederate territory started to fall under Union control in 1862, many areas were left to be reconstructed. Aside from addressing the physical destruction caused by four years of warfare that had laid waste to large swaths of the South and shattered the region's economy and infrastructure, the United States confronted two burning political and social questions. First, how and under what terms would the rebellious states be brought back into the Union? Second, what would be the fate of African Americans in the postslavery South? Answers to these questions were forged in all parts of American society, not least in the everyday lives of the men and women in the Southern states who are the subjects of the chapters in this book. At the national level, President Abraham Lincoln; his successor, Andrew Johnson; and the Republican-dominated Congress proceeded with a succession of different schemes, ranging from the conservative to the radical, to reintegrate the former Confederate states into the Union. Additionally, they strived, with varying degrees of success and sincerity, to extend civil and political rights to those who were formerly enslaved and to facilitate adjustment to the postslavery world through federal intervention in the South. At the same time as politicians in Washington, D.C., provided a legislative framework for Reconstruction, in local communities and at the state level across the former Confederacy, African Americans and white Southerners struggled, often violently, to renegotiate race relations and political power in the wake of the abolition of slavery. It was amid this tumult of local and national political conflict, violence, and social upheaval that individuals strived to fashion a place and a future for themselves and their families.

As a coherent political process directed by the federal government, Reconstruction dated from the middle years of the Civil War through to 1877, when the last Union troops left the South. The early course of Reconstruction was set by the Republican presidents Lincoln and Johnson. In its first stage, beginning in 1862, presidential Reconstruction involved the appointment by Lincoln of military governors to the Confederate states of Louisiana, North Carolina, and Tennessee, all of which had fallen to Union forces early in the war. In 1863, Lincoln issued the Emancipation Proclamation, a document arguably motivated in the short term by military expediency as much as ideological commitment to blacks' freedom. The proclamation freed all slaves in areas under Confederate government but kept in bondage those in Union-controlled lands, such as Kentucky, Maryland, and parts of Tennessee and Louisiana. Despite its limitations, the Emancipation Proclamation was symbolic of Union war aims shifting to encompass abolition in addition to the previously established objective of reunion. Also in 1863, Lincoln laid out the terms under which seceded states would be readmitted to the Union. Rather than seeking to punish the South for secession, Lincoln offered generous conditions to the rebellious states that aimed to bring about a speedy reunion. Among the key provisions of Lincoln's Reconstruction policies was the requirement that, in order for a seceded state to resume its former status and rights within the Union, one-tenth of the state's electorate as registered in 1860 had to pledge allegiance to the United States. Lincoln also demanded that newly constituted Southern state governments rescind their secession ordinances and recognize the abolition of slavery.

Lincoln's approach to Reconstruction provoked opposition from within his own party. Led by antislavery advocates such as Charles Sumner and

Thaddeus Stevens, Republicans in Congress criticized Lincoln's leniency toward the Confederacy and called for a more punitive strategy that would not only reunify the nation but also ensure the destruction of the old Southern political and social order. For some, this meant preventing the former slaveholding elite from retaining their dominance of the South; for others, it encompassed, in addition, a redistribution of land to the formerly enslaved and extending the right to vote to African American men.

Buoyed by a series of Union victories on the battlefield, Lincoln was able to resist the opposition to his Reconstruction plans and win reelection in 1864, but over the next four years, the conflict between radical and conservative Republicans intensified and many congressmen fiercely opposed the policies of Lincoln's vice-president and successor, Andrew Johnson. Although Johnson's plans for Reconstruction did not diverge radically from the course that Lincoln had set while the nation was still engulfed in war, they were increasingly at odds with the prevailing mood within the Republican Party. Like Lincoln, Johnson adopted lenient policies toward the Southern states and sought to reconstruct the Union in ways that belied Confederate defeat and surrender and were of little benefit to the formerly enslaved. In plans outlined in May 1865, just weeks after Lincoln's assassination, Johnson offered to pardon all but the most prominent Confederates who pledged allegiance to the Union and support for the abolition of slavery. Johnson also decreed that Confederate states would be readmitted to the Union once they had declared secession illegal and sanctioned the abolition of slavery. However, nowhere in his policies did Johnson address the civil rights of the freedpeople, and by 1866, this absence put him at odds with Congress.

Events in the South, including widespread white violence against African Americans and the passage of draconian Black Codes in several states that limited African American freedoms, had convinced a majority of Republican congressmen that the federal government had to adopt a more activist approach to secure full civic and legal equality for the freedpeople. During the spring and summer of 1866, Republicans in the House of Representatives introduced a raft of bills that were intended to give real meaning to African American freedom and revolutionize Southern social and race relations, but Johnson repeatedly used his presidential veto to block this legislation. Johnson vetoed a civil rights act that would have granted full citizenship to all persons born within the United States, and he also threw out the Freedmen's Bureau Bill, which proposed extending federal aid and support for the formerly enslaved, claiming that it was unconstitutional and would prove too expensive to implement.

The midterm elections of November 1866 heralded a fundamental shift in the course of Reconstruction. Benefiting from Northern apathy toward the president and opposition to the immediate restoration of the Southern states to the Union, Radical Republicans won a huge majority of seats in Congress, which they used to override the presidential veto and force through many of their ambitious plans for a radically changed South; this signaled the end of the presidential Reconstruction era and the onset of radical, also known as congressional, Reconstruction. Within months, Republican congressmen passed the Civil Rights Act of 1866 and a modified version of the Freedmen's Bureau Bill. In addition, they introduced the Fourteenth Amendment to the U.S. Constitution in order to protect a clause in the Civil Rights Act that guaranteed African American citizenship rights. With the exception of Tennessee, every former Confederate state refused to ratify the Fourteenth Amendment, and in response, Congress passed the first Reconstruction Act in March 1867, making ratification a precondition of states resuming their participation in Congress.

Over the following months of 1867, further Reconstruction legislation divided the former Confederacy into five military zones, each under the control of a Union general. Johnson condemned the Military Reconstruction Acts, and his view that neither the military nor African Americans should hold political sway in the South was shared by a majority of Northerners. Even so, Congress retained the upper hand in its struggle with the president, and in early 1868, matters came to a head over Johnson's attempt to fire his secretary of war, Edwin Stanton. Stanton had been working with Radical Republicans to undermine Johnson's Reconstruction plans, but his removal from office violated the recently passed Tenure of Office Act and provided the excuse that the radicals had been waiting for to remove Johnson from power. On February 24, 1868, the House of Representatives voted to initiate impeachment proceedings against the president, and a Senate trial commenced four weeks later. Senators ultimately failed to convict Johnson by a single vote, but the president had suffered a fatal political wound, and when the Republican Party came to choose its nominee for president later in the year, it turned to Union war hero Ulysses S. Grant.

As the debates and disputes over federal government policy played out in Washington and at the community level in the South, Reconstruction proceeded according to local dynamics that were shaped, but not set, by the national context. From as early as 1865, tens of thousands of African Americans participated in local politics, joining Union Leagues, organizing statewide conventions, and standing for election to public office. In 1867 and 1868, hundreds of black candidates were elected to serve at constitutional conventions, where they worked with white Republican delegates to draw up new state constitutions in line with the requirements of congressional Reconstruction policy. In some states, when the new constitutions were put into practice, African Americans won numerous local and state offices, and a small number were even elected to Congress.

In many communities during the mid to late 1860s, African Americans' political and civil rights were actively protected by federal troops and Freedmen's Bureau agents. However, few white Southerners were willing to accept racial egalitarianism and black political participation, and they used diverse tactics, ranging from legal protests against federal laws to brutal acts of violent repression, in an effort to maintain their social, political, and economic dominance of the region. So widespread was violence against African Americans in the Reconstruction South that it was as if a new civil war was taking place within the former Confederacy. In some of the most notorious incidents, such as the race riots in Memphis and New Orleans in 1866 and the massacre in Colfax, Louisiana, in 1872, hundreds of people, mainly African Americans, were wounded, and several scores were murdered.

The aim of white violence in the South was, above all, to crush the agency and power of the black electorate and Republican politicians. Although the Ku Klux Klan was resisted by African Americans from its inception and effectively suppressed by the federal government in the early 1870s, other paramilitary groups continued to perpetrate atrocities that contributed to the Democratic Party regaining political control of the South during the 1870s. This process of transition away from Republican governments in the South was known as Redemption, and it was facilitated by developments throughout the nation as well as in Southern communities. In the Northern states, voters previously sympathetic to the abolition of slavery were far less enthusiastic about the prospect of racial equality, and especially as reports of Republican political corruption emerged in the early 1870s, they grew disenchanted with the radicals' policies. A major economic depression pushed Reconstruction farther down the political agenda in the North and made class conflict, rather than racial matters, the more pressing issue of the day. A majority among the influential Northern white electorate was also keen that the nation's Civil War wounds be healed as rapidly as possible and was opposed to African American civil rights inhibiting the reunion of North and South.

By the time that the Republican candidate, Rutherford B. Hayes, won the disputed and drawn-out presidential election of 1876, Reconstruction as a national political process was at an end. In 1874, the Democrats had won control of Congress for the first time since the Civil War, bringing to a close the era of radical ascendancy. In the South, meanwhile, Republican governments were swept from power in one state after another over an eight-year period beginning in 1869. The final states to be "redeemed" were Louisiana and South Carolina, where rival Republican and Democratic administrations vied for authority following contested elections in November 1876. Eventually, as part of an informal agreement between Democrats and Republicans in Washington that secured the White House for Hayes, the new president withdrew from the disputed states the federal troops upon whom the Republicans' claim to power depended. The short era of Republican governance in the South was over, the region was redeemed for Democratic rule, and in the following decades white Southerners were able to entrench African Americans' second-class citizenship largely free of federal interference.

In most histories that focus on national politics, the year 1877 marks the end of Reconstruction. Yet Southern society did not change overnight, and from the perspective of social and local history, this traditional periodization is somewhat arbitrary and misleading. While the return of Democratic "home rule" in the South was of no small consequence, it did not immediately resolve the profound questions about how Southern society and race relations would function in the postslavery era. On the contrary, African Americans' struggle to define the meaning of freedom and to construct a place for themselves within American society persisted long after 1877, albeit on altered political terrain. Processes of black community and institution building continued, growing numbers of educated and skilled black workers moved into new forms of employment, and African Americans of all backgrounds relocated throughout the United States in search of enhanced economic and social opportunities. Furthermore, the brutal racial violence of lynchings and the inhumane systems of convict leasing that were established across the South to limit black autonomy and secure for white employers a subservient labor force were subject to criticism and protest led by African Americans and later supported by sections of Northern white society.

The Historiography of Reconstruction

Historical interpretations of the post–Civil War era had a powerful political influence in the years after Reconstruction, and few periods in American history have provoked such historiographical controversy and debate. Early historians of Reconstruction were mostly sympathetic to the white supremacist cause and constructed a narrative based on assumptions of black inferiority that depicted Reconstruction as a tragic time when white Southern rights were compromised by a corrupt and overbearing federal government supported by the votes of African Americans who were ignorant and easily manipulated by disreputable white "carpetbaggers" and "scalawags." This view of Reconstruction was rooted in the Lost Cause ideology that emerged in the 1870s as Southerners attempted to come to terms with Confederate defeat and African American freedom. Although the South had lost the war, the popular view was that its cause had been honorable and just. In the view of influential historians such as William Archibald Dunning (1857–1922), African Americans, Northern radicals, and Southern white supporters of the Republican Party had attempted to bring about a "contemptible" reordering of the Southern social and political structure during Reconstruction and had set the region's political system on a course of corruption and misgovernment. Associations such as the United Daughters of the Confederacy worked to promote this view of Southern history through memorials and meetings, while films such as *The Birth of a Nation* (1915) were instrumental in popularizing and normalizing the Lost Cause view of the Civil War and Reconstruction across the United States. Based in part on Thomas Dixon's hugely popular novel *The Clansman, The Birth of a Nation* glorified the Ku Klux Klan and promoted white supremacy. Even so, the film's racist politics were endorsed and legitimized by President Woodrow Wilson, who hosted the movie's premiere at the White House.

The Lost Cause myth was the dominant view of Reconstruction throughout the late 19th century and the first half of the 20th century, but dissenting voices were always present, most notably from African American spokespersons and historians. In the 1870s and 1880s, Frederick Douglass, one of the most politically prominent African Americans of the age, defined the Civil War and Reconstruction as ideological battles fought on the Union side for emancipation, racial equality, and progress, and on the Confederate side for slavery and barbarism (Blight 1989, 1163). Several decades later, W. E. B. Du Bois (1910) published a seminal essay in the *American Historical Review* that outlined the many positive aspects of Reconstruction, among which Du Bois included the constitutional amendments that extended fundamental civil rights to all American citizens, as well as the educational progress of the formerly enslaved and the participation of the freedmen and freedwomen in politics. Building on this essay, in 1935, Du Bois published a monograph, *Black Reconstruction*, in which he refuted the notion that the failures associated with Reconstruction were due to

African American ignorance and instead applauded the efforts of the black community to create a new South based on education, democracy, and civil and legal rights for all.

When first published, much of Du Bois's research on Reconstruction was ridiculed by fellow historians, and it did little to dent the hegemony of the Dunning school. During the civil rights era, however, it became apparent that Du Bois's scholarship, despite some limitations, had been ahead of its time. In the 1960s and 1970s, the increasing participation in the historical profession of people from a variety of racial and ethnic backgrounds and the concurrent rise of social history prompted a shift in the focus of Reconstruction research that provided fresh insights into key historical actors who had been excluded from previous accounts. In many of the new histories, the experiences of the formerly enslaved took center stage as historians reflected on how African American lives had changed during the era of emancipation. Scholars such as Leon Litwack (1979) wrote about the experience of African Americans as they embraced freedom throughout the South. Others, such as Herbert Gutman (1976), focused on the black family and its capacity to weather the harsh realities of freedom experienced in the Reconstruction era.

Aside from this reassessment of the freedpeople, revisionist historians were also more sympathetic than their predecessors to the political achievements of Radical Republicans, but such new ways of thinking about Reconstruction had their limitations. The influence of revisionist histories was for a long time confined to academic circles and in school textbooks and the popular imagination, traditional views of Reconstruction persisted well into the civil rights era. Furthermore, the revisionists perhaps overstated their case in emphasizing the achievements and radicalism of Reconstruction. In contrast, works published in the 1970s and 1980s that are sometimes labeled "postrevisionist" suggested that continuity rather than change was the hallmark of post–Civil War American society. Historians such as Michael Benedict (1974) and Jonathan Wiener (1976) argued for an analysis of Reconstruction that stressed the inherently conservative tendencies of the era reflected, for example, in the persistence of the antebellum political elite and the limited ambitions of even so-called radicals to bring about fundamental restructuring of Southern society and to secure meaningful political and economic progress for African Americans.

In 1988, the publication of Eric Foner's *Reconstruction: America's Unfinished Revolution, 1863–1877* marked the culmination of the historiographical shift away from the Dunning interpretation of Reconstruction. Foner placed African American agency at the center of his analysis and highlighted the revolutionary implications of emancipation not only for the formerly enslaved but also, more broadly, for the meaning of freedom in the United States. Despite the "violent reaction" of the white South that curtailed the immediate achievements of Reconstruction, Foner argued that Reconstruction was a revolutionary moment that represented Americans' "first attempt to live up to the noble professions of their political creed" (Foner 1988, xxv).

In the past 20 years, research on Reconstruction has developed in new directions. In particular, historians have focused increasingly on the diverse experiences of women, Native Americans, former slaveholders, and Northerners. Laura F. Edwards (2000) and LeeAnn Whites (2005) have drawn connections between the political and social lives of women, rich and poor, black and white, during Reconstruction. Those authors concerned with Native American history during the post–Civil War era, such as Christine Bolt (1987), have charted federal campaigns to assimilate Native nations into the "American way of life" and considered how American Indians resisted this process. Scholars such as Nina Silber (1993) have written accounts of how the North faced the challenges of reunification with the South, while Heather Cox Richardson (2001, 2007) has reflected on the significance of class as a concept for understanding Northern society during this time as well as the interconnections between the North, South, and West in the process of Reconstruction. Scholars have also examined the African American experience in new ways, notably through several ambitious local studies that reveal the diversity of black labor and society and that highlight the interconnections of community life and politics at the grassroots level.

The chapters in this book reflect many of these recent developments in Reconstruction historiography. Their focus is on the ways in which eight different groups of people experienced the post–Civil War era in the Southern states. Three chapters look at the African American experience from the very different perspectives of men, women, and those who lived in cities. Two other chapters consider the lives of Southern whites, focusing specifically on how former planter-class slaveholders and white women adjusted to the new realities of the postslavery world. The remaining chapters examine Reconstruction from the standpoints of Native Americans, Northerners who lived and worked in the South, and Civil War veterans from both sides of the sectional conflict. Accompanying each chapter are sidebars that offer a closer look at a representative individual or a particularly significant incident or idea related to the group in question, while a detailed chronology of the Reconstruction era, a series of primary documents, and an extensive encyclopedia-style reference chapter provide further ways to explore the history of this critical period in the American past.

Though they do not encompass all of the people who found themselves in the South during Reconstruction, the chapters and other materials in this book do reveal the diversity of everyday life in the region. They also highlight the interplay of categories of race, class, gender, and geography in shaping the lived experiences of Reconstruction-era Americans, and they bring to light the interaction of the personal and the political events at the local and national level. They show that the course of Reconstruction was set not only by politicians in Washington, D.C. and Southern state governments but also by ordinary people working and living their lives in the fields, homes, and public spaces of the South. To write the social history of Reconstruction, therefore, is to contribute to an understanding of far more than what might generally be defined as society, for in this violently contested era of intense social change and upheaval, the lives of ordinary people throughout the Southern states—their social histories—were inherently and powerfully political.

James M. Campbell and Rebecca J. Fraser

References and Further Reading

Benedict, Michael. 1974. "Preserving the Constitution: The Conservative Basis of Radical Reconstruction." *Journal of American History* 61:65–90.

Blight, David W. 1989. "'For Something beyond the Battlefield': Frederick Douglass and the Struggle for the Memory of the Civil War." *Journal of American History* 75 (4): 1156–1178.

Bolt, Christine. 1987. *American Indian Policy and American Reform: Case Studies of the Campaign to Assimilate the Indians.* London: Allen and Unwin.

Brown, Thomas J. 2006. *Reconstructions: New Perspectives on the Postbellum United States.* New York: Oxford University Press.

Du Bois, W. E. B. 1910. "Reconstruction and Its Benefits." *American Historical Review* 15 (4): 781–799.

Du Bois, W. E. B. 1935. *Black Reconstruction: An Essay toward a History of the Part which Black Folk Played in the Attempt to Reconstruct Democracy, 1860–1880.* New York: Harcourt Brace.

Dunning, William A. 1907. *Reconstruction: Political and Economic, 1865–1877.* New York: Harper and Bros.

Edwards, Laura F. 2000. *Scarlett Doesn't Live Here Anymore: Southern Women in the Civil War Era*. Urbana: University of Illinois Press.

Foner, Eric. 1988. *Reconstruction: America's Unfinished Revolution, 1863–1877*. New York: Harper and Row.

Gutman, Herbert. 1976. *The Black Family in Slavery and Freedom, 1750–1925*. Oxford, UK: Blackwell.

Library of Congress. 2001. Interview with W. L. Bost. *Born in Slavery: Slave Narratives from the Federal Writers' Project, 1936–1938*. North Carolina Narratives, vol. 11, pt. 1, 138–146. http://memory.loc.gov/cgi-bin/ampage?collId=mesn&fileName=111/mesn111.db&recNum=141&itemLink=S?ammem/mesnbib:@field(AUTHOR+@od1(Bost,+W++L+))

Litwack, Leon. 1979. *Been in the Storm So Long: The Aftermath of Slavery*. New York: Alfred A. Knopf.

Richardson, Heather C. 2001. *The Death of Reconstruction: Race, Labor, and Politics in the Post–Civil War North, 1865–1901*. Cambridge, MA: Harvard University Press.

Richardson, Heather C. 2007. *West from Appomattox: The Reconstruction of America after the Civil War*. New Haven, CT: Yale University Press.

Silber, Nina. 1993. *The Romance of Reunion: Northerners and the South, 1865–1900*. Chapel Hill: University of North Carolina Press.

Whites, LeeAnn. 2005. *Gender Matters: Civil War, Reconstruction, and the Making of the New South*. New York: Palgrave Macmillan.

Wiener, Jonathan M. 1976. "Planter Persistence and Social Change: Alabama, 1850–1870." *Journal of Interdisciplinary History* 7 (2): 235–260.

About the Editors and Contributors

James M. Campbell is a lecturer in American history at the University of Leicester in the United Kingdom. He is the author of *Slavery on Trial: Race, Class, and Criminal Justice in Antebellum Richmond, Virginia* (University Press of Florida, 2007). He has also published articles in *Slavery and Abolition* and *American Nineteenth Century History* and is currently researching issues of race, law, and violence in the post–Civil War Northern United States.

Nichola Clayton is a departmental lecturer in American history at the University of Oxford in the United Kingdom and has previously taught at the universities of Sheffield and Leeds. She is currently finishing her doctoral thesis, which is an examination of U.S. Civil War debates about confiscation and land redistribution.

David Deverick teaches American history at the University of Nottingham in the United Kingdom. He has a particular interest in the U.S. Civil War period and the battle for civil rights of the 1950s and 1960s.

Kate Dossett is a lecturer in North American history at the University of Leeds in the United Kingdom. She is the author of *Bridging Race Divides: Black Nationalism, Feminism and Integration 1896–1935* (University Press of Florida, 2008) and has an article forthcoming in the *Journal of Women's History.*

Rebecca J. Fraser is a lecturer in American history at the University of East Anglia in the United Kingdom. She is author of *Courtship and Love among the Enslaved in North Carolina* (University Press of Mississippi, 2007). She has also published journal articles in the *Journal of Southern History* and *Slavery and Abolition.*

Susan-Mary Grant is a professor of American history at Newcastle University in the United Kingdom. She is the author of *North Over South: Northern Nationalism and American Identity in the Antebellum Era* (University Press of Kansas, 2000) and *The War for a Nation: The American Civil War* (Routledge, 2006) and has edited several volumes on the Civil War–era United States. She is the current editor of *American Nineteenth Century History.*

Bonnie Laughlin-Schultz is a PhD candidate in history at Indiana University. She is completing a dissertation about the wife and daughters of abolitionist John Brown and American memory of antislavery violence.

Gabriella Treglia is a lecturer at Durham University in the United Kingdom, where she specializes in modern Native American sociocultural history. She is currently working on a monograph analyzing the sociocultural dimension of the Indian New Deal (1933–1945). She has previously published work on this topic in *Place and Native American Indian History & Culture,* edited by Joy Porter (Peter Lang, 2007).

Chronology

1860   **November 6**   Republican Party candidate Abraham Lincoln is elected president of the United States.

December 20   Interpreting Lincoln's election as an unacceptable threat to slavery and its rights as a state, South Carolina secedes from the Union following a unanimous vote by eight delegates at a convention held in Charleston.

1861   **January 9–February 1**   Delegates vote for secession at conventions held in the Deep South states of Mississippi, Florida, Alabama, Georgia, Louisiana, and Texas.

February 9   Delegates from the seven seceded states meet in Montgomery, Alabama, to form the Confederate States of America. Jefferson Davis is named the new nation's provisional president, and Montgomery, Alabama, is established as the Confederate capital.

March 4   Abraham Lincoln is inaugurated as president of the United States and restates his aim to maintain both slavery and the Union.

April 12   The Civil War begins in Charleston, South Carolina, when Confederate General Pierre Beauregard orders troops to fire on Fort Sumter. Union Major Robert Anderson surrenders the fort the following day.

April 17–May 20   In the wake of events at Fort Sumter and Lincoln's call for volunteer troops to join the Union army, Virginia, Arkansas, Tennessee, and North Carolina secede from the Union and join the Confederate States of America. Under military and political pressure from Washington, D.C., the four other slave states of Delaware, Kentucky, Maryland, and Missouri remain loyal to the Union.

May 29   The Confederate capital is relocated to Richmond, Virginia.

November 7   Union troops under the command of Thomas W. Sherman occupy Port Royal. In the following days, the rest of the South Carolina Sea Islands fall under Union control. Resident white planters desert the Islands, most leaving behind their African American slaves.

1862   **May**   Union troops led by Benjamin Butler occupy New Orleans. During the remaining years of the Civil War, the city serves as a test ground for Republican Reconstruction policies.

May 20   Congress passes the Homestead Act.

July 1   Congress passes the Pacific Railway Act with the aim of creating a railroad and telegraph line stretching from the Missouri River to the Pacific Ocean.

July 17   Congress passes the second Confiscation Act and the Militia Act, empowering the president to seize Confederate property and to grant pardons and amnesties to individuals involved in the rebellion against the Union according to "such conditions as he may deem expedient for the public welfare." The act provides a legal basis for presidential Reconstruction and paves the way for African American troops to serve in the United States armed forces.

September 22   Days after the Battle of Antietam leaves nearly 5,000 men dead and 18,000 wounded, Lincoln issues the preliminary Emancipation Proclamation declaring that all slaves in Confederate-controlled territories will be freed on the first day of 1863.

1863   **January 1**   Lincoln signs the Emancipation Proclamation into law.

February   The pro-Union Cherokee National Council abolishes slavery. The law has little practical impact as most Cherokee slaveholders remain loyal to the Confederacy.

June 20   West Virginia becomes a state of the Union after adopting a new constitution that provides for the gradual emancipation of slaves.

July 1–3   At the Battle of Gettysburg, Union forces led by General George Meade turn back the Confederate advance into Pennsylvania.

November   Free men of color in New Orleans issue appeals to the state's governor, military governor, and President Lincoln requesting that they be permitted to register and vote.

December 8   Lincoln issues the Proclamation of Amnesty and Recon-struction, in which he lays out policies for reincorporating the seceded states into the Union.

1864   **February**   The Wade-Davis Bill is introduced in Congress as a more radi-cal alternative to Lincoln's moderate plans for Reconstruction.

February 22   In accordance with the principles of Lincoln's Proclamation of Amnesty and Reconstruction, Michael Hahn is elected governor of Louisiana. African Americans in the state are excluded from participation in the ballot.

March 4   Arkansas ratifies a new constitution in line with Lincoln's terms for readmission to the Union.

July 21   Louis and J. B. Roudanez found the *New Orleans Tribune,* the first daily black newspaper in the United States.

July 23   Louisiana adopts a new constitution that will remain in force un-til 1870.

October 4–7   A National Convention of Colored Men held in Syracuse, New York, calls for the abolition of slavery and equal civil and voting rights for African Americans. The convention also establishes the National Equal Rights League.

November 8   Abraham Lincoln is reelected president of the United States, defeating the Democratic candidate, General George B. McClellan. Andrew Johnson, former governor of Tennessee, becomes vice-president.

November 15   Union armies under the command of General William T. Sherman leave Atlanta and begin a six-week march to Savannah, Georgia. En route, the troops liberate thousands of slaves.

1865   **January 16**   General Sherman issues Special Field Order Number 15 re-distributing to freed slaves 400,000 acres of land along the eastern coast of the United States from Charleston, South Carolina, to northern Florida. Later in 1865, President Andrew Johnson overturns the order and restores the land to its previous, white owners.

January 31   Congress approves the Thirteenth Amendment abolishing slavery in the United States.

March 3   The Bureau of Refugees, Freedmen, and Abandoned Lands (Freedmen's Bureau) is created.

April 2   The Army of Northern Virginia and the Confederate government abandon Richmond following a nine-month siege of the city by General Ulysses S. Grant's Army of the Potomac.

April 3   Union troops led by the 36th U.S. Colored regiment enter Richmond, where they are met by jubilant African Americans celebrating freedom.

April 9   Commander of the Confederate armies, Robert E. Lee, surrenders to General Grant at Appomattox Court House, Virginia.

April 14   Abraham Lincoln is shot by actor John Wilkes Booth at Ford's Theatre in Washington, D.C. Lincoln dies the following morning and Andrew Johnson becomes president of the United States.

May 29   President Johnson lays out his plans for Reconstruction in two proclamations. The first offers pardons to white southerners willing to pledge allegiance to the Union and support abolition. Excluded from this provision are the very wealthy, those who held senior Confederate military or political posts, and those who had demonstrated hostility to the Union during the war. The second proclamation provides for the readmission of ex-Confederate states to the Union once new constitutions have been established repealing the ordinances of secession and abolishing slavery.

May 29–July 13   President Johnson appoints Unionist provisional state governors in North Carolina, South Carolina, Mississippi, Texas, Georgia, Alabama, and Florida.

July 4   In towns and cities across the Southern states, African Americans celebrate emancipation and peace with processions, songs, speeches, and dinners. In many places, documents such as the Declaration of Independence and the Emancipation Proclamation are read; black political leaders are introduced to large crowds, and protests are made against discrimination and abuse by federal soldiers. Throughout the rest of 1865, black political organization continues apace, often under the Republican Party auspices of the Union Leagues and Equal Rights Leagues.

August 14   In accordance with the terms of President Johnson's Reconstruction proclamations for readmission to the Union, Mississippi holds a convention at which a new constitution is written that repudiates secession and the Confederate debt and formally outlaws slavery. Other Southern states take similar steps in the following months.

Summer–Fall Freedmen's conventions are held in states across the South to articulate and organize African American political interests and concerns.

Fall Rumors spread in the Deep South that African Americans, led by Union veterans, are planning an insurrection at Christmas. White fears include the onset of an all-out race war, the redistribution of white property to the formerly enslaved, and a labor shortage resulting from African Americans' reluctance to work for white employers. Fears of rebellion prove groundless, though they are encouraged and used by white Southerners as an argument against land redistribution and to justify repressive and often violent treatment of African Americans.

October 14 The Arapaho and Cheyenne Indian tribes sign a treaty with the United States according to which they give up their claims to ancestral lands that include most of Colorado. The treaty also establishes a reservation for the tribes along the Arkansas River.

October 19–21 The first annual meeting of the National Equal Rights League is held in Cleveland. The meeting is attended by black delegates from 10 states in both the North and South.

December 2–21 Newly elected conservative governments enact Black Codes in the former Confederate states of Mississippi and South Carolina. The legislation restricts the civil and labor rights of the freedpeople and establishes repressive mechanisms of criminal justice intended to perpetuate white supremacy. In the following months, similar codes are established in other Southern states. Although less overtly discriminatory than the Mississippi example, they serve an equally repressive purpose. Many sections of the Black Codes are ruled invalid by Freedmen's Bureau agents and other Union authorities on the ground and, subsequently, by the Civil Rights Act of 1866.

December 4 The 39th Congress convenes in Washington, D.C. President Johnson recommends that elected officials from the ex-Confederate states be readmitted to the House of Representatives and the Senate as soon as their state ratifies the Thirteenth Amendment. Republicans in Congress reject this proposal.

December 6 The Thirteenth Amendment abolishing slavery is formally ratified by the states.

December 13 Congress establishes the Joint Committee on Reconstruction to investigate conditions in the ex-Confederate states.

1866 **January–February** After the federal government fails to redistribute Southern lands to the freedpeople, thousands of African Americans who have, until this time, refused to enter into labor contracts begin to accept terms to work for white landowners in agricultural occupations.

February 19 Legislation is passed in Congress to extend the life of the previously temporary Freedmen's Bureau indefinitely and to expand its powers. Reflecting the growing conflict between the president and Congress, Andrew Johnson vetoes the measure.

March 27 Johnson vetoes the Civil Rights Act after it is passed by Congress.

April 9 Radical and moderate Republicans in Congress unite to pass the Civil Rights Act over Johnson's veto.

April 28 The Joint Committee on Reconstruction reports back to Congress and recommends the continued exclusion of the ex-Confederate states from the federal government.

May 1–3 Rioting in Memphis leaves 46 African Americans and 2 whites dead. At least 90 African American stores and homes, as well as 4 churches, are destroyed in the violence.

June 13 Congress approves the Fourteenth Amendment, which defines citizenship to include all persons born or naturalized in the United States and guarantees all citizens equal rights and protection of the laws.

June 21 Congress passes the Southern Homestead Act.

July 16 A revised version of the Freedmen's Bureau Bill is passed by Congress over the president's veto.

July 19 Congress passes legislation granting 160 acres of land in the territory of Oklahoma to all Cherokees, free African Americans, and former slaves who choose to reside there within six months. Many Cherokees are not informed of the opportunity to acquire land until after the cutoff date of January 19, 1867.

July 24 Tennessee becomes the first ex-Confederate state readmitted to the Union.

July 30 Rioting in New Orleans leaves 34 African Americans and 3 white Republicans dead and more than 100 people injured.

August 28–September   President Johnson undertakes his "swing around the circle tour" in a disastrous attempt to bolster support for his Reconstruction policies in advance of midterm congressional elections.

November   Across the Northern states, Republican candidates opposed to the conservative Reconstruction policies of President Johnson emerge victorious from the midterm elections. When the new Congress convenes in 1867, Radical Republicans control more than two-thirds of both houses and are able to force through their plans for Reconstruction over the presidential veto.

1867   **January 8**   The National Convention of Colored Soldiers and Sailors convenes in Philadelphia.

March 2   Congress passes the First Reconstruction Act over President Johnson's veto. The act divides the former confederacy into five military districts and requires states to adopt the Fourteenth Amendment as a condition of readmission to the Union. On the same day, Congress passes the Army Appropriations Act and the Tenure of Office Act. These pieces of legislation constrain, respectively, the president's control of the armed forces and power to remove Senate-approved civil officeholders from their posts.

March 23   Congress passes the Second Reconstruction Act.

May 4   Crowds of African Americans gather in New Orleans to protest segregation on the city's streetcars. On May 5, racial violence breaks out across the city as African American men and women force their way into cars reserved for whites. Desegregation of the New Orleans streetcars occurs over the following days. Later in 1867, African Americans in other cities, including Charleston, Nashville, and Richmond, use diverse tactics including sit-ins and legal challenges to enforce the desegregation of streetcars, railroads, and steamboats.

July 19   Congress passes the Third Military Reconstruction Act.

August 12   President Johnson suspends Secretary of War Edwin Stanton and appoints General Ulysses Grant as an interim replacement. This action leads to Johnson's impeachment, as Radical Republicans argue that it violates the Tenure of Office Act.

November   Elections of delegates to state constitutional conventions are held across the former Confederacy. In Alabama, Mississippi, Louisiana, and Texas, at least 80 percent of eligible African American voters participate in the elections. With many white Southerners refusing to go to the polls, a large majority of the elected delegates are Republicans, and, although considerable variation is seen in different states, in total, more than 25 percent of all delegates are African Americans. Over the following months, constitutional conventions are held and Radical Reconstruction policies begin to affect black life in the South, as African Americans in ex-Confederate states are appointed to serve on municipal police forces, in fire departments, and in other city offices. Additionally, Union Leagues in the South, which hitherto have mostly been centered in towns and cities and often dominated by whites, begin to recruit larger numbers of African Americans from rural plantation regions.

Democratic legislatures are elected in the northern states of Connecticut, New York, Ohio, and Pennsylvania.

1868   **March 5**   President Johnson is impeached by the House of Representatives. On May 26, he is acquitted by the Senate by a single vote.

March 11   The Fourth Reconstruction Act comes into law. It provides for the ratification of state constitutions by a simple majority of votes cast, rather than by a majority of all registered voters, as had previously been required by the Second Reconstruction Act.

April 29   The Treaty of Fort Laramie is signed by the United States and the Lakota (Sioux) Nation. The treaty guarantees Lakota control of the Black Hills, but this provision is violated in 1874 when forces led by General George Custer enter the territory.

June 22–July 14   Arkansas, Florida, Louisiana, North Carolina, South Carolina, and Alabama are readmitted to the Union after ratifying the Fourteenth Amendment.

July 4   President Johnson issues an amnesty proclamation pardoning all ex-Confederates except those indicted for certain felonies, including treason.

November 3   The Republican candidate and former Union General Ulysses S. Grant is elected president, defeating his Democratic rival, Horatio Seymour. In elections held in the readmitted ex-Confederate states, Republican administrations, supportive of radical Reconstruction, are returned to power. Although whites dominate in a majority of high-ranking government positions, in some states African American candidates are elected in substantial numbers, notably in South Carolina, where they win 55 percent of seats in the state legislature.

1869   **January 1** The Freedmen's Bureau ceases all operations except those concerning education and payments to black veterans.

February 26 The Fifteenth Amendment to the Constitution is passed by Congress. The amendment prohibits the federal government or any state from denying or abridging the right of U.S. citizens to vote.

March 4 Ulysses S. Grant is inaugurated president of the United States.

April 12 The U.S. Supreme Court rules in the case of *Texas v. White* that secession is illegal. Republican Reconstruction policies are consequently deemed constitutional.

November The South's first Democrat-controlled "Redeemer" government is elected in Tennessee. By 1871, conservative rule has also been restored in Virginia, North Carolina, and Georgia.

1870   **January 26–July 15** Virginia, Mississippi, Texas, and Georgia become the final ex-Confederate states readmitted to the Union.

February 3 The Fifteenth Amendment receives final ratification.

February 25 Hiram Revels of Mississippi becomes the first African American sworn into office as a U.S. senator.

May 31 Responding to a Senate committee report that reveals continuing widespread Ku Klux Klan violence in the South, Congress passes the first Enforcement Act outlawing conspiracies that aim to deprive citizens of their civil rights.

July 14 Congress passes a second Enforcement Act providing for special deputy marshals to police elections in cities with populations in excess of 20,000 people.

1871   **January 3** Congress passes the Indian Appropriations Act. The act abolishes the status of Indian tribes as independent sovereign nations and defines all Native Americans as "wards" of the federal government.

February 28 The first Enforcement Act is amended by Congress, and new regulations are introduced for the conduct of congressional elections, including federal supervision of voting.

April 20 The third Enforcement Act (also known as the Ku Klux Klan Act) is passed by Congress to combat widespread acts of violent vigilantism perpetrated by white supremacists in the South. The same day, a joint congressional committee is established to investigate conditions in the ex-Confederate states. Over the next 10 months, the committee hears testimony from all segments of Southern society, including former slaves and Klansmen. When it reports back to Congress in February 1872, the committee advocates the need for continued federal protection of civil rights in the South.

October 10 Three African Americans are killed and many more injured when race riots erupt in Philadelphia as Pennsylvania allows African Americans to vote for the first time since 1838.

October 17 Widespread Ku Klux Klan violence in the South Carolina Piedmont region leads President Grant to declare martial law and suspend the right of habeas corpus in the state.

1872 **May** Congress passes the Amnesty Act, restoring the political rights of more than 150,000 former Confederate soldiers who had been barred from voting or holding political office since 1865. The act boosts the political power of the Democratic Party in the South.

June 10 Congress votes to abolish the Freedmen's Bureau, effective from the end of the month, and also passes the final Enforcement Act to expand federal oversight of rural elections.

November Ulysses S. Grant is elected president of the United States for the second time, defeating Horace Greeley, a candidate backed by both Democrats and members of the Liberal Republican Party who were opposed to continued federal government intervention in the issues of Reconstruction. Northern public apathy toward Reconstruction is widespread by this time, and Grant's election victory owes more to economic prosperity and his first-term achievements in foreign affairs than to popular support for his policies toward the South and black civil rights.

In Louisiana, rival Fusionist and Radical Republican state governments are set up after a disputed gubernatorial election in which victory is claimed by both William P. Kellogg, the Republican candidate, and John McEnery, the Democrat and Liberal candidate.

1873 **April 13** More than 100 African Americans are killed by white vigilantes in Colfax, Louisiana. The massacre is part of an ongoing campaign of white violence in the region following the disputed state elections of November 1872.

April 14 The U.S. Supreme Court rules in the so-called Slaughter-House Cases that the protection of individual civil rights is the responsibility of state governments. Although the Slaughter-House Cases themselves concern the rights of butchers in New Orleans, the court's decision has the effect of limiting the power of the federal government to guarantee equal rights for African Americans.

May 22   President Grant sends federal troops to support the administration of Republican William P. Kellogg in Louisiana and to put down the rival government of John McEnery.

September 18   The Panic of 1873 begins, sending hundreds of firms into bankruptcy and causing mass unemployment. As the U.S. economy enters a depression that will last for several years, Northern concern with the plight of African Americans in the South continues to wane.

1874   **April 27**   The White League, a paramilitary organization opposed to radical Reconstruction and the government of William Kellogg, is formed in Louisiana.

June 28   The Freedman's Savings Bank collapses as a result of the continuing economic depression and financial mismanagement. The small investments of thousands of African Americans are wiped out.

November   In midterm congressional elections, Democrats win control of both the House of Representatives and the Senate for the first time since before the Civil War. The process of "redeeming" the Southern states continues, as Alabama and Arkansas return to Democratic Party control.

December   President Grant sends federal troops to Vicksburg, Mississippi, following a series of violent racial incidents in the area.

1875   **January**   Five Democrats illegally attempt to take seats in the Louisiana statehouse and are ejected by federal troops led by General Philip H. Sheridan. A nationwide public outcry against Sheridan's actions reflects growing popular disillusionment with Reconstruction.

March 1   Before the Democrats assume control of Congress, the outgoing Republicans pass a new enforcement act and a civil rights act that guarantee African Americans equal treatment in public places and on transportation. An additional provision to prohibit segregated schooling is struck from the final legislation. Section 1 of the act, relating to segregated public facilities, will be declared unconstitutional by the U.S. Supreme Court in 1883.

October   The U.S. Supreme Court delivers its ruling in the case of *United States v. Cruickshank*, which involved the prosecution of 98 white men for participation in the Colfax Massacre of April 1873. The defendants were indicted under the Enforcement Act of 1870 with conspiracy to violate African Americans' constitutional rights, including the right to assemble, bear arms, and vote. In a unanimous decision that undermines the power of the federal government to protect the rights of African Americans in the South, the Supreme Court rules that the Fourteenth Amendment can be enforced only against state authorities and not against private citizens.

November   Mississippi becomes the eighth Southern state redeemed by the Democrats following state government elections marred by violence, intimidation, and fraud.

1876   **July 8**   In the town of Hamburg, South Carolina, hundreds of armed white men, led by Democratic politician General Matthew C. Butler, attack the local black militia company. A local black marshal is killed along with 5 other African Americans who are among 25 militiamen captured by the white mob. The massacre was prompted by a court case in which a local white farmer was charged with contempt of court after he had accused the black militia of blocking his right of way on a local road. Over the following months, the campaign of General Wade Hampton, the Democratic Party candidate for governor in South Carolina, is supported by acts of violence and intimidation against black voters, perpetrated by thousands of white supremacists who are organized into as many as three hundred paramilitary groups across the state.

November 7   In the presidential election, Republican candidate Rutherford B. Hayes and Democratic candidate Samuel Tilden both claim victory, amidst disputes over the results of elections in the unredeemed states of Florida, Louisiana, and South Carolina. In the race for governor in South Carolina, both Wade Hampton and the incumbent Republican governor, Daniel Chamberlain, claim victory and establish competing legislatures. A similar situation develops in Louisiana, where rival governments are set up under Democrat Francis Nicholls and Republican Stephen Packard.

1877   **March 4**   Rutherford Hayes is inaugurated as president following a deal that sees the Republican Party agree to abandon Reconstruction policies and remove the small numbers of federal troops remaining in the ex-Confederate states. With federal support withdrawn, the Republican administrations in Louisiana and South Carolina are disbanded, and Democrats Francis Nicholls and Wade Hampton are confirmed as the states' respective governors. The last remaining Republican state governments in the South are toppled, and white supremacist rule is restored throughout the region.

1879 **November** The Readjuster Party wins control of the Virginia General Assembly.

1880 **March 1** In the case of *Strauder v. West Virginia*, the U.S. Supreme Court affirms the right of African Americans to serve on juries.

1883 **May 21** The Choctaw Indian nation grants citizenship to former slaves.

October 15 Ruling in five cases known collectively as "the Civil Rights Cases," the U.S. Supreme Court declares the Civil Rights Act of 1875 unconstitutional.

November 3 Four African Americans and one white person are killed in rioting in Danville, Virginia. Democrats blame Readjuster policies for the riot, and, in state elections held three days later, the Democrats regain control of the General Assembly.

1890 **November 1** Mississippi introduces literacy tests as a means to disenfranchise African American voters. Over the next two decades, other Southern states adopt similar measures, as well as poll taxes, and all-white primaries to undermine black voting rights.

1894 **September 10** The National Association of the Daughters of the Confederacy is formed in Nashville. In 1895, the organization changes its name to the United Daughters of the Confederacy.

1896 **May 18** In the case of *Plessy v. Ferguson*, the U.S. Supreme Court gives federal sanction to racial segregation throughout the nation.

1902 **May 29** Virginia adopts a new constitution that disenfranchises almost all remaining African American voters in the state and halves the size of the white electorate. The constitution is not put to a public ballot for fear that it will be rejected.

1915 **February 18** After hosting a screening of *The Birth of a Nation* at the White House, President Woodrow Wilson is reported to have declared that the film "[was] like writing history with lightning." Wilson's endorsement helps to cement the film's racist and negative interpretation of the Reconstruction era in America's historical memory.

The Meaning of Freedom for African American Men

1

Rebecca J. Fraser

For the enslaved black man and woman and the African American community as a whole, the Civil War effected a major change in their world—life would never be the same again. Yet the realities of freedom during the era of Reconstruction were far less tangible than most African Americans had hoped. Freedom brought new responsibilities to the African American community that were increasingly difficult to shoulder in the Reconstruction South. In the aftermath of emancipation, families separated during slavery were reunited, and the confusion and chaos confronting those whose spouses remarried in the belief that they would never see their husband or wife again caused much heartache and grief. In addition, the shortages of the Civil War hit the African American community harder than other Southerners. Typically clinging to the lowest rung of the Southern social ladder, African Americans' recently won freedom imposed new economic burdens upon them. Although rumors abounded that the federal government would provide each newly freed slave with 40 acres of land and a mule, such talk proved to be unfounded, and Reconstruction provided little in the way of economic remuneration for the emancipated African American.

It is perhaps unrealistic to believe that slavery and its ideological underpinnings could have been destroyed by the catalog of legislative acts and constitutional amendments witnessed during the early years of Reconstruction. This chapter considers the multiple ways in which freedmen defined their own concepts of freedom within the contexts of their personal worlds:

An enslaved African American man is sold and taken away from his family. (Library of Congress)

marriage, family, and household. It also underlines the difficulties freedmen encountered in reconstructing their lives during the era of Reconstruction. These difficulties were primarily a direct consequence of the system of slavery, which perpetuated negative stereotypes of enslaved men that persisted into the Reconstruction era. Just as African Americans sought to define their own understanding of freedom in the New South, so white Southerners sought to reassert their racial superiority and create a social and economic system that could be understood as slavery by another name.

Experiencing a Sea of Change

African Americans attempted to seize their newfound freedom with both hands, and they worked hard to define the extent of their changed status, maintaining institutions that had been fostered under the system of slavery, such as marriage and the family, which could now legally flourish in the postbellum South. In addition, African Americans developed new means to

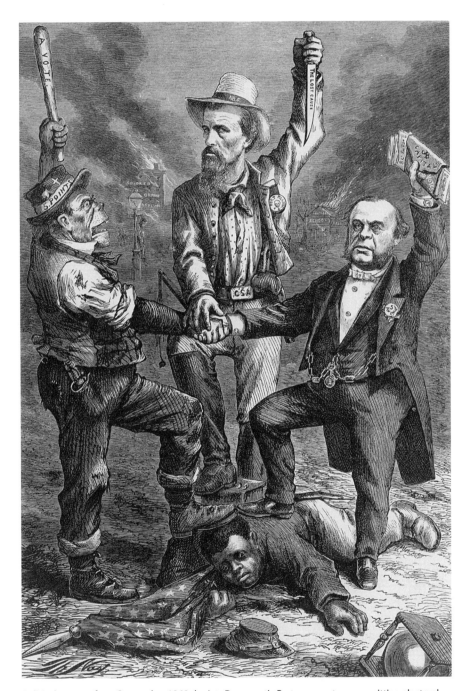

Political cartoon from September 1868 depicts Democratic Party supporters committing electoral fraud and violently resisting the Reconstruction Acts. (Library of Congress)

further define and express their freedoms. Frederick Douglass, a former slave and an acclaimed abolitionist, stated in 1858 that "The vital question at stake in the great sectional crisis is not whether the South shall be extended or limited, whether the South shall bear rule or not . . . but whether the four million now held in bondage are *men* and entitled to the rights and liberties of men" (cited in Blight 1989, 13, emphasis added). Despite the fact that Douglass was extremely gender blind in his assertion, he raises an interesting point concerning enslaved masculinity and the rights and privileges of citizens, who at this point in time were defined as white men. As historian Laura Edwards argues, securing their place as men would prove far more difficult for African Americans than it would have done for white males in the Reconstruction era. Black skin had been irrefutably conflated with dependence and enslavement, and, freedmen found themselves struggling to turn the concepts of freedom and liberty into concrete realities (Edwards 1997, 161).

The Civil War constituted a much more fundamental change for enslaved men than it did for Southern or Northern white men. The war opened the possibility that black men in slavery might be able to acquire the material basis for manhood in their own right and lay claim to rights and privileges that had previously been the exclusive domain of free white men. In many ways, as LeeAnn Whites asserts, the Civil War represented a conflict of masculinity as white Southern men fought to keep the black man in his place and thus sustain their own sense of identity (Whites 1992). The free black communities in the North and the South also viewed the Civil War as a test and a means for establishing the manhood of those in their communities. Surely, they reasoned, if the free black man was to stand by the Union at this critical juncture, his efforts would be recognized and he could no longer be denied full rights to citizenship.

Defining Freedom

As Susan-Mary Grant argues in Chapter 8 of this volume, concerning former Union and Confederate soldiers, the Civil War was a complex experience for those free and formerly enslaved black men who enlisted in Union ranks. It allowed them to reach beyond the assumptions and stereotypes of the antebellum period and attempt to set to rest the racist ideals that dictated that African American men were childlike and dependent. By enlisting in the Union ranks, these men hoped to prove these stereotypical images wrong. Importantly, enlistment also allowed formerly enslaved men to claim a sense of agency and authority over the uses to which they put their own bodies rather than having to be subjected to the ultimate authority of the slaveholder. Indeed, these African American soldiers acted as "apostles of black equality" as they spread ideals of freedom amongst the formerly enslaved, defined in measures such as landownership and civil and political rights (Foner 1988, 80). However, racism pervaded the Union ranks, and older ideas persisted regarding African American inferiority. Once enlistment of African American men became official policy, after January 1, 1863, the federal government ordered that all such regiments should have only white commissioned officers, thereby denying African American men the opportunity to advance in status. In several cases, African American soldiers were paid only half of white soldiers' wages, and they were usually given the more deadly or monotonous duties in the ranks.

In response to such treatment, they began to reassert their growing sense of freedom and liberation. Several colored regiments protested their unfair wages and stressed the fact that they, too, had wives and sweethearts, just as the white soldiers did, who depended upon them for an income. Several petitions were written by regiments protesting the inequality of the pay received by black soldiers. The 54th Massachusetts infantry refused all pay for 18 months until the federal government agreed to end this particular policy. They were joined by other African American units in the Union ranks and consequently achieved a reversal of this policy by mid-1864. Others protested the treatment of their families, whom they had left under the care of contraband camps. The camps were established as a result of the Confiscation Act of 1862, which decreed that all properties seized from the Confederacy during the war could be used in supporting the war efforts of the Union. As property, slaves were considered as contrabands of war once they had crossed Union-occupied lines. Soldiers of the 36th United States Colored infantry, stationed in Virginia, wrote to Gen. Oliver Howard, commissioner of the Freedmen's Bureau, to protest the suffering of their wives, children, and parents who lived in the contraband camps in Roanoke Island, North Carolina. They argued that although they had served faithfully in the army, stressing their duty to the Union, their families had suffered in the process: "When we were enlisted in the service we were promised that our Wifes and family's should receive rations from government. The rations for our Wifes and family's have been (and are now cut down) to one half the regular ration. Consequently three or four days out of every 10 days, they have nothing to eat" (Smith 1997, 57).

After the end of the Civil War and in the early years of Reconstruction, the enslaved were legally emancipated with the passage of the Thirteenth

Amendment on January 31, 1865, and guaranteed the full privileges of republican citizenship. Despite these rights of full membership in the United States, the majority of African American men were more concerned with defining freedoms within the realities of their own lives than with participation in the political process. Freedmen often expressed their freedom simply through their attitude, the way they acted, and the way they dressed. Others found more concrete ways to do so. Several appended a surname and a title to their name, symbolizing that with freedom they now expected to be treated with as much respect and dignity as white men. When Jourdan Anderson wrote to his former master, Col. P. H. Anderson, declining his offer to return as a laborer on his plantation, Jourdan drew upon this very aspect of freedom. He reported in a letter written on August 7, 1865, and published in the *Cincinnati Commercial,* that he was "doing tolerably well here. I get $25 a month, with victuals and clothing: have a comfortable home for Mandy (the folks here call her Mrs. Anderson), and the children, Milly, Jane and Grundy, go to school and are learning well; the teacher says grundy has a head for a preacher" (Mintz 2007).

Jourdan Anderson thus underlined the concrete realities of freedom that both he and his family were expressing by rejecting Colonel Anderson's invitation. Emancipation for freedpeople meant, above all, independence from white control. In his defiant attitude and remarks ("the folks here call her Mrs. Anderson"), Jourdan Anderson was defining his (and by extension, his family's) sense of freedom, underlining the fact that the old regime of slavery had been destroyed and that Colonel Anderson could never again expect to call Jourdan's wife by anything but her full title. The fact that some of Colonel Anderson's female relatives would also have been known as "Mrs. Anderson" only serves to reinforce the complex ways in which the dynamics of power shifted in these early years of Reconstruction. Although the hopes and aspirations of freedmen in the immediate aftermath of the Civil War proved mostly unfulfilled by 1877, these early years of Reconstruction did communicate to white Southerners the determination and desire of African Americans to define and express their rights to freedom in ways that were entirely independent from white authority.

Reclaiming Marriage

One of the most meaningful ways that freedpeople could communicate and express their freedom was through validating the legal standing of their marriages, which had been created under slavery. The enslaved, as a form of property, were not legally entitled to marry, although many did have quasi-

Special Order Number 15

In the immediate period after emancipation, thousands of African Americans chose to reaffirm their commitment to each other by validating their marriage in front of a preacher. John Eaton, the superintendent of Contrabands in the Department of Tennessee and Arkansas, issued a military edict, Special Order Number 15, in March 1864, which instructed Union army clergy to "solemnize the rite of marriage among freedmen."

Special Order Number 15 did not require that those slaves who already considered themselves to be "married" renew their marriage ties. Some amongst the formerly enslaved did not register their marriage under this order or at the end of the Civil War. They believed that they had already affirmed their commitment to one another on a very public stage through a marriage ceremony conducted during slavery.

Thus, they did not see why they should have to prove their love for one another a second time. Despite such attitudes, at the end of the Civil War, many freedmen and freedwomen did choose to register their marriage with local government officials, with most paying around 25 cents for the privilege.

Radical Republicans (see the introduction to this book) in Congress and numerous activists for African American civil and political rights used these examples of freedmen and freedwomen validating their marital ties as evidence that their relationships could now be counted on an equal footing with the marriages of free white men and women. Therefore, these politicians argued, was it not reasonable and just to grant freed African Americans the same political and civil rights as well?

marriage ceremonies, performed by either the master or the local preacher. During the Civil War, Union officials began to recognize the fact that African American soldiers were not legally married to those they claimed as their wives. In order to remedy this situation, various officials began passing regulations such as Special Order Number 15, which directed army clergy in Tennessee and Arkansas to solemnize the marriages of all freedpeople.

In the immediate emancipation period, thousands of African Americans chose to reaffirm their commitment to each other in front of officiating clergy; 4,627 formerly enslaved people in and near Davis Bend, Vicksburg, and Natchez, Mississippi, registered their marriage (Gutman 1976, 18). Through the ritual of a wedding ceremony and the opportunity to solemnize their vows in front of a preacher, they were acting out their own definitions of what it meant to be free. However, such characterizations of freedom would take on new meaning in the immediate aftermath of the Civil War and during Reconstruction, when African American families tended to the massive scars and festering wounds that slavery had dealt upon their familial relationships.

Reuniting Families

Formerly enslaved men and women desperately searched the South for loved ones sold and separated from them during slavery. The results of such searches could at times reveal complicated familial bonds. Often, finding a spouse or sweetheart was as heartbreaking and traumatic as the initial separation. This outcome was especially poignant for those men and women who remarried in the belief that they would never see their former spouse again, or for children who had never met, or had little recollection of, their parents, being sold away from them at such a young age. The worlds of the freedmen reunited with wife and children were often turned upside down, as they were forced to confront complex questions of commitment, fidelity, and trust; such were the legacies of the internal slave trade developed in the South following the official closure of the transatlantic trade with Africa in 1808. Take, for example, Laura Spicer's husband, who wrote to her shortly after the end of the Civil War, expressing his grief at the fact that Laura and their children had been sold away from him during slavery and his inner turmoil regarding his current situation. He had subsequently remarried in the belief that he would never see Laura or their children again, and, as he explained to her, "I am married, and my wife have two children, and if you and I meets it would make a very dissatisfied family." He did request that she send some of the children's hair in a separate piece of paper with each of their names so that he had something to remember them by. As for Laura; his new wife, Anna; and himself, he concluded that "I had rather anything to had happened to me most than ever to have been parted from you and the children. As I am I do not know who I love best, you or Anna . . . . Laura I do love you the same. My love to you have *never* failed" (Gutman 1976, 7).

Black newspapers often ran advertisements for those searching for loved ones. Many of these ads featured formerly enslaved men who were attempting to locate their wife and children in the aftermath of the Civil War. Husbands and fathers often held out little hope of ever seeing their family reunited, although some were willing to offer substantial rewards for any news. Ben East and his wife, Flora, offered a $200 reward for anybody who might provide news of their daughter, Polly, and son, Geo[rge] Washington, who were "carried away from this city to the state of Mississippi, and subsequently to Texas." Ben and Flora promised $100 each to any person who "will assist them, or either of them, to get to Nashville, or even just to get word to them of their whereabouts" (Smith 1997, 51).

Several freedmen wrote to the Freemen's Bureau for help in tracking down their "lost" family members. Others wrote to the former masters and mistresses of their kin, requesting that these family members should now be regarded as free. Pvt. Spotswood Rice, an African American soldier fighting for the Union, wrote to his daughter's mistress, Kitty Diggs, while he was hospitalized with chronic rheumatism in the fall of 1864. He had been informed that she was refusing to let him see his daughter, Mary, and had also accused him of trying to steal Mary away from her. Spotswood Rice's response was fierce and angry, reinforcing the point that by holding Mary in slavery, Kitty Diggs was fighting a war that she could not and would not win. Even though Rice had offered to buy the child's freedom previously, he admits that he is glad that she did not take him up on his offer. Now the whole government supported him in his aim of emancipating the enslaved, his daughter included. He warned Kitty that "I have no fears about getting mary out of your hands this whole Government gives chear to me and you cannot help your self" (Berlin and Rowland 1996, 197).

Reconstructing Households

In addition to attempting to validate and recreate their familial relationships, freedmen sought a degree of control over their households. During enslavement, the authority of enslaved men had been denied and negated in the context of the household by the white slaveholding population. However, during the early years of Reconstruction, freedmen sought to reassert their position as heads of household. Various institutional measures helped to reinforce this position. The very fact that some had fought alongside Union troops during the Civil War meant that they had actively participated in defining their own claims to freedom. This expression was also communicated through the gender roles and identities that freedmen and freedwomen assumed during the Reconstruction period. In the early years of Reconstruction, freedwomen focused upon their home and their families, withdrawing their labor from the market when they could afford to do so and thus limiting the authority of white employers. Although it has been suggested that freedwomen tended to quit work altogether in the immediate Reconstruction period as a means to resist their previous status as slaves, in fact this was not the case. The majority of freedpeople's households could not sustain the financial impact that they would have incurred as a result. Freedwomen did work during the Reconstruction period, but they refused to work on the terms that their white employers and federal officials demanded. Instead, they negotiated their own working arrangements and conditions and limited the time they spent engaged in waged work. Moreover, as Laura Edwards has underlined, such assumptions devalued the labor performed by freedwomen in the context of the household and in the task of caring for other family members. Through these means, they were able to balance the work they performed outside of the household with those domestic labors vital for the support and maintenance of their family, such as tending vegetable plots, raising poultry, making clothes, and caring for the young and elderly (Edwards 2000, 138).

Labor Issues

Many white Southerners bemoaned the resultant decrease in the potential supply of labor and accused African American women of attempting to "play the lady." In contrast, freedmen witnessed this situation with pride and wore it as a badge of honor. It communicated to Southern society in particular, and to the United States in general, that freedpeople were now trying to support themselves through household economies that mixed paid employment and productive labor within their own home. It also proved that freedmen were assuming the role of chief breadwinner in their household. In distancing themselves from white employers, freedpeople were enhancing their ability to live their lives on their own terms.

Several freedwomen remembered the Reconstruction era as a period in which their menfolk provided for their families in the best ways that they could. This mentality helped to reinforce the notion of the male breadwinner in African American households and helped to strengthen positive perceptions of fatherhood within the context of the families of freedpeople. For example, an African American washerwoman recalled that her dead husband had been "a good husband and father and provided for his family as best he could" (cited in Edwards 1997, 168). During slavery, the role of the father had been marginalized in the context of the enslaved family through the slaveholder's disregard for such ties. Enslaved men were not regarded as the heads of their household and had no formal power over family members. Enslaved men often lived on a different plantation from that of their wife and children. Although they would usually be able to get permission from the slaveholder to visit their family during their off-time, their absence from the family invariably caused them to be concerned about the safety and care of their wife and children at the hands of the slaveholder, the overseer, and other enslaved men.

During the early Reconstruction era, the question of child labor figured prominently in African Americans' struggles to gain some sense of influence in their children's lives. Apprenticeship laws enacted through the

The plantation police, or Home Guard, examine African American passes on the levee road below New Orleans (1863). Under the Black Codes, whites aimed to continue regulating African Americans' freedom of movement after emancipation. (Bettmann/Corbis)

Black Codes, which regulated and restricted the labor of the freedpeople, allowed for former slaveholders to bind black children to unpaid labor until they reached adulthood. Not only did such a situation revive older notions of white slaveholding power over the labor and lives of freedpeople's families and, by extension, their communities, it also deprived them of a vital labor source themselves. The labor of children was as essential to the support of the freedpeople's households as it was to the material enterprise and domestic comfort of the former slaveholders. In a circular published in Maryland on December 6, 1864, a warning was issued against the illegal apprenticing of African American children. It stated that Brig. Gen. Henry H. Lockwood had arrived in eastern Maryland with the express intention to "BREAK UP the practice now prevalent of apprenticing Negroes without the consent of their parents, to their former masters or others." The circular threatened arrest for anyone found guilty of such practices and offered all parents affected who could not afford the upkeep of their children a free passage to the Freedman's Home, an institution for African Americans of "friendless" status or those of colored soldiers (Berlin and Rowland 1996, 212). The Union army challenged these apprenticeship laws in order to reiterate the status of freedpeople to the former Confederacy. It was also, in

Shelter for Orphans of Colored Soldiers and Friendless Colored Children

The Shelter for Orphans of Colored Soldiers and Friendless Colored Children was established as part of a Freedmen's Bureau initiative in Baltimore in 1867. It was one of numerous such institutions established during Reconstruction for the care of African American orphans and those from the poorest families whose parents were unable to support them. Such shelters were endorsed by the likes of Brig. Gen. Henry H. Lockwood, who had commanded troops in Maryland during much of the Civil War and had issued a circular warning against the illegal apprenticing of African American children to "former masters or others" without the consent of their parents. If the parents of the reclaimed children could not maintain them, the circular offered all parents a free passage to the Baltimore Freedman's Home, a precursor of the Baltimore orphanage of 1867 and wider projects throughout the former Confederacy. However, despite widespread support from the white as well as the African American population, the day-to-day running of the Baltimore shelter was, like many other African American institutions of the time, financed directly by contributions from the black community, many of which were raised by local church groups.

After Reconstruction, support for the shelter at the state level waned, and in an act passed by the Maryland legislature in 1882, the children's shelter was merged with the Shelter for the Aged and the Infirm Colored Citizens of Baltimore in 1882. According to the terms of the merger, the orphanage was required to pass on and use all of its property and proceeds to the Shelter for the Aged and Infirm.

the process, emphasizing the notion that freedmen and freedwomen were not to be dependent upon the federal government for their care; they were to assume the full responsibilities of freedom, including care of their children. Freedmen were usually only too willing to embrace their new responsibilities. Not only did they recognize the economic importance of their children to their family's survival, they also, within the expressions of love and commitment that they communicated to their children, conveyed a valid statement concerning the right of African American fathers to care for their own family and household.

Land Ownership

Probably the most significant aspect of freedpeople's struggle to define the extent of their liberty was rooted in the question of landownership. This struggle was particularly manifested in the way that freedpeople began to reorganize their households based on kinship rather than antebellum ownership. Julie Saville notes that, during the early years of Reconstruction, freedmen living in the interior of South Carolina often quit their antebellum "homeplace" to be reunited with their family on another plantation owned by a different landowner (Saville 1994, 103). Following the dissolution of the Black Codes and the failure of Gen. William T. Sherman's temporary order to grant each freed family 40 acres of tillable land on the South Carolina Sea Islands and on the coast of Georgia, the federal government promoted a free-labor policy. Under this ideal, African Americans would become agricultural wage workers on land owned by white planters. Concepts of freedom in relation to landownership as a result of this policy consisted of the right to contract labor and receive pay for it, not for African Americans to own the land that they had worked upon for years and to receive the full harvested benefits from their labor. With African American men at the forefront of their reconstructed families, familial units thus became the chief bargaining tool in establishing working relationships with employers. Freedmen were regarded by the Freedmen's Bureau as the voice of authority within the household, and it was they who signed labor contracts for members of their family, including their wife and their children. Under the system of sharecropping that subsequently developed across the Southern states, land was rented to freedpeople's families, who in return were required to give a share of the crop that they produced to the landowners. In theory, such a system would bolster freedpeople's ability to control their own lives, as it would free them from the direct control of white employers; would satisfy their desire for land; and would possibly allow for some upward social mobility, depending on the profitability of crops they produced.

However, this ideal of economic autonomy was not to be realized. Previously, sharecropping had allowed for tenants to pay a specific amount to work the land for a given time while retaining control over their lives, labor, and produce. However, as increasing numbers of African Americans became sharecroppers, the status of this position declined and Southern law turned sharecroppers into common laborers. Employers were given complete control over the production process and produce, and by law, the tenant or worker could be arrested if he or she attempted to sell any of the produce. In order to prevent economic independence, legislation was also developed to prevent grazing, hunting, fishing, and trespassing on "private" lands. The economic crisis produced by the Civil War hit freedpeople particularly hard, and several were forced to borrow resources and obtain credit at inflated rates of interest in order to produce the crops.

This situation led inevitably to a cycle of debt, desperation, and destitution. Although legally free, many African American families were now enslaved by their own powerlessness and poverty. The crash of the cotton market soon after emancipation and the economic effects of the Civil War served to compound their problems, and several freed families were thrown into a cycle of debt and despair from which they seemed unable to escape. Various fraternities and associations had been established during Reconstruction by African Americans to aid freedmen and freedwomen in realizing their quest for social, economic, and political freedom. Many of these associations were very vocal when it came to the issue of land redistribution and the failure of the Republican Party-controlled government to fulfill its promises to freedpeople regarding economic parity and equality with whites. Writing under the pseudonym "Kush" and speaking for the African American group, one member of the Young Men's Progressive Association complained in 1872 that after seven years of Reconstruction, few South Carolina blacks owned their own lands. Kush pointed out that "Four hundred thousand people who were slaves before the war do not even now own their own labor. Their labor is owned by the land owner who controls and directs it." Kush also argued that white Republicans had deceived freedpeople into believing that they would acquire land. He insisted that there was "nothing in slavery as mean as this because slavery was honest in its intentions and purposes and meant what it said and did; but this is open contempt, and he who, among us, submits to it, should be despised by the whole colored race, as unworthy of its confidence" (Smith 1997, 83). While many freedmen and freedwomen had originally looked to the land as a sure route to secure their freedom, it seemed to many others as if the system of sharecropping had replanted the old mechanisms of control and authority that had existed under slavery. The majority of freedmen's families working under this system were forced to eke out a meager existence, enslaved by economic policies that seemed to contradict their newly acquired free status.

Other Social Barriers to Freedom

This was, of course, only part of the story. Some freedmen and freedwomen were able to negotiate the complex economic problems of the Reconstruction period to emerge as professionals, skilled artisans, and farm owners. Several freedpeople also chose to migrate to the Southern cities, where the majority hoped to make a decent and an honest living. Relocat-

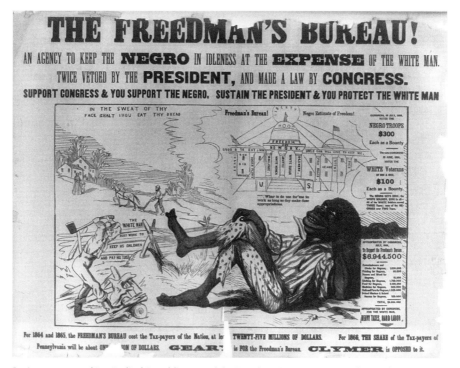

Racist poster attacking Radical Republicans and the Freedmen's Bureau, 1866. (Library of Congress)

ing to the city seemed to many freedmen as a means to get closer to free-dom, a way to communicate and express their newly claimed liberties by traveling where and how they wanted. By contrast, former slaveholders, the Freedmen's Bureau, and the federal government saw this population's migration during Reconstruction as evidence of the fact that freedpeople saw freedom as an opportunity for idleness and vagabondage. This charac-terization was especially applied in the case of freedmen who were deemed to be the chief breadwinner of their household by government agencies. In fact, those who left their home in the South usually had good reason to do so. As well as reflecting the wartime displacement and disorientation of many African Americans, the decision to move expressed the extended boundaries of their newfound freedom, which allowed them full geograph-ical and social mobility.

As Eric Foner points out, "Reconstruction witnessed the rise of a new urban geography," but this growth was not always a positive experience for those living within it. The massive influx of people flooded the urban labor market, and as result, most freedpeople who migrated to the cities were forced into low-wage, menial positions (Foner 1988, 81–82). In Chapter 3 of this volume, concerning urban black life during Reconstruction, James Campbell underscores that many freedpeople who moved into the cities after emancipation faced hostility from those African Americans who were already occupying them. Coupled with this rejection was the problem of finding decent employment, and consequently, many freedmen and freedwomen housed themselves in poor accommodation, creating shanty towns where poverty and squalor were rife (Foner 1988, 81–82).

One of the most potent and troubling opponents of freedmen's attempts to define and express their freedoms was the Ku Klux Klan. The activity and violence of the Klan varied across the former Confederacy. Some states or particular counties experienced rabid activity while other areas experienced little Klan-related violence. For those African Americans who were subject to attacks by the Klan, it was a horrifying and fearful experience. The Klan's methods typically were cruel and callous, paying little regard for human dignity and respect. Interracial relationships between African American men and white women were a particular point of grievance for the Klan, and it consequently targeted these unions, often dragging the "offending" couple from their bed in the dead of night to face their punishments. During slavery, Southern white society had done all it could to denigrate and degrade the enslaved man's sense of masculinity. While male slaveholders and their male relatives raped slave women with impunity, enslaved men who entered into a relationship with a free white woman, consenting or not, were subjected to harsh legislative punishments.

During Reconstruction, however, with formerly enslaved men now legally free, it was feared by the majority of white Southerners that the freedmen would begin expressing their freedom by taking certain liberties with white women. The desire of the Klan to resurrect and reinforce racial superiority for white society thus extended into the domestic and personal worlds of African American men in particular, as they faced increasingly brutal measures inflicted upon their bodies. In one case, recounted in the Ku Klux Klan reports, a black man and white woman were accused of cohabitation in Georgia. The man was subsequently taken out to the woods, where a hole was dug in the ground and a block buried in it. His penis was then nailed to the block and a large knife was laid by his side. Wood was piled up around him and set on fire. He was thus left with the choice to either burn to death or use the knife to cut his penis off and escape with his life—he chose to live (cited in Hodes 1997, 156).

Interracial relationships were not the only grievance that the Klan held against African American men, but they could often result in the most

In 1871, Congress enacted the Ku Klux Klan Act to confront the rising tide of Klan violence in the South. This political cartoon links the Klan to the ideals of the Confederate States of America and the Democratic Party. (Bettmann/Corbis)

macabre of punishments. The slightest infraction could result in Klan retaliation and reprisal. Former slave Ben Johnson recalled that Klan violence could be meted out for a whole host of offenses. In one case that Ben remembered with particular clarity, Ed and Cindy, who had previously been enslaved, refused to remove themselves from the place that they had regarded as home on their master's plantation. The Klan was swift in its punishment of this "flouting" of white racial superiority and authority. As Ben explained, "Hit wuz on a cold night when dey come an' drugged de niggers out'n bed. Dey carried 'em down into the woods an' whup dem, den dey throws 'em in de pond, dere bodies breakin' de ice. Ed come out an' come ter our house, but Cindy ain't been seed since" (Library of Congress 2001, 10–11). It was in the silent screams of the victims of these brutal and often fatal attacks that the Klan revealed their complete disregard for morality, respectability, and humanity.

Within their personal worlds, then, freed African American men struggled to define and make concrete their own sense of freedom during Reconstruction. The reasons for this struggle were multiple and varied, but they all came down to the fact that the majority of white Americans in the North and South during the Reconstruction era relied upon stereotypical images of freedmen and freedwomen that stretched backward into the antebellum period and slavery. These assumptions, focusing upon African African men, defined them as incapable of looking after themselves or their families. The majority of white society viewed freedpeople, in general, and freedmen, in particular, as a problem; they had been unshackled from the paternalistic care of the master and could not cope with the pressures that freedom thrust upon them. What white society failed to consider, however, was that it was precisely due to the fact that freedmen had been forced to live under the institution of slavery that they entered Reconstruction in a position of ultimate dependency. Enslaved men and women had seen their families torn apart by sale and separation; enslaved men had had their masculinity negated in the context of the family and the household; and enslaved communities had been denied the right of ownership to the crops that they had sown, cultivated, and harvested. This was the "peculiar institution," a distinctive feature of Southern society in the pre-civil war period, which defined the southern economy, its social hierarchy, the southern way of life. It was a system whereby slaveholders and traders got rich through the backbreaking labor of those they enslaved and thus, in the aftermath of the Civil War and African American emancipation, white Southerners sought new ways to maintain the Southern social order.

Conclusion

During the early years of Reconstruction, the majority of freedmen expressed hopes and aspirations of freedom that were intimately related to their own families and communities. Sometimes these expressions of freedom were simple, reflected in the slightest gesture or remark that would have previously overstepped the boundaries separating master from slave. Freedom was also symbolized through freedmen's attitudes, the clothes that they could now choose to wear, and the adoption of a title and a surname claimed as a sign of respectability. Moreover, other expressions of freedom were more formalized. Freedmen sought to legalize and validate their marital unions, which had not been recognized under slavery; to reconstruct their familial bonds with wife and children who had been sold and separated from them; to reorganize their household economies so that their wives and children were not subject to the overall control of white employers; and to purchase their own land and property in order to signal to white Southern society that they were now heads of their own households. The personal was indeed political for freedmen during this period. Their hopes and aspirations of the early years of Reconstruction rapidly faded from the horizon in the latter years as Southern states were "redeemed" by the Democrats (see the Introduction to this volume). Nevertheless, many freedmen held onto the glimmer of light that the concept of freedom held out to them and attempted to transform it into a reality in the best way that they could.

References and Further Reading

Berlin, Ira, and Leslie S. Rowland. 1996. *Families and Freedom: A Documentary History of African American Kinship in the Civil War Era.* New York: New Press.

Blight, David W. 1989. *Frederick Douglass' Civil War: Keeping Faith in Jubilee.* Baton Rouge: Louisiana State University Press.

Edwards, Laura F. 1997. *Gendered Strife and Confusion: The Political Culture of Reconstruction.* Urbana: University of Illinois Press.

Edwards, Laura F. 2000. *Scarlett Doesn't Live Here Anymore: Southern Women in the Civil War Era.* Urbana: University of Illinois Press.

Foner, Eric. 1988. *Reconstruction: America's Unfinished Revolution, 1863–1877.* New York: Perennial.

Gutman, Herbert G. 1976. *The Black Family in Slavery and Freedom, 1750–1925.* New York: Vintage.

Hodes, Martha. 1997. *White Women, Black Men: Illicit Sex in the Nineteenth Century South.* New Haven, CT: Yale University Press.

Library of Congress. 2001. Ex-slave story. *Born in Slavery: Slave Narratives from the Federal Writers' Project, 1936–1938.* North Carolina Narratives, vol. 11, pt. 2, 8–13.

Mintz, S. 2007. "African American Voices: Jourdan Anderson." In *Digital History.* (Online information; retrieved 3/06.) http://www.digitalhistory.uh.edu/black_voices/voices_display.cfm?id=80.

Saville, Julie. 1994. *The Work of Reconstruction: From Slave to Wage Labor in South Carolina, 1860–1870.* New York: Cambridge University Press.

Smith, John David. 1997. *Black Voices from Reconstruction.* Gainesville: University Press of Florida.

Whites, Leeann. 1992. "The Civil War as a Crisis in Gender." In *Divided Houses: Gender and the Civil War,* ed. Catherine Clinton and Nina Silber.

White Women in | 2
Reconstruction

Bonnie Laughlin-Schultz

Two days after Confederate General Robert E. Lee's surrender to Union General Ulysses S. Grant at Appomattox Courthouse in Virginia marked the end of the Civil War, President Abraham Lincoln delivered his last public address. Instead of merely rejoicing in the triumph of the Union, Lincoln encouraged Northerners and Southerners to put aside their differences and acknowledged that Reconstruction had the potential to be "fraught with great difficulty" (Lincoln 1865). To white women of the South, Lincoln's words rang very true in the aftermath of the war and prior to Reconstruction, though for very different reasons than those that informed the president's speech. While Lincoln was preoccupied with healing the sectional divide and securing African American freedom, Southern white women struggled to recreate their families and lives against a backdrop of physical destruction and loss of life. Many white women worked to make sense of a world that they perceived as turned upside down by the South's defeat and the demise of slavery.

Southern white women's lives were diverse and changing during Reconstruction. Class was an important source of division among white women, but these women also shared much common ground based on their race and gender. This chapter underlines the wide range of Southern white women's experiences and addresses a number of important questions related to white women's lives and labors during the Reconstruction era. What changes did the Civil War bring, and, more importantly, how did white women make sense of these changes? How did women's labor

Women dressed in black approach a shell of a four-story building, gutted by fire in the "Burnt District," Richmond, Virginia, ca. 1865. (Library of Congress)

transform during Reconstruction, and how did women respond to such changes? How did elite white women struggle to reassert power over former slaves, and how did such struggles play out in family households throughout the South? Beyond the confines of the household, how did Southern white women enter into the public realm of associations? And how did Southern ideology change in the face of a civil war that disrupted the gender-, race-, and class-based norms that had structured antebellum society?

The World the War Wrought: A Hopeless Future?

The Civil War brought chaos and confusion to the lives of many Southern white women. Louisiana native Kate Stone was just 21 when the war broke out. With her brothers away fighting, Kate and her mother had managed Brokenburn, the family plantation, and more than 150 slaves, but in the middle of the war, Kate and her mother (along with other planter families) fled to Texas to wait out the conflict. In late May 1865, nearly six weeks after Lee's surrender, Stone remained unsure of whether the war had ended and noted in her diary that rumors of the Confederacy's defeat were making many of the planter families anxious (Anderson 1955, 342). Elvira Seddon, who lived less than 40 miles from the Confederate capital of Richmond, Virginia, also did not learn about Lee's surrender for more than a month and was frustrated by the suspense in which she waited (Culpepper

Illustration of Kate Stone, who authored *Brokenburn,* a journaled account of a well-educated and patriotic Southern girl's experiences during the Civil War. (Library of Congress)

Gertrude Thomas

Next to Mary Boykin Chesnut, Ella Gertrude Clanton Thomas (1834–1907) may be the most famous diarist of the Civil War and Reconstruction eras. Thomas kept her diary from 1848 until 1889, offering historians and students alike a unique window into how white Southern women experienced the tumultuous decades she chronicled. Before the Civil War, Thomas, daughter of a wealthy planter, had been the quintessential Southern belle in Augusta, Georgia, but the Civil War and its aftermath radically transformed her life. When her husband fell into debt during the war, Thomas, like many other women of her class, was forced to take on new roles. She found work for a time as a teacher, contemplated writing for a living, and was also forced to assume the duties of housekeeper and cook, a transition that symbolized a considerable loss of status with which she was hard pressed to cope.

2002, 11–12). Stone could hardly believe that the war was ending, confiding in her diary that the reports were too awful to believe.

Once the war was officially over (and known to be so), women such as Stone and Seddon responded with an array of emotions, ranging from relief to shock and despair. Some women were happy to know the soldiers would return home and were eager to reclaim husbands, sons, and brothers. In her diary, Gertrude Thomas, concerned about the safety of her male relatives, as well as the economic plight she faced at home, noted that she was thankful that the hard days of the war were ending (Culpepper 2004, 218). Some scholars contend, in fact, that it was the withdrawal of Confederate women's support for the Southern cause that partially contributed to the South's defeat.

But the reasons for Southern defeat were not so simple to Thomas and many other white women of the South. While eager for menfolk to return and resume work on behalf of their families, white women such as Thomas also engaged in what the historian Laura Edwards describes as a genuine mourning stemming from the defeat and the humiliation suffered at the hands of the North. Gertrude Thomas reported weeping into her pillow after the May 1865 capture of Confederate president Jefferson Davis and even found comfort in fantasizing about writing a taunting letter to Union general William T. Sherman's wife (Edwards 2000, 66, 181). Revealing similar emotions, Kate Stone recorded her joy upon learning that Abraham Lincoln was dead and noted that she thought his assassin, Southern nationalist John Wilkes Booth, was much braver than the man he had killed (Anderson

At the time Thomas's diary ended in 1889, she was still struggling to come to terms with her continuing economic distress and trying to make sense of the New South she inhabited. As historian Nell Irvin Painter points out, Thomas could be more open-minded than many of her peers in Southern society, but more often she responded to the post–Civil War world in language that was both racist and elitist (Painter 1990, 21). At the same time, the postwar world opened up new opportunities for women like Thomas. In the 1880s and 1890s, she became active in literary clubs as well as the Augusta chapter of the Women's Christian Temperance Union and women's suffrage reform. As a writer and reformer, Thomas gained a new kind of status in her community, albeit one that was far removed from that she had imagined for herself as a young woman.

1955, 333). Throughout the federal Reconstruction era, Southern white women resented the presence of "Yankee" soldiers as well as the loyalty oaths that were required from Southerners before their states would be readmitted to the Union. Some, such as Ellen House, went so far as to state that the South was now enslaved to the North (Culpepper 2004, 219).

Common white women—farming women or landless women—may have met the end of the war with an even deeper ambivalence than their more wealthy sisters. Many had been hit hard by the war and were living in poverty by the time of the Confederate surrender. The situation was compounded by the 1865 planting season, which began late and yielded a small crop because of the chaos surrounding the war's end. Some poor women never found their way out of this poverty. Sarah Guttery of Alabama, for instance, took in sewing and did fieldwork with her daughter after her husband was killed in the war, but despite their efforts, the Guttery women were never able to escape debt and impoverishment (Edwards 2000, 149).

The experiences of women such as Sarah Guttery are much harder for historians to recapture than those of elite women. Because the sources and scholarship related to them are so much more plentiful, this chapter focuses primarily on the experiences of elite white women from planter families. While these elite women were an undeniably small percentage of Southern society, they left behind the bulk of the historical accounts of Southern women's experiences during Reconstruction. Additionally, to a degree out of proportion to their actual size, elite men's and women's ideas about what the New South should be shaped the Southern future, for better and for worse.

Regardless of their status, most white women shared, at the war's end, Sarah Guttery's profound sense of loss: material, social, cultural, and political; the military defeat and the tragic fatalities of the war compounded this loss. Kate Stone's grief was so great that she foresaw a hopeless future. Returning to her family's plantation after the war ended, she confided to her diary that it hardly even seemed to be the same place that she had left (Anderson 1955, 340, 364).

In part, Stone's sense of despair stemmed from the sheer scale of Union and Confederate losses on the battlefields. In Chapter 8 of this volume, Susan-Mary Grant underlines the extreme physical and psychological adjustments that soldiers of the Confederacy faced when returning home. Scholars estimate that 620,000 soldiers were killed in the Civil War. Of this figure—staggering in contemporary times as well as in the present—258,000 of the men who died had fought on behalf of the Confederacy. An additional 129,000 Confederate soldiers returned from the war with some type of disability (Culpepper 2004, 228–229). In Georgia alone, an estimated 20,000 women were widowed and 60,000 children were orphaned by the war, and 300,000 slaves were freed (Culpepper 2002, 47). Similar figures in other Southern states meant that marriage patterns as well as broader social relations would be radically altered in the South for decades to come. The 1870 census reported that there were 25,000 more women than men in North Carolina, 36,000 more women than men in Georgia, and 15,000 more women than men in Virginia—in large part due to the Civil War casualties (Scott 1970, 106).

Like all Americans, Southern women were staggered by the number of Civil War dead. Additionally, like their northern, western, and midwestern counterparts, white Southern women also mourned their personal losses. Susan Sillers Darden of Fayette, Mississippi, for instance, confided to her diary her grief over the wartime losses of her son and brother. Her oldest son, Buckner, had died in 1862 of wounds sustained in battle, while her brother Joseph had died of smallpox after being taken prisoner by the Union army (Culpepper 2002, 244). For some women, mourning endured throughout the Reconstruction period. Rachel Creighton, whose brother Bud died from wounds at the Battle of Perryville, used her diary as an outlet for her anger and grief. Her consciousness of the number of weeks that had passed since his death persisted for years, and, 134 weeks after his passing, Rachel reported that she still wore a mourning veil (Culpepper 2002, 33).

Confederate women send their men to war, *Frank Leslie's Illustrated Newspaper,* May 23, 1863. (Library of Congress)

In addition to this personal grief, white Southern women also reckoned with more tangible losses in the early period of Reconstruction. During the war, much of the South had been devastated by the Northern armies. Union general William T. Sherman's famous (or, to Southern women, infamous) "March to the Sea" had resulted in tremendous damage, and the combined war approach of Sherman and Grant had devastated physical dwellings, land, and Southern infrastructure. Two hundred miles of railroad tracks lay in ruins; fields, crops, and buildings were destroyed; and 60,000 horses and innumerable livestock had been confiscated by the Union army (Culpepper 2002, 49).

Sydney Andrews, a Northern journalist, traveled south to describe the impact of the war in Georgia and the Carolinas. In his reporting, he described food shortages and extensive deprivation due to the lost labor and widespread destruction. Additionally, he wrote of the economic fluctuations of the late 1860s. The year following the war was marked by harsh weather, inflation, and crop failures, and succeeding years brought more of the same problems. As a result, Andrews reported, the sight of widows wandering the streets begging was a common phenomenon (Edwards 2000, 150–151).

Southern women, especially elites facing economic distress for the first time, described the postwar world as one turned upside down. Diarist Eliza Anderson Fain, an eastern Tennessee woman, recognized by May 1865 that she would have difficulty supporting a family given the destruction caused by the war (Fain 2004, 338). And her words proved prophetic: after the war, Fain attempted to hold onto her family farm by relying on her sons and some former slaves she had hired, but they were not able to sustain it and eventually lost the property.

White Women's Changing Labors, In and Out of the Household

The 19th century was a time of profound changes for American women's labor and leisure. Prior to the Civil War, many Northern women had begun to teach school, work in urban textile factories, or take advantage of ready-made cotton cloth, but it was only after the Civil War that Southern white women's labors began to be similarly transformed. The profound losses of the war, coupled with the emancipation of African American slaves upon whose labor the planters had built their lavish lifestyle, meant that many elite women now had to undertake household chores for themselves. Instead of managing food production and overseeing household slaves, many

White woman hanging laundry to dry on an outdoor clothesline, assisted by a girl holding a basket of clothespins, ca. 1870. (Library of Congress)

elite and yeoman women now had to tackle cooking and cleaning. Cornelia Spencer, a young Southern woman, acknowledged that due to the war and emancipation, many "delicate" women who had been raised in affluent circles now had to work for a living, and in June 1875, the *New Orleans Picayune* published a series of articles on the rising number of women now working not just inside their home but also outside the home for wages (Culpepper 2002, 56; Scott 1970, 124). Poor and common white women continued to undertake domestic chores as they always had, but in the higher echelons of white society, too, more and more women ventured outside of the household and took paid positions as teachers, clerical staff, typesetters, and writers. These new vocations in turn inspired more attention to education throughout the South. As African Americans embraced freedom by founding schools and claiming literacy, white women also coveted better education to deal with a changing world. This was evident in a letter from a group of women published in *DeBow's Review* in 1870. With their husbands dead and their land ravished, the women appealed for the establishment of a school to teach them printing, wood carving, gardening, bookkeeping, and telegraph operating, skills that they now needed to find employment (Weiner 1998, 218).

Ironically, when white women faced up to life without enslaved domestic servants, they found themselves as helpless as they had deluded themselves that slaves would be in the postemancipation world (Weiner 1998, 193). While proslavery ideology had preached that African Americans were naturally inferior and dependent on paternalistic masters, the reality was that the slave masters and mistresses had been dependent on African American labor.

Cooking, washing, and ironing—unpleasant and time-consuming tasks in the 19th century—were all new to Gertrude Thomas, and like many Southern white women, her early attempts at undertaking household chores led only to fumbling and frustration. Writing in her diary, Thomas recounted the story of the first time she made cakes for her family's supper, noting that her children had stood around to watch the novel sight (Edwards 2000, 172). Raised in an elite Georgia planter family, she had been accustomed to a household with many slaves who undertook all of her chores, from washing to cooking to cleaning and beyond. Now, instead of supervising slaves performing such tasks, she, like many other once-elite southern women, had to fill a pot of water, build a fire under it, slosh clothes around in the boiling water, wring them, and hang them awkwardly to dry (Culpepper 2002, 126). By 1870, Thomas had become accustomed to the household chores but was still struck by how her postwar life differed from her antebellum experiences. She ruefully acknowledged that she thought the choice to have three meals a day was unwise now that she knew all the preparation and cleanup that such meals required (Edwards 2000, 173). In the antebellum world, undertaking such chores would have signaled that she was not a "lady," and Thomas confided in her diary that she felt denigrated by the task.

Adapting to the need to perform household chores was particularly overwhelming for the older generations of white women who had grown to adulthood against the backdrop of slavery and antebellum luxury. The younger generations, those born after 1820 and especially after 1850, found it easier to adapt to the new household regimes under which they lived. The rearrangement of Southern kitchens in the Reconstruction era demonstrates how some younger women adapted. As Southern women took over the kitchen after the freeing of the slaves, a physical migration took place as the kitchen was incorporated into the house rather than being in a separate building (Censer 2003, 79).

But even as they adapted, some elite women worried about what messages these changes were sending to the next generation of Southern women, black and white. Longing for their former status, some white women struggled to assert renewed control over former slaves whom they hired as paid domestic servants. Some also worried about their own children's place in society. Eliza Rhea Anderson Fain described how she was glad to be strong enough to handle washing day but worried about her daughter, Fannie, who was reluctant to help with household cleaning. Eliza added that she feared that her daughter had taken in the wrong notions about the chore she was unwilling to do (Fain 2004, 330). Fannie might simply have been belligerent, but the passage in her mother's diary makes it seem that, instead, Fannie struggled to come to terms with the new expectations that her mother, and society, had for her.

During Reconstruction, more Southern women engaged in paid wage work outside the home than ever before. Women's work in the South was transformed during the war and continued to change in the aftermath of the conflict. For poor white women, wage labor became more and more necessary; some found work as domestics and laundresses in positions that had formerly been held by slaves. Additionally, many poorer women worked alongside their husbands in fields as sharecroppers. By 1880, one-third of all white Southerners worked as sharecroppers, and such work often demanded that both male and female hands toiled in the fields (Edwards 2000, 164). Elite women were not exempt from the expansion of wage labor. With many men away fighting, upper- and middle-class women began working as postmistresses, clerical workers, governesses, and typesetters. Historian Jane Turner Censer describes the occupations held by two unmarried sisters during Reconstruction as somewhat typical: Saidie Mason worked as a companion and housekeeper, while Susan worked as a library clerk at the Washington Naval Library (Censer 2003, 181).

Other women turned to teaching as a source of income, including Rebecca Latimer Felton, a Georgia woman, who opened a school in January 1866 (Scott 1970, 93). A system of common schools reliant on a teaching corps of young women had emerged in the North by the 1830s. It was only after the Civil War that such a change occurred in the South. Historian Anne Firor Scott describes the period as a revival of education (Scott 1970, 111). During the war itself, some institutions for higher learning, such as Trinity College in North Carolina, allowed women to occupy the seats left empty by Confederate soldiers. After the war, many schools began looking

Photo of Rebecca Latimer Felton taken between 1909 and 1932. (Library of Congress)

to provide young Southern women with an education that was not just ornamental but that included academic subjects that would better prepare them for some degree of economic independence.

Accompanying this revival of schooling was the growth of a female teaching force. During the Civil War, the percentage of female teachers in North Carolina rose from 10 percent to 40 percent. This figure dropped upon soldiers' return to 25 percent, but by 1880, for the first time in Southern history, the majority of schoolteachers were female rather than male (Censer 2003, 156; Faust 1996, 251). During Reconstruction, many elite and middle-class white women taught in public schools, opened private schools, or worked at the female academies that had long existed for elite girls.

As had occurred in the antebellum North, teaching became a socially acceptable way for elite and middle-class women to engage in paid labor. Kate DeRosset Meares, whose husband had been killed in the Seven Days' Battle, worked as a teacher (and ultimately a principal) for 15 years while bringing up her three sons without attracting criticism for her dual public and private roles (Censer 2003, 166–167). Southern women also recognized that the education they offered was preparing younger women to earn a living later in life. Mary Louisa Carrington, a widow in Virginia who turned to teaching to support herself and her two daughters, made sure that her daughters, Willie and Bessie, received schooling so that they, too, could live independently if necessary (Censer 2003, 17). In 1884, the Mississippi legislature established the state's Industrial Institute and College to provide industrial preparation, teacher training, and all-around education to women. It was the first state-supported college for women in the United States and served as an indication of how much had changed since the Civil War.

In addition to teaching, some educated Southern women turned to writing as a means of generating income. Southern women could aspire to write for local newspapers; regional magazines such as *Southern Magazine* or *The Land We Love*; or even national forums such as *The Nation, Atlantic Monthly*, and the *North American Review*. Additionally, some Southern women such as Augusta Jane Evans wrote novels. Evan's novels included *Macaria; Or, Altars of Sacrifice* (1864) and *St. Elmo* (1866). Paid work as writers also gave white women an outlet for their (sometimes racist) feelings about Reconstruction. Mary Tucker Magill, for instance, published a short story in 1871 about households in Virginia that featured ungrateful slaves who had run away during the war (Censer 2003, 274).

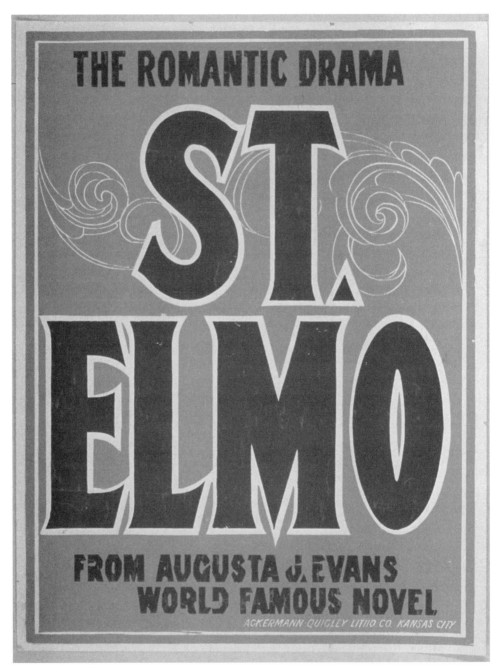

Poster for *St. Elmo,* the world-famous novel by Augusta Jane Evans. (Library of Congress)

Augusta Jane Evans

Augusta Jane Evans Wilson (1835–1909) was one of the most prominent Southern woman writers of the 19th century. During her lifetime, Evans wrote a total of nine novels, of which the most famous, *St. Elmo* (1866), appeared during Reconstruction. Evans originally turned to writing as a means to make money for her family, and her widespread popularity brought her family some financial relief from the hardships of the Reconstruction era.

Evans staunchly supported the Confederacy during and after the war. Legend has it that she even broke off her engagement in 1860 because her fiancé supported Lincoln, and her pro-Southern attitudes and visceral hatred of the Republican Party were reflected in her writing at the time. In the late years of the Civil War, Evans (already known for writing two previous novels, the first when she was just 15) published *Macaria; or, Altars of Sacrifice* (1864), which historian Jane Turner Censer identifies as the most important Confederate novel published. Evans intended her work to

rally Southern men and women to the floundering cause (Censer 2003, 210–211). In the novel, Evans detailed the Battle of Manassas and encouraged female devotion to the cause and to their soldiers. At the war's end, Evans was devastated by the Confederacy's defeat, and in her Reconstruction-era novels she idealized the world of the Old South as it crumbled around her. *St. Elmo,* a novel populated with sentimental heroines and heroes, became a best seller of such popularity that even towns were named after it.

Evans married a wealthy widowed planter in 1868 and continued to write, publishing five more sentimental novels before her death in 1909. One of her last novels, *A Speckled Bird* (1902), glorified a Confederate widow heading up the Maurice family. In the book, a Maurice daughter who had married a Yankee died—a fitting punishment, according to Evans, whose anger over her perception of Northern aggression during Reconstruction had not faded with time.

White Women and the Transformation of White Supremacy

On the eve of war, 4 million African Americans—33 percent of the Southern population—were enslaved (Edwards 2000, 49). In the war's aftermath, African Americans embraced freedom, fleeing plantations, embracing education, and trying to create new lives for their families. Many elite white women, trapped in the twisted, racist logic of antebellum proslavery thought, found dealing with former slaves challenging. To women such as Gertrude Thomas and Kate Stone, it seemed as though all the foundations of society had been shattered by the war and emancipation. Southern white women were by no means exempt from racist beliefs and practices. They worked stubbornly to reassert supremacy over African American domestic servants and poor white women, and in the process they helped to undermine Reconstruction.

Looking ahead during the Civil War, some white women had exhibited concern over the loss of African American domestic labor. Betty Herndon Maury recorded her distress when she heard her small daughter, while playing house, complaining about how all the slaves had run away (Culpepper 2002, 123–124). During the early years of Reconstruction, Gertrude Thomas grew increasingly frustrated by her inability to hire live-in domestic help. When one of her former slaves was unwilling to stay on (without her children) to work and live at Thomas's house for 25 cents a week, Thomas was dismayed, and her reaction was not atypical. By 1870, 28 percent of former large slaveholders in Fauquier County, Virginia, had no live-in servants, and by 1880, this figure had risen to 50 percent (Edwards 2000, 173; Censer 2003, 71).

In addition to being confronted by African Americans' refusal to "live in," white women also resentfully contended with a labor force that could now bargain for wages and terms of employment, and even quit. In her study of African American women in Atlanta, Tera Hunter describes the effects that African American laundresses' newfound power to negotiate had on white women accustomed to issuing commands rather than striking bargains. When Virginia Shelton offered a job to Hannah, an African American with a reputation as a skilled cook and laundress, Hannah bargained for an additional job for her laborer husband. Shelton offered her 5 dollars a month for her services and 10 for her husband's, but Hannah successfully insisted on earning 8 and 15 dollars, respectively (Hunter 1997, 30–31). An 1881 strike by Atlanta's washerwomen further demonstrated this newfound bargaining power—and white women's sense that this assertiveness on the part of African Americans threatened their status.

Many elite white women like Gertrude Thomas seemed genuinely bewildered at what they perceived as a loss of respect from their former slaves. Some were surprised and then angered when freedmen and freedwomen asserted their independence. In her eastern Tennessee community, Eliza Fain observed a quarrel that a neighbor, a woman she identified only as Mrs. N, had with a servant. In her diary, Fain dryly interpreted the strife that resulted from the racial equality forced on white Southerners by the war and added that she prayed that God would show African Americans their obligations to the former slaveholders who had once protected them (Fain 2004, 331). Fain's lack of ability to accept African American equality was not uncommon, among both elite and common white women (and men) in the South.

Some scholars point to the wistful creation of a "mammy" figure as a response to this lack of acceptance, a symbol used by white Southerners to convince themselves that such a dutiful slave had once existed.

Laura Edwards asserts that by the 1870s, a tense truce had developed between elite white women and black women, but she acknowledges that relations were always on edge and that some white women even participated in the violence that African Americans increasingly faced (Edwards 2000, 174). Although some black workers, such as the aforementioned Hannah, bargained successfully with would-be employers for higher pay, not all African Americans who asserted their rights were so fortunate. Eliza Jane Ellison, an African American domestic, was shot by an employer when she demanded extra wages for doing additional laundry, and other domestics faced similar abuse (Hunter 1997, 31). Although some white women of the South did work on behalf of former slaves or for the Republican Party (whom the Ku Klux Klan also targeted), more often white women condoned the violence that emerged during Reconstruction and the lynching campaigns that followed in the 1890s. For example, Southern women stitched robes for husbands or fathers who were members of the Ku Klux Klan, an organization that was founded ostensibly to "protect" white women. One woman, Elizabeth Avery Meriwether, even attended planning sessions for the Memphis chapter of the Klan that was founded by her husband (Hodes 1997, 159; Culpepper 2002, 4).

While white women negotiated relationships with African American women in the changing world of Reconstruction, they also negotiated new relationships with white men, especially within their own household. Scholars have described an antebellum ideal of female dependence, a Southern "belle" whose status was exemplified by her dependent position in the social structure of the antebellum South. It was as if such a woman, historian Anne Firor Scott famously wrote, was on a pedestal.

During the Civil War, Southern women had taken charge of plantations, labored in fields, and worked in hospitals, becoming independent out of necessity. Even elite Southern belles were forced into independence, and as a result, their relationships with the men on whom they had formerly depended shifted. Historian Joan Cashin describes the wartime experience of Kate and William McLure. While William was away at war, Kate became increasingly confident in her ability to manage their Upcountry plantation. Cashin argues that upon William's return from war in 1865, he was surprised to find that the wife he thought of as delicate was no longer so. Southern manhood was also challenged by the economic situation that meant that the majority of Southern men could no longer afford dependent

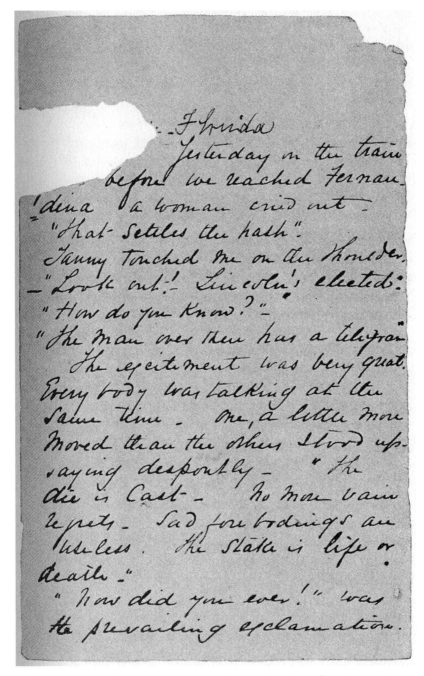

Leaf from Mary Boykin Chesnut's Civil War diary. (Chesnut, Mary, *A Diary from Dixie,* 1905)

wives. Though famous diarist Mary Chesnut's husband originally mocked her plans for a butter and eggs business, in the hardship of the early days of Reconstruction, he later sought to borrow money from her profits (Culpepper 2002, 228). The Reconstruction era thus witnessed a breakdown of antebellum traditions of courtship and propriety, as the very notion of the belle shifted to encompass more active and independent women.

As a result of such developments, according to LeeAnn Whites, the years between 1860 and 1890 were marked by a "crisis in gender" (Whites 2005). Other historians point to a broader crisis, as the Civil War disrupted many antebellum race- and gender-based ideologies. Laura Edwards has persuasively argued that the household was at the center of this crisis and redefinition of gender ideals. In *Gendered Strife and Confusion,* Edwards describes how, prior to the Civil War, relationships between masters and slaves and husbands and wives had structured Southern society. After the war, the ideal of the belle on a pedestal was no longer feasible, and it was replaced by new ideals of domesticity and "worthy womanhood" (Edwards 1987, 130). Magazines, newspapers, and novels highlighted the need for "cheerful wives" to create "cheerful homes" (Edwards, 2000, 182). In embracing Victorian ideals of domesticity, which they deemed common white and African American women to be incapable of achieving, the white Southern elite attempted to regain the upper hand and reinscribe white supremacy. In addition to violence and ideas of "worthy" womanhood, the law was also employed to shore up boundaries between the races (Bardaglio 1995, 184). After emancipation, the Southern states enacted the Black Codes, which discriminated against African Americans, and attempted to restrict their social, political, and economic mobility. Even personal relationships were politicized, as laws were passed to prohibit interracial marriage, a development that Martha Hodes explains as resulting from the growing white male fear that in a world without slavery, sex between white women and African American men would become more common (Hodes 1997).

Southern White Women, Voluntary Associations, and a Growing Public Sphere

The 1890s and subsequent decades would be marked by Southern devotion to the "Lost Cause," a mythical vision that conceived of the prewar South as a harmonious society that brave soldiers had defended in the face of tyrannical Northern states. Through the United Daughters of the Confederacy

(UDC), which was founded in 1894, Southern women played an important role in creating and popularizing the Lost Cause. The work that women did in the UDC built upon their earlier participation in memorial associations during the late 1860s and 1870s. During Reconstruction, white Southern women were active in other organizations, too. Like their Northern counterparts, they played a much more prominent role than before the war in the public sphere through their work in reform societies, churches, and even suffrage associations. Historians debate the extent to which the Civil War and its aftermath affected Southern white women's self-perceptions, but there is little debate that after the war, voluntary associations gained a vibrancy that they had not previously possessed.

What Marilyn Culpepper labels "battlefield pilgrimages" began almost immediately after the Confederate defeat. In March 1866, Sarah Carter and her friends visited several sites, including that of the Seven Pines battle, and such pilgrimages soon morphed into broader commemorative work (Culpepper 2002, 191). For example, in October 1866, Floride Clemson participated in a memorial ceremony for Confederate dead in Pendleton, South Carolina. There, 50 women paraded with banners emblazoned with dead soldiers' names and the dates and places of their deaths. Following the parade, the women laid wreaths on graves in the local cemetery (Culpepper 2002, 232). Similar scenes occurred in various locations across the South in the 1860s and 1870s.

In the spring and summer of 1866, Southern women organized chapters of the Ladies Memorial Association (LMA) in many locales. Through the LMA, they worked to preserve Confederate cemeteries, recover bodies, and honor the dead. Their work in the LMA marked the first major instance of Southern women's embrace of association work. A typical example comes from Winchester, Virginia. There, after a farmer found the remains of two dead soldiers, women formed a memorial society to take care of their reburial (Censer 2003, 191–192). Similarly, in Petersburg, Virginia, a chapter of the LMA was founded in May 1866. Originally organized to identify and move remains of Confederate soldiers, the chapter sent several female members to convince the president of a railroad company to transport Confederate corpses for free. By December 1866, the LMA had located 5,000 graves and had ordered more than 600 headstones to mark them. The following February, the women solicited bids for preparing 4,000 more headstones. Additionally, they worked with the Petersburg Common Council to construct a 500-grave cemetery. By June 1868, the LMA treasurer recorded having spent $1,000 on moving and reburying bodies (Censer 2003, 194–195).

Women pay respects at Confederate cemetery, Charleston, South Carolina. The Ladies Memorial Association (LMA) strove to preserve Confederate cemeteries in southern states throughout the 1860s and 1870s. (Library of Congress)

The work of bringing home, burying, and memorializing the dead was difficult. Southern cemeteries were in disarray following the war, and locating remains could be a logistical nightmare. But Southern women embraced work in the LMA, and its chapters had the largest membership of any women's organization in the South in the 1870s and 1880s (Whites 2005, 87). While prominent men performed many of the organizational tasks (such as managing finances and delivering public speeches), Southern women subtly assumed some power in the public sphere through participation in the LMA. Just as women in the antebellum North had justified antislavery work on the basis of women's moral capacity and religious devotion, through their work in LMA and its successor groups, like the UDC, white Southern women worked to preserve the memory (as well as the grave sites) of the Civil War dead (Whites 2005, 90). In doing so, they laid a foundation for the claim—which flourished in the 1890s—that Southern men had been noble soldiers fighting for liberty and a way of life that had been harmonious, orderly, and happy.

Many white Southern women soon became active in other women's clubs and reform organizations. Throughout the 1870s and 1880s, a variety of reforming associations were formed in the South. Some of these organizations stemmed from work in churches, and some, like the LMA, grew directly from the war. In Charleston, South Carolina, Mary Amarintha Snowden (also president of the local LMA) worked to found the Home for Mothers, Widows, and Daughters of Confederate Soldiers, which at one time housed 70 people and educated 50 children (Whites 2005, 91). Similarly, the New Orleans Ladies Benevolent Association staged balls for honoring the dead and for the benefit of women who were orphaned, widowed, and wounded (Culpepper 2002, 231).

In the 1880s and 1890s, Southern women also joined reform associations linked to temperance and suffrage. In 1874, the Women's Christian Temperance Union was founded by Frances Willard, who built on women's temperance campaigns in small midwestern towns. In the 1880s and 1890s, Southern women (including Gertrude Thomas) became active in temperance work. Jane Turner Censer points out that in some temperance societies, African American and white Southern women even worked side by side to achieve the goal of prohibiting alcohol. Additionally, women of all classes became involved in the grange movement of the 1860s and 1870s. An organization founded for education and advancement of farmers, the grange offered membership to women as well as to men.

By 1870, a few Southern women took their newfound independence and reforming voice even further and began to work for women's suffrage. The Virginia Suffrage Association was founded in 1870, a year after suffrage resolutions were read at constitutional conventions in Texas and Arkansas. In 1870, a women's rights convention was held in Columbia, South Carolina. Elizabeth Avery Meriwether, whose husband worked to found the local chapter of the Klan and who edited the prosuffrage *Tennessee Tablet*, suggested that white women should have the vote in order to counter black power at the ballot box (Scott 1970, 173–174). By 1881, Meriwether was traveling and lecturing throughout New England on the women's suffrage issue, but she stayed away from the subject in the South, where she kept to the more conventional and less controversial topic of temperance. Although some Southern women such as Gertrude Thomas would become active in the suffrage movement by the 1890s, there was no widespread suffrage sentiment in the South in the late 19th century. Most Southern women declined to participate in either the National Woman's Suffrage Association or the American Women's Suffrage Association, which were founded by Northern reformers Elizabeth Cady Stanton, Susan B. Anthony, and Lucy Stone, respectively.

Conclusion

The Reconstruction era brought widespread changes to the lives of white Southern women. Many elite women, whether by force or choice, abandoned the ideal of the sheltered Southern belle and began to undertake domestic chores, seek a degree of financial independence, and work in reform associations. Large numbers of common women also worked in reform societies and, more than ever, engaged in paid labor and sharecropping. Some women found the transformations invigorating, but many resented the newfound freedom that African Americans enjoyed. As a result, even while their lives were changing, some white Southern women, like others in the United States, worked to strengthen the ideology of white supremacy that Southern society and race relations had been founded upon.

References and Further Reading

Anderson, John Q., ed. 1955. *Brokenburn: The Journal of Kate Stone, 1861–1868*. Baton Rouge: Louisiana State University Press.

Bardaglio, Peter W. 1995. *Reconstructing the Household: Families, Sex, and the Law in the Nineteenth-Century South*. Chapel Hill: University of North Carolina Press.

Censer, Jane Turner. 2003. *The Reconstruction of White Southern Womanhood, 1865–1895*. Baton Rouge: Louisiana State University Press.

Culpepper, Marilyn Mayer. 2002. *All Things Altered: Women in the Wake of Civil War and Reconstruction*. Jefferson, NC: McFarland.

Culpepper, Marilyn Mayer. 2004. *Women of the Civil War South: Personal Accounts from Diaries, Letters, and Postwar Reminiscences*. Jefferson, NC: McFarland.

Edwards, Laura F. 1997. *Gendered Strife and Confusion: The Political Culture of Reconstruction.* Urbana: University of Illinois Press.

Edwards, Laura F. 2000. *Scarlett Doesn't Live Here Anymore: Southern Women in the Civil War Era.* Urbana: University of Illinois Press.

Fain, John N., ed. 2004. *Sanctified Trial: The Diary of Eliza Rhea Anderson Fain, a Confederate Woman in East Tennessee.* Knoxville: University of Tennessee Press.

Faust, Drew Gilpin. 1996. *Mothers of Invention: Women of the Slaveholding South in the American Civil War.* New York: Vintage.

Hodes, Martha. 1997. *White Women, Black Men: Illicit Sex in the Nineteenth Century South.* New Haven, CT: Yale University Press.

Hunter, Tera W. 1997. *To 'Joy My Freedom: Southern Black Women's Lives and Labors after the Civil War.* Cambridge, MA: Harvard University Press.

Lincoln, Abraham. 1865. "Last Public Address." In *Abraham Lincoln Online: Speeches and Writings.* (Online information; retrieved 4/28/08.) http://showcase.netins.net/web/creative/lincoln/speeches/last.htm.

Painter, Nell Irvin. 1990. "Introduction: The Journal of Ella Gertrude Clanton Thomas: An Educated Southern White Woman in the Era of Slavery, War, and Reconstruction." In *The Secret Eye: The Journal of Ella Gertrude Clanton Thomas, 1848–1889,* ed. Virginia Ingraham Burr. Chapel Hill: University of North Carolina Press.

Scott, Anne Firor. 1970. *The Southern Lady: From Pedestal to Politics, 1830–1930.* Chicago: University of Chicago Press.

Weiner, Marli F. 1998. *Mistresses and Slaves: Plantation Women in South Carolina, 1830–80.* Urbana: University of Illinois Press.

Whites, LeeAnn. 2005. *Gender Matters: Civil War, Reconstruction, and the Making of the New South.* New York: Palgrave Macmillan.

African Americans in Southern Cities $\quad$ 3

James M. Campbell

In the spring and summer of 1866, race riots erupted in the cities of Memphis and New Orleans. Dozens were killed, mainly African Americans murdered by white mobs, and property worth hundreds of thousands of dollars, including black churches, schools, and homes, was destroyed. The riots were products of urban racial tensions and evidence of the dangers that black Southerners faced in the cities of the former Confederacy. Nevertheless, for most African Americans, such dangers were outweighed by the opportunities presented by city life.

From Richmond, Virginia, to New Orleans, Southern cities held for African Americans enticing prospects of employment, a rich community life, education, the chance to participate in political organizations, and a substantial degree of personal autonomy. Lured by these features of the urban environment, African Americans moved to cities in the thousands in the years after the Civil War and carved out lives for themselves that challenged notions of white supremacy in ways that were rarely possible in the rural South. Even after the restoration of Democratic Party rule in the South, urban race relations remained distinct from plantation and farming regions. Urban black communities were not always united on all issues, but they were strong and resourceful. This adaptability was due to several factors, including the distinctive legacy of urban slavery; the large numbers of free African Americans who had lived in cities during the antebellum era; and, especially in the early years of Reconstruction, the stationing of Freedmen's Bureau agents and federal soldiers in cities. Moreover, the long-standing but informal structures of race relations that continued to

Scenes in Memphis, Tennessee, during the riot: burning a Freedmen's schoolhouse and shooting down African Americans on May 2, 1866. (Library of Congress)

shape black-white interactions in traditional rural communities were less effective at maintaining white social dominance in the dynamic and changing urban world, where they were challenged by the demands and culture of the market economy and extensive interracial relationships that flourished, especially among the lower classes.

Urbanization in the North and South

In the mid-19th century, many of the social and economic developments that occurred in Southern cities were common to urban areas throughout the United States. For example, Southern merchants, manufacturers, and municipal governments shared the concern of their Northern counterparts with profits and progress. Southern cities also introduced services ranging from fire and police protection to public streetcars and sewage systems that were features of city life across the nation. Likewise, social dislocation plagued cities on either side of the Mason-Dixon Line. For millions of poor urban Americans, black and white, life in the mid-19th century was marked by crime, poverty, and overcrowded and unsanitary living conditions, as well as unstable and low-paid employment.

Yet, even though Southern cities were part of a national urban culture that transcended the sectional divide, they were also marked by the distinctive influence of their region (Kimball 2000, xviii). Several factors tended toward the emergence of Southern urban societies that would have seemed alien to residents of New York or Chicago. In comparison with Northern cities, the leading urban centers of the South during Reconstruction typically had much larger black populations, fewer European immigrants, and relatively underdeveloped manufacturing and industrial sectors. Southern cities were also infused with the values, culture, and concerns of the white planters who dominated the antebellum era and fought to regain their political power and assert white supremacy throughout the Reconstruction years. Finally, the legacies of slavery and emancipation, the impact of federal Reconstruction policies, and the challenge of rebuilding infrastructures and economies that were left shattered by the war all gave a uniquely regional flavor to life in Southern cities.

Population Growth in the Urban South: From Slavery to Freedom

Throughout the 19th century, Southern cities were anomalous locations within a region that was overwhelmingly agricultural. In 1860, only

7.1 percent of Southerners lived in towns or cities, in comparison with almost 20 percent of Northerners. While the economies and populations of Northern cities like New York, Boston, Philadelphia, and Chicago boomed on the back of mass immigration from Europe and the expansion of industry and manufacturing, New Orleans and Louisville were the only cities in the Confederacy with populations greater than 50,000. On the eve of secession, other leading Southern cities, such as Richmond, Virginia; Charleston, South Carolina; Savannah, Georgia; Mobile, Alabama; and Memphis, had populations of between 20,000 and 40,000 people, and both during the antebellum period and throughout Reconstruction, towns with populations of less than 4,000 people represented the characteristic Southern urban settlement (Wade 1964, 326–327).

The limited rate of urban expansion that occurred in the antebellum South has been explained by many historians as a consequence of slavery: slaveholders rooted in the aristocratic cultural traditions of plantation society were slow to invest in the new industries that fueled urban growth in the mid-19th-century North. Furthermore, the demands of the Southern economy, almost wholly dependent as it was on staple crop production, encouraged the development of small towns rather than great metropolises. In addition, several factors discouraged slaveholders from keeping slaves in city environments. Uppermost among the concerns of many slaveholders were the more extensive opportunities for slave resistance that existed in cities in comparison with rural regions (Takagi 1999, 6; Wade 1964, 243). Moreover, even if slaves could be adequately disciplined in cities, slaveholders often concluded that greater profits could be made from employing slaves in agricultural pursuits rather than in urban occupations (Goldin 1976, 9).

In the years of the Civil War and Reconstruction, the population of Southern cities grew steadily, but overall rates of urbanization in the region continued to lag far behind the rest of the United States and, in particular, the Northeast. In part, this lag reflected the colonial nature of the North-South economic relationship and the rapid evolution of the national railroad system that enabled Southern producers to transport goods directly to Northern cities, bypassing Southern ports (Goldfield 1981, 1016). Overall, by 1890, approximately 35 percent of the U.S. population lived in towns and cities of more than 2,500 people. In the South, however, urban residents were just 13 percent of the total population. Nevertheless, individual cities had experienced substantial growth. Typical of this trend was Richmond, the capital city of the Confederacy, which saw its population increase from 38,000 in 1860 to 51,000 in 1870. Ten years later, Richmond's population stood at almost 64,000, an increase of more than 50 percent in just 20 years. During the same period, the population of other long-estab-lished Southern port cities such as New Orleans, Charleston, Savannah, and Mobile grew at a similar rate, but the most accelerated population ex-pansion of all occurred in interior towns, such as Atlanta and Nashville, that flourished as a result of the postwar boom in railroad construction (Rabinowitz 1996, 19).

African Americans accounted for most of the increase in the South's urban population during Reconstruction. While the white population stag-nated and in some cities even declined, the number of black Americans in Southern cities doubled in the five years after the war's end. In Raleigh, North Carolina, and Charleston, blacks were a majority of the population by 1870, while in many other cities, including Atlanta, Savannah, Rich-mond, and Montgomery, Alabama, there were almost as many blacks as whites. The largest urban black population was in New Orleans, where the number of African Americans doubled during the 1860s to 50,495, or 26 percent of the city's total population (Rabinowitz 1996, 19; Blassingame 1976, 221, 324).

No longer confined by slavery to their owners' farms and plantations, for many freedpeople, moving to a city was a symbolic assertion of their liberty, but it was also a means to more pragmatic ends. Almost all rural migrants arrived in cities hoping to improve the material conditions of their lives, whether though finding new forms of employment; involving them-selves in black community groups, schools, and churches; or simply obtain-ing food and other forms of poor relief from the Union army or Freedmen's Bureau. For many others, the most pressing motivation was to trace family members from whom they had been separated by the cruel vagaries of the domestic slave trade. Charles Maho arrived in Richmond with the Union army in April 1865, hoping to find the family he had left behind when he was sold to a Mississippi cotton planter in the late 1850s. But his search had a bittersweet conclusion; although reunited with his daughter, Maho learned upon reaching Richmond that his wife had died years before (Rachleff 1989, 15).

The influx of rural migrants to Southern cities contributed to the for-mation of urban black communities that were more diverse, developed, and divided than was typical in agricultural parts of the South. While white Southerners tended to negate the significance of differences within the African American community, marked variations in class and skin color could be found among nonwhite urban residents that were both a symbol of black social advancement and also, at times, a cause of division and disunity among African Americans. This division was in part a legacy of the antebellum era and the distinctive experiences of urban slaves, but it also reflected the extensive economic, social, educational, and political opportunities that opened up to many African Americans in Southern cities after the Civil War.

Several distinct groups of African Americans existed within urban society in the Reconstruction South. Most numerous were freedmen and freedwomen who had been enslaved in cities and emancipated during the war years. Their lives as slaves had not been easy (see Chapter 1), yet those freedpeople who had been enslaved in cities before the war were more likely than plantation laborers to have lived and worked independently of their owners and often had exploited the greater freedom the city allowed to earn a small wage, learn a trade, and obtain a degree of literacy. These antebellum experiences placed urban freedpeople in a better position than those from rural areas to benefit from the new opportunities for employment and education that emancipation offered. For their part, rural migrants to Southern cities were sometimes met with hostility by established black residents who resented the additional competition for the limited resources of urban relief agencies and the competition they created for jobs and school places. In the aftermath of the Memphis race riot in 1866, established black residents even called for the removal of former slaves recently arrived from the countryside whom they held responsible for increasing racial tensions in the city (Foner 1988, 262).

A substantial minority of the black men and women in Reconstruction-era Southern cities had been free before the Civil War. Legal and customary restrictions on black employment and civil rights forced most antebellum free blacks to live in poverty, yet, even so, on the eve of Reconstruction they were more likely than recently freed African Americans to be literate, to be financially stable, and to work in skilled trades. In the war's immediate aftermath, those African Americans whose freedom predated emancipation assumed many of the leadership positions within the black community and played an integral role in the expansion of institutions such as black churches, schools, labor unions, benevolent societies, and political organizations.

In some cities, a legacy of mutual ambivalence and distrust characterized relations between historically free African Americans and those who obtained their liberty only at the end of the Civil War. This was especially true in the Gulf Coast cities of New Orleans and Mobile, as well as in Charleston, where skin color as well as free status had traditionally delineated divisions within the African American community. In these Deep

South cities, light-skinned free mulattoes, some with ancestral links to Spanish and French colonists, had constituted an African American elite during the antebellum decades, and many feared that emancipation would undermine their social standing. This fear was reflected in the persistence in postwar Charleston of the Brown Fellowship Society, an organization founded in the antebellum period that specifically excluded dark-skinned African Americans from its membership. Some mulattoes who had been free before the war also aligned themselves politically against the freed-people, while others refused to send their children to primarily black schools.

The Course of Reconstruction in Southern Cities

Southern cities embarked on Reconstruction at different times and in contrasting states of disrepair that reflected their varying experiences of the Civil War. On the eve of Richmond's eventual capitulation to Gen. Ulysses S. Grant's Army of the Potomac, the city's business district was burned to the ground by fleeing Confederates. Similarly widespread damage followed the arrival of Union troops in Atlanta and Columbia, South Carolina, while Gen. William T. Sherman himself reported that the town of Meridian, Mississippi, barely still existed, so thoroughly had his men destroyed its railroads, storehouses, hospitals, and offices (Shank 1964, 282). By contrast, Mobile, Alabama, and Austin, Texas, were among towns left mostly unscathed by the arrival of Union forces. Still other cities, like Nashville, New Orleans, and Vicksburg, Mississippi, had experienced at least two years of Union rule by the time the war ended, though Vicksburg had scarcely begun to recover from the siege that precipitated its fall in 1863.

In all Southern cities, the defeat of the Confederacy left economic and political instability and promised social upheavals that were met with trepidation by whites and unprecedented expectancy among African Americans. Across the South, urban black communities celebrated emancipation with parades and festivities, but this optimism, which characterized the weeks immediately following Gen. Robert E. Lee's surrender at Appomattox, soon gave way to dismay at the early course of municipal Reconstruction. Although occupying forces in Southern cities enforced emancipation, during the summer of 1865 Union occupiers introduced policies to deal with urban migrants and refugees that seemed more in tune with the interests and ideals of former slaveholders than the needs and demands of the freedpeople.

The most pressing issues for Union commanders were to secure the loyalty of the white population and to provide food and provisions for the tens of thousands of urban residents and refugees driven to destitution by the war. As many as 10,000 families in New Orleans were dependent on army provisions during the final two years of the war, while in Richmond, within three weeks of the conflict's end, an army-operated relief commission was feeding more than 15,000 people (O'Brien 1981, 269). In counties around Atlanta, up to 50,000 people faced starvation in the spring and summer of 1865, as men, women, and children walked many miles to the city in the hope of obtaining relief (Thornberry 1974, 237).

For the most part, army-distributed federal aid in Southern cities was directed toward whites. Union officials feared that providing African Americans equal access to poor relief would attract more rural black laborers to Southern cities, exacerbating problems of urban overcrowding and further undermining labor control on plantations where white landowners were struggling to adjust to the newly liberated status of their workforce. In light of these concerns, throughout the summer of 1865, federal troops enforced repressive measures that restricted aid to African Americans and limited their freedom of movement and employment in cities. For example, rural black migrants in Charleston were warned to return to their farms and threatened with forced labor if found to be unemployed in the city (Jenkins 1998, 51). In Richmond, African Americans were forced to sign labor contracts before receiving economic relief, while freedmen who could not present a pass signed by a white person attesting to their identity and employment were subject to arrest by Union soldiers (Foner 1988, 154; O'Brien 1981, 271).

In addition to the limitations on black rights imposed by the Union armies, in the months after the end of the war African Americans were further disadvantaged by the rapid return to municipal power of the antebellum ruling elite. As early as May 1865, in Mobile, the Mayor's Court, which investigated all crimes committed in the city and imposed punishments for minor offenses, resumed operations, enforcing much the same oppressive regulations against the city's black population as it had prior to emancipation (Fitzgerald 2002, 32). The following month in Richmond saw the return to office of Joseph Mayo, who had served as mayor for 13 years until the city's surrender to Grant's army and was renowned for the brutal whippings he imposed on slaves during the 1850s. In a petition submitted to President Andrew Johnson and reprinted in the *New York Tribune* requesting protection from Mayo's regime, black Richmonders recorded the repression they endured in the summer after emancipation: "The military and police authorities will not allow us to walk the streets by day or night, in the regular pursuit of our business or on our way to church, without a *pass,* and passes do not in all cases protect us from arrest, insult, abuse, violence and imprisonment" (Holt and Brown 2000).

With such conditions prevailing in Southern cities in the summer of 1865, and notwithstanding the presence of black federal troops, the conduct of the Union army was met with approval by at least some Southern whites. Seventeen-year-old Emma LeConte of Columbia, South Carolina, wrote of the manner in which the local Union commander, Colonel Haughton, had governed the city since its surrender. While reluctant "to admit anything good of a Yankee," LeConte acknowledged that Houghton had been "all kindness and consideration to the [white] citizens" (LeConte 1998, 82). The *Commercial Bulletin* was similarly complimentary about the occupying forces in Richmond, praising their "forebearance, moderation, courtesy and benevolence" (cited in O'Brien 1981, 270).

Throughout 1866, the position of the African American community in urban societies remained precarious. Despite the presence of federal troops, Freedmen's Bureau agents, and missionaries associated with Northern religious and benevolent associations, the influence of the antebellum white elite remained strong, and black political influence and civil rights were severely constrained. During this era of presidential Reconstruction, African Americans were unable to vote, were rarely appointed to city government posts, and were almost entirely excluded from serving on city police forces. Reports of police brutality against freedpeople remained widespread, and city courts rarely provided protection for African Americans from any form of white violence except, in some cases, under pressure from the Freedmen's Bureau. Following the Memphis riot of 1866, for example, reports filed with the Freedmen's Bureau noted that "although many of the perpetrators are known, no arrests have been made, nor is there now any indication on the part of the Civil Authorities that any are meditated by them" (Bureau of Refugees, Freedmen, and Abandoned Lands 1866). Such attitudes reflected the existence of racial tensions between African Americans and lower-class whites in Southern cities, as well as the continued political dominance of the former slaveholding class.

Only with the passage of the Civil Rights Act of 1866, the Military Reconstruction Acts the following year, and ratification of the Fourteenth Amendment in 1868 did municipal politics in the South begin to respond to the interests of the African American community. Empowered with the ballot, urban black voters helped Republican candidates win municipal elections across the South in 1867 and 1868. For the first time, too, African

The Memphis Riot of 1866

On April 30, 1866, all troops in the three black Union regiments stationed in Memphis were discharged at the expiration of their terms of service. The following day, a crowd of between 30 and 60 of these former soldiers, most still wearing their blue Union army uniforms, gathered on South Street, in Memphis' Sixth Ward, to rescue from police custody a fellow black veteran. The police and white civilians began firing on the black crowd, and several hours of conflict ensued. After nightfall, the veterans sought refuge at Fort Pickering, on the outskirts of the city, where they were subsequently confined on the orders of Gen. George Stoneman, commander of the Union forces in Memphis.

Over the next two days and nights, while federal troops stood by, white mobs subjected Memphis's African American community to a reign of violent terror. By May 3, when General Stoneman belatedly ordered the enforcement of martial law, 46 African Americans lay dead. All had been unarmed at the time they were killed. White rioters had also raped six black women, committed countless robberies and assaults, and burned to the ground property worth in excess of $100,000, including 4 black churches, 12 schools, and 91 private homes.

Americans won seats on city councils, and in many localities black officers also began to serve on the police force and in the fire department. In Mobile, the first African American police officers were appointed in July 1867, and by the time that the city's first Republican mayor, Gustavus Horton, left office the following year, black men accounted for 20 of the city's 67 officers (Fitzgerald 2002, 103). In Charleston, Montgomery, and Vicksburg, African Americans comprised between 40 and 50 percent of the police force by 1870, proportions broadly similar to their share of those cities' total populations. There were also substantial numbers of black policemen in Mobile, New Orleans, and Portsmouth, Virginia, although in other leading Southern cities, including Richmond, Savannah, and Louisville, African Americans remained excluded from the police force throughout Reconstruction (Rousey 1985, 359).

Republican city governments held great promise for African Americans, yet Radical rule was short-lived in most of the urban South. As a result of violence at the polls, voter registration irregularities, gerrymandering, and the strength of Democratic Party appeals to white supremacy, Republicans lost control of Nashville's city council as early as 1869. Within two years, both Richmond and Atlanta had also reverted to Democratic governance, although in some municipalities, Republicans clung to office for longer periods. In Raleigh, Democrats did not return to power until 1875, while

Two white men were also killed in the rioting, one by a stray bullet and another by his own, misfiring pistol.

The Memphis riots were caused by several factors. A large number of the rioters were Irishmen who lived in Memphis's Sixth Ward. Lower class but upwardly mobile, these men felt their prospects of economic and social uplift threatened in the year after the end of the Civil War by the growing number of rural freedpeople in the city, as well as the presence of black Union troops and Freedmen's Bureau agents. The rioters were further incited by Democratic Party–controlled newspapers, such as the *Memphis Argus,* and they acted with the tacit endorsement of Memphis's white elite. Moreover, their resort to collective violence was a product of their experiences serving in the Confederate Army and a consequence of a heritage in which ritualistic violence was an important form of social control.

In the months following the riot, Radical Republicans in Congress used the events in Memphis, as well as similar mob violence in New Orleans, to help win support for greater federal advocacy and protection for African American civil rights.

Charleston was not "redeemed" (see the Introduction to this book) until the time of Wade Hampton's state gubernatorial victory in 1876. Even after this time, when Democratic power was secure across the South and federal intervention in the former Confederate states had ceased, African Americans continued to serve in city government posts, but they did so in smaller numbers and with their political influence severely curtailed. This limitation was reflected in the makeup of Southern police forces, which, under conservative regimes, were purged of most, and in many cases all, of their black officers.

Work and Labor Organizations

The rise and decline of the Republican Party as a force in city elections during the late 1860s and 1870s provided the political context within which urban African Americans adjusted to the new social and economic realities of freedom. Radical rule provided increased opportunities for black men and women to improve their economic status, develop strong community institutions, move forward the struggle for civil rights, and secure protection from white violence. Yet Republican political power was not a precondition for these developments. Urban black life had its own internal dynamics, and throughout Reconstruction, change in Southern cities was driven by African Americans' organizational strength and their ambitions as individuals, families, and communities.

As had been the case during the antebellum era, during Reconstruction, most African Americans in Southern cities worked in unskilled laboring jobs or as domestic servants. In New Orleans in 1880, African American men accounted for 44 percent of the nearly 15,000 laborers in the city, even though they were only 24 percent of the city's total male labor force. Smaller numbers of men worked as domestic servants; black women dominated this profession. Immediately after emancipation, many freedwomen refused to work as domestics for white employers, considering such labor symbolic of servitude. However, economic necessity soon forced a reconsideration of this stance. Not only were black male incomes frequently insufficient to support a family but also urban black populations tended to have a higher number of female-headed households than either white city residents or African American rural residents in the South. This caused black women to enter the labor market far more frequently than their white counterparts. In Charleston in 1870, more than 50 percent of adult black women were gainfully employed, compared with only 14 percent of white women (Jenkins 1998, 99).

To a far greater extent than in rural areas, cities provided opportunities for African Americans to work as skilled artisans and, on rare occasions, in professional occupations. In all cities, there were substantial numbers of black tradesmen, although racial discrimination meant that skilled black workers were often concentrated in a small number of occupations, typically including barbering, carpentry, shoemaking, and baking. In cities with a developed manufacturing base, such as Richmond and New Orleans, African Americans also found work in tobacco factories, while throughout the urban South they kept groceries, saloons, and boardinghouses. The success of these service-sector businesses contributed to an increase in black property holding during Reconstruction. In Atlanta, the value of black-owned taxable property increased sevenfold between 1869 and 1874 to more than $250,000 (Rabinowitz 1996, 94). Similarly, the number of black landowners in Savannah rose from 96 in 1870 to 648 in 1880 (Blassingame 1973, 468).

While urban black property holders increased in number during Reconstruction, for most black workers, low wages, poor working conditions, and persistent racial discrimination remained the rule. One response to this situation within the black working community was the establishment of labor unions. Prior to the Civil War, slavery had undermined the development of unions in the Southern states, but even so, in most cities a workers' movement was emerging by the late antebellum decades, albeit overwhelmingly dominated by whites. After the Civil War, black workers, too, became active participants in labor organizations. Depending on the industry in which they worked and the city where they lived, some black workers were able to join existing white unions. However, motivated by an incipient black nationalism, as well as racial discrimination of the type that would undermine the labor movement in the United States for decades to come, other African Americans either chose or were forced to establish independent labor organizations.

Repeatedly during Reconstruction, black workers in cities instituted work stoppages as a means to obtain higher wages and improved working conditions, including shorter hours. The most organized workers in many cities were the longshoremen, who worked on the docks loading and unloading cargo. In September 1869, the Charleston Longshoremen's Protective Union Association (LPUA), formed the previous year, struck successfully for higher wages and a closed-shop agreement. The following month, a second LPUA strike led to the rehiring of a white longshoreman fired for his involvement in the Republican Party (Jenkins 1998, 67). Evidently, black industrial action could be motivated by political as well as explicitly economic considerations.

Apart from the workers' conviction and organizational strength, the success of black strike action was dependent on external factors, in particular, the availability of an alternative source of labor to break the strike. Here, the black longshoremen were at an advantage over workers in other occupations, for their labor was not only strenuous but also traditionally associated with slavery, which made it difficult for employers to hire whites to break the strike (Hine 1984, 505). Nevertheless, black workers in other occupations also organized themselves into unions and engaged in industrial action. Tailors and painters followed the longshoremen's lead and stopped work in Charleston in the fall of 1869, while in New Orleans between 1865 and 1880, at least 15 workers' associations were formed by African Americans. As well as longshoremen, these included organizations that represented steamboatmen, porters, and cigarmakers. Apart from improved pay and conditions, these unions provided social services and financial aid to members and their families (Blassingame 1976, 64).

Notwithstanding the efforts of labor unions, black employment patterns in cities fluctuated in accordance with changing political and economic circumstances. During years when cities had Republican administrations, more jobs typically became available to blacks through patronage, notably in the construction industry. By the mid-1870s, however, not only had most Southern cities been redeemed by Democratic election victories but also the Panic of 1873 and ensuing depression further constrained black economic prospects. For tens of thousands of African Americans, the economic outlook deteriorated still further in 1874 with the collapse of the Freedman's Savings Bank. Established in 1865, this institution attracted mainly small deposits from African Americans who were encouraged to invest by Northern officials and Southern black newspapers that promoted habits of thrift and saving as necessary to the economic uplift of the race. Few black investors ever recovered any of the money they had deposited with the Freedmen's Bank, and years would pass before many were willing to trust the banking system with their limited savings again.

Urban Living Conditions

In all cities, the unskilled nature of most black employment meant that household incomes were typically low. Low wages led to numerous repercussions for black family life and standards of living. Rarely able to purchase property of their own and discriminated against by whites opposed to integrated housing, urban black workers were often forced to rent cheap accommodation, and this trend gradually promoted the growth of predominantly black residential areas that often were found on the outskirts of cities. A stark change in urban residential patterns occurred as a result, for as slaves before the war, African Americans had commonly lived near their white owners, frequently on the same lot and often in rooms in the same house.

Independent black housing was an important mark of free status, yet living standards in black residences were usually poor. Records from Nashville show that in the late 1870s, most black houses were built of wood at a time when white residences were more commonly brick structures. Moreover, very few African Americans had private baths or water closets, even though such facilities were increasingly common in white houses. In 1877, for example, all but 4 of the 562 private water closets in Nashville were located in white properties (Rabinowitz 1996, 118). This low quality of life was in part a consequence of the inattention to black neighborhoods shown by Southern city councils. Basic municipal services, including sewage systems and clean water, as well as street lighting and protection from fire and crime, were only slowly extended into black communities. Together with malnutrition, also a consequence of poverty, poor housing conditions contributed to the periodic outbreak of cholera, smallpox, and yellow fever epidemics and were a primary cause of a black mortality rate that was in some cities double that of the white population. White commentators often dismissed the high death rates among urban African Americans as due not to environmental factors but rather to the weaker constitution of the black body (Lane 1991, 40). However, Freedmen's Bureau agents took some steps to improve standards of living in black neighborhoods. In Washington, D.C., for example, the Bureau built new tenements, ordered the cleansing of black residences, and provided new homes in healthier environments outside the city (Harrison 2006, 81–84).

Religion and Education

Economic hardship and social deprivation plagued African Americans in Southern cities during Reconstruction, yet strong urban black communities evolved throughout the region. Even before abolition, cities were centers of black institutional life in the South. Churches, schools, labor unions, secret fraternal orders, debate clubs, temperance societies, and burial societies were just some of the diverse organizations that African Americans formed in Southern cities as early as the Revolutionary War era, and they became more numerous and significant than ever before during Reconstruction. By the mid-1870s, Richmond was home to more than 400 black clubs and societies, and even in smaller cities, like Memphis and Savannah, African Americans soon formed in excess of 200 social organizations (Foner 1988, 95). These institutions provided the urban black community with a degree of cohesiveness and self-support that was integral to individual blacks' struggles to give meaning to their free status and to resist the persistent and virulent strains of racist thought and violence within Southern society.

The most prominent black organization during Reconstruction was the church. Far more than the focus of African American religious activity, churches were a fulcrum of black social life and additionally served important political and economic functions, especially for the incipient black middle class. In the antebellum era, most slaves and free blacks in Southern cities were forced to attend services in white-controlled churches, and only a small number of urban black congregations existed. In Richmond, for example, four African Baptist churches were formed by 1860, while in Savannah, five black churches with a combined property value of $63,000 were testament to the religious commitment of that city's black community on the eve of emancipation. However, while the South remained a slave society, even black churches were subject to white control. Many black churches had white ministers, and although services were attended by thousands of black congregants, others in the black community dismissed the church as just another pillar of the slaveholders' rule. This ambivalent attitude toward white-controlled churches was evident in 1865 when emancipation prompted a mass exodus of African Americans from their traditional places of worship and the establishment of independent black churches. Most African Americans joined Baptist or Methodist churches, although some among the urban black elite were attracted to the more disciplined services of the Congregationalists (Foner 1988, 100–101).

African Americans invested a substantial proportion of their limited financial resources into the construction of church buildings. By 1866, blacks in Charleston had erected 10 new churches. These included Morris Street Baptist Church, which from an initial membership of just 73 in 1865 grew to attract more than 3,000 congregants by the mid-1880s. The African Methodist Episcopal (AME) Church was equally successful. As early as the fall of 1865, black Methodists in Charleston had raised more than $1,500 toward a new church building that, when finished, would seat 2,500 people (Jenkins 1998, 114–119).

As rapidly as urban African American communities organized independent churches in the period immediately after emancipation, so, too, did they work to establish freedmen's schools. Deprived of formal education as slaves, African Americans embraced the opportunity to learn to read and write during Reconstruction. Old as well as young black men and women attended classes that were conducted often in makeshift accommodations, including churches, confiscated Confederate property, and even old slave auction houses. Soon after Nashville fell under Union occupation in 1862, 1,200 black pupils were attending schools in the city, and within five years, the number had increased to more than 3,000. Similarly, schools in Richmond were teaching more than 1,000 black pupils within a month of Lee's surrender at Appomattox.

In the early years of Reconstruction, African American schools were supported by Northern missionary societies and the Freedmen's Bureau, but they were also dependent for funding on blacks' own limited financial resources. In Little Rock, Arkansas, for example, African Methodist Episcopal churches opened banks accounts for a book fund to support Wilberforce University, an AME school, and a ladies aid society (Lovett 1981, 327). Likewise, in Savannah, African Americans raised $900 to finance two schools founded in January 1865 by the American Missionary Association and attended by 500 black pupils. Later that same year, 1,877 African Americans attended 13 schools across the city and surrounding Chatham County, though in future years, Savannah's black community would struggle to maintain such extensive educational provisions. By 1870, when the Freedmen's Bureau had been scaled down and Northern philanthropic interest in the fate of Southern blacks had declined, only 5 schools remained in Savannah and the black student body had declined to just 672 pupils. In 1872, the Chatham County Board of Education, which oversaw schooling in Savannah, started for the first time to make provisions for black public education, but by 1875, still less than two-fifths of black children attended school (Blassingame 1973, 471).

Whether schools were privately or publicly funded, they were invariably segregated. As in the realm of religion, where African Americans embraced the opportunity to worship independently of whites, school segregation did not cause undue concern within the black community. However, other aspects of urban race relations during Reconstruction were more contested. Although shaped by the white supremacist culture that pervaded the entire South, the crowded and socially mobile and diverse urban context was less conducive than rural areas to the persistence of traditional social and racial hierarchies. Particularly during radical Reconstruction, but in many cases after that time, too, limited interaction of blacks and whites in public accommodations was tolerated in Southern cities, and in some cases, African Americans actively and successfully challenged segregation.

In the antebellum period, African Americans had been excluded from many public accommodations and urban spaces, including schools, hospitals, almshouses, parks, and squares. During Reconstruction, civil rights legislation enacted at the federal level proscribed discrimination in public facilities on the basis of race. However, in practice, while African Americans gained access to all areas of urban life, in many cases they did so only on segregated terms. In New Orleans, for example, hotels and restaurants routinely barred African Americans, while in theaters and on steamboats, separate and inferior facilities were provided for black patrons. Similar patterns were repeated in other Southern cities, although New Orleans bucked the regional trend for segregated education by establishing integrated schools that served as many as one-third of the city's pupils.

In several cities, African American communities organized to oppose discrimination in the provision of public transportation and city services. The first successful black protest movements against segregation in the urban South occurred on streetcars. During the Civil War and the years of

Magazine cover for the American Missionary Association, September 1882. (Courtesy of Cornell University Library, Making of America Digital Collection)

presidential Reconstruction, African Americans in Southern cities were either prohibited from riding on streetcars altogether or permitted only to stand on the outside of the carriages. Through petitioning military officials; staging sit-ins on white-only cars; and, on occasion, assaulting white drivers, African Americans in New Orleans protested streetcar segregation from 1862 until 1867, when the city's streetcar company agreed to accept black passengers as equal customers (Blassingame 1976, 189–190). Also in 1867, streetcars were desegregated in Nashville, Richmond, and Charleston following black protests and with the support of local Union army commanders. In Charleston, coordinated sit-ins on the streetcars were organized at a mass meeting attended by up to 2,000 local African Americans on March 26, 1867. Over the following month, city police officers arrested blacks involved in the sit-ins, prompting sometimes violent conflicts with the black community. At the same time, blacks pursued integration through the courts, and by June, these twin policies of direct action and legal challenges had brought about an end to segregation not only on Charleston's streetcars but also on its railroads and steamboats. Within weeks, public transportation in Charleston was integrated in practice as well as theory and it remained so in many Southern cities until the early years of the 20th century (Jenkins 1998, 143–144; Rabinowitz 1996, 184).

Broader questions about associations between African Americans and whites in Southern cities remained politically contentious throughout Reconstruction. Urban poverty and social dislocation were no respecters of established racial hierarchies, and lower-class whites, as well as blacks, struggled to find work and provide for their families, particularly during the economic depression of the mid-1870s. In addition, many lower-class leisure activities were conducted on at least partially integrated terms. For example, although some saloons were segregated, many drinking and gambling establishments served customers of all racial backgrounds, and blacks and whites also encountered each other on the race track, on the baseball diamond, and in the boxing ring (Somers 1974, 34). The fear of the white elite was that the common economic plight of blacks and working-class whites, as well as their social interaction in the bars, streets, and even brothels of Southern cities, could lead to the development of mutual political sympathies and social relationships that transcended racial boundaries and threatened to compromise the ideology of white supremacy. Although this fear was never fully realized, interracial working-class politics remained viable in the urban South until the 1890s, largely as a result of the common social experiences of the black and white poor.

Conclusion

During Reconstruction, the Southern urban environment was conducive to great change in African American life, and cities bore witness to fierce contests over the meaning of black freedom and its implications for Southern race relations. There were several reasons why the transition from slavery to freedom proceeded in a distinct manner in urban areas. First, the guiding hand of the federal government, in the form of troops and the Freedmen's Bureau, was more prominent in the urban South than elsewhere in the region. Especially during radical Reconstruction, this federal presence offered some protection for black voting rights and a limited degree of personal security from white violence. Second, cities provided opportunities for black economic upward mobility and the development of strong community institutions that were the basis of black political participation. Third, in contrast to large parts of the rural South, the urban context encouraged more fluid race relations that enabled African Americans to utilize public services, frequent stores, and engage with poor whites with at least a semblance of equality, even if the threat of white violence underlay almost all interracial encounters throughout the era. The fact that the South's growing urban African American populations coexisted with substantial numbers of white working-class men and women, whose living standards and economic status were much like their own, presented a continual challenge to the traditional political appeal of Southern elites to notions of white supremacy and racial solidarity across class lines. Significantly, this challenge was eventually met by ever more pervasive segregation laws in cities, for the very presence of these laws on municipal and state statute books was evidence that segregation could not be maintained in cities by custom alone.

By the mid-1870s, black political power had been comprehensively eroded in most Southern cities. Federal troops were withdrawn from the region in 1877 following the election of President Rutherford B. Hayes, and black voters were increasingly kept from the polls by both legal means and organized violence and intimidation. However, the gains that urban African Americans had made during Reconstruction in terms of property ownership, education, employment, and community organization were not reversed. On the contrary, they provided social experiences, material resources, and organizational structures that would continue to subvert white supremacy in Southern cities throughout the era of Jim Crow.

References and Further Reading

Blassingame, John. 1973. "Before the Ghetto: The Making of the Black Community in Savannah, Georgia, 1865–1880." *Journal of Social History* 6 (4): 463–488.

Blassingame, John. 1976. *Black New Orleans, 1860–1880.* Chicago: University of Chicago Press.

Bureau of Refugees, Freedmen, and Abandoned Lands. 1866. "Report of an Investigation of the Cause, Origin, and Results of the Late Riots in the City of Memphis Made by Col. Charles F. Johnson, Inspector General States of Ky. and Tennessee and Major T. W. Gilbreth, A. D. C. To Maj. Genl. Howard, Commissioner Bureau R. F. & A. Lands." National Archives Microfilm Publication M999, roll 34. (Online information; retrieved 4/28/08.) http://freedmensbureau.com/tennessee/outrages/memphisriot.htm.

Fitzgerald, Michael W. 2002. *Urban Emancipation: Popular Politics in Reconstruction Mobile, 1860–1890.* Baton Rouge: Louisiana State University Press.

Foner, Eric. 1988. *Reconstruction: America's Unfinished Revolution.* New York: Harper and Row.

Goldfield, David R. 1981. "The Urban South: A Regional Framework." *American Historical Review* 86 (5): 1009–1034.

Goldin, Claudia Dale. 1976. *Urban Slavery in the American South 1820–1860: A Quantitative History.* Chicago: University of Chicago Press.

Harrison, Robert. 2006. "Welfare and Employment Policies of the Freedmen's Bureau in the District of Columbia." *Journal of Southern History* 72 (1): 75–110.

Hine, William C. 1984. "Black Organized Labor in Reconstruction Charleston." *Labor History* 25:504–517.

Holt, Thomas C., and Elsa Barkley Brown, eds. 2000. "African Americans in Richmond, Virginia, Petition President Andrew Johnson, 1865." In *Major Problems in African American History: From Freedom to "Freedom Now," 1865–1990s.* Boston: Houghton Mifflin.

Jenkins, Wilbert L. 1998. *Seizing the New Day: African Americans in Post–Civil War Charleston.* Bloomington: Indiana University Press.

Kimball, Gregg D. 2000. *American City, Southern Place: A Cultural History of Antebellum Richmond.* Athens: University of Georgia Press.

Lane, Roger. 1991. *William Dorsey's Philadelphia and Ours: On the Past and Future of the Black City in America.* Cary, NC: Oxford University Press.

LeConte, Emma F. 1998. *A Journal Kept by Emma Florence LeConte, from Dec. 31, 1864 to Aug. 6, 1865, Written in her Seventeenth Year and Containing a Detailed Account of the Burning of Columbia, by One who was an Eyewitness.* (Online transcript; retrieved 4/28/08.) http://docsouth.unc.edu/fpn/leconteemma/leconte.html.

Lovett, Bobby L. 1981. "Some 1871 Accounts for the Little Rock, Arkansas Freedman's Savings and Trust Company." *Journal of Negro History* 66 (4): 326–328.

O'Brien, John T. 1981. "Reconstruction in Richmond: White Restoration and Black Protest, April–June 1865." *Virginia Magazine of History and Biography* 89 (3): 259–281.

Rabinowitz, Howard N. 1996. *Race Relations in the Urban South, 1865–1890.* Athens: University of Georgia Press.

Rachleff, Peter J. 1989. *Black Labor in Richmond, 1865–1890.* Urbana: University of Illinois Press.

Rousey, Dennis C. 1985. "Yellow Fever and Black Policemen in Memphis: A Post-Reconstruction Anomaly." *Journal of Southern History* 51 (3): 357–374.

Shank, George Kline, Jr. 1964. "Meridian: A Mississippi City at Birth, during the Civil War, and in Reconstruction." *Journal of Mississippi History* 26 (4): 275–282.

Somers, Dale A. 1974. "Black and White in New Orleans: A Study in Urban Race Relations, 1865–1900." *Journal of Southern History* 40 (1): 19–42.

Takagi, Midori. 1999. *"Rearing Wolves to Our Own Destruction": Slavery in Richmond, Virginia, 1782–1865.* Charlottesville: University of Virginia Press.

Thornberry, Jerry. 1974. "Northerners and the Atlanta Freedmen, 1865–69." *Prologue* 6 (4): 236–251.

Wade, Richard C. 1964. *Slavery in the Cities, 1820–1860.* New York: Oxford University Press.

Northerners in the Reconstruction South

4

Nichola Clayton

Writing shortly after the end of the Civil War, the editors of the *New York Times* confidently declared that the thorny question of how to reconstruct Southern society might be settled by one single solution: Northern migration. "Half a million Northern farmers and mechanics, carrying with them Northern methods of labor, Northern systems of popular instruction, and Northern habits of independent thought" would, predicted the *Times*, prove sufficient to strike the final death blow to the last vestiges of slavery (*New York Times,* June 26, 1865). Although the presence of Northerners in the postwar South did not ultimately prove to be the panacea for the many problems that beset Reconstruction, this optimistic outlook was shared by many north of the Mason-Dixon Line during and immediately after the war.

Almost all Northerners who ventured southward during those years—often referred to as "carpetbaggers"—regarded themselves as agents of Southern regeneration, as missionaries of one kind or another. Even if a majority were drawn by economic opportunities rather than any desire to assist newly emancipated African Americans, they believed that their experience of managing wage labor and their ability to impart Northern values and attitudes would effect a transformation of Southern society. Their presence would bring about the establishment of free schools, a free press, and other benefits, and most importantly of all, Northerners would demonstrate to a skeptical white South that African Americans would work more effectively under the new system of free labor than they had done as

A Thomas Nast caricature of a carpetbagger, a man from the North who traveled to the South after the Civil War to take advantage of the new political, social, and economic conditions in the former states of the defeated Confederacy. The derogatory term came from the popular story that the opportunists arrived in the South carrying all their worldly possessions in a carpetbag. (Bettmann/Corbis)

Carpetbaggers: The Traditional View

Coined by the political opponents of Reconstruction, the term *carpetbagger* was a derogatory label given to Northerners who decamped to the South after the end of the Civil War, allegedly in pursuit of wealth and political power. The stereotypical carpetbagger was a poorly educated man with little property—hence his ability to carry all of his possessions in a single carpetbag—who sought to exploit and manipulate the supposedly ignorant former slaves for his own aggrandizement. According to conservative Southern whites, carpetbaggers were to blame for much of the corruption and scandal that plagued the reconstructed state governments, while their political alliance with African Americans was seen as an ominous threat to the racial status quo. For Southerners who opposed the postwar settlement, the rapacity and malevolence of these Northern interlopers was matched only by that of the "scalawags", or Southern-born whites who supported the Republican Party and, in doing so, were accused of betraying both their race *and* their section

(or region). Although historians writing in the early 20th century largely accepted this portrayal of the villainous carpetbagger, subsequent authors have almost completely rewritten the traditional understanding of the motives that brought Northerners to the Reconstruction South. Many were indeed drawn by the prospect of economic gain, and some carpetbagger politicians were indisputably corrupt. Yet the aspirations of these transplanted Northerners were far more complex than the simple lure of profit or political office; certainly the men and women who traveled south to engage in missionary and educational activities among former slaves sought no such rewards. Carpetbaggers motivated by economic gain generally entered politics only after their initial plans had been frustrated by falling cotton prices, and many of those who went on to hold office displayed a progressive outlook, endeavoring to promote political and social reform as well as economic development.

slaves. Without doubt, Northern idealism had its limits. Few of these economic migrants were fully convinced that blacks and whites were equal in all respects, yet they hoped to prove that economics, at least, could be color blind.

Most carpetbaggers failed to fit the stereotype of entirely unprincipled and self-seeking adventurers; a significant number of Northerners who relocated to the Reconstruction South did so for noneconomic reasons and saw themselves as missionaries of a less ambiguous sort. Hundreds of men and women, both black and white, left their homes in the North to teach in the freedmen's schools run by benevolent societies under the aegis of the Freedmen's Bureau. While their motives differed somewhat from the more material-minded brand of carpetbagger, both shared a similar expectation

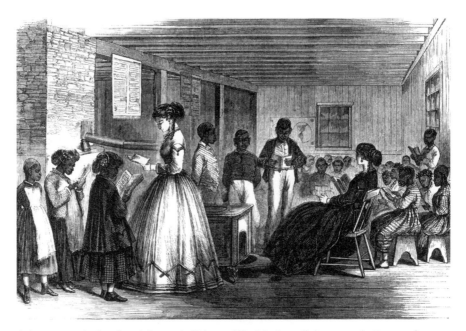

A classroom at the Freedmen's Bureau in Richmond, Virginia. Formally known as the Bureau of Refugees, Freedmen, and Abandoned Lands, the Freedmen's Bureau was a federal agency within the War Department that was charged with supervising the transition from slavery to freedom in the Confederacy. (Library of Congress)

that the "Northernization" of black and white Southerners was a desirable and an attainable goal. With the advent of congressional Reconstruction in 1867, carpetbaggers of all stripes became involved in Southern politics, and Republican officeholders would include not only Northerners who had engaged in cotton planting but former missionaries, teachers, and bureau agents as well. Relations with white Southerners were often complex, ranging from guarded cordiality to outright hostility, and Northerners who engaged in educating former slaves and participated in Republican politics in particular found themselves subject to violence, which on occasion proved to be fatal. Black Southerners too had their own ideas regarding social and economic relations in the New South, and they often resisted the demands of their Northern employers and resented the interfering behavior of well-meaning Northern teachers and missionaries. Though some carpetbaggers adjusted to these challenges and remained in their adopted homes, for many, Reconstruction brought financial failure, personal frustration, and a growing disillusionment with the lofty goals they believed had propelled them southward in the first place.

Wartime Beginnings

As with the process of Reconstruction itself, the presence of Northerners in the South began long before the war ended at Appomattox. Between 1861 and 1865, thousands of Northern men gained their first glimpse of Dixie as soldiers in the Union army. Indeed, a majority of those who would attempt to establish themselves as cotton planters after 1865 had spent at least part of the war in military service. During these years, Union military occupation of Southern territory had also brought in its wake a trickle of Northern civilians, whose expectations and experience would provide a taste of things to come. As the number of freed slaves behind Union lines grew, Northern religious and benevolent associations began to send missionaries southward to administer relief and to establish freedmen's schools. The American Missionary Association (AMA) the largest and most influential of these organizations, dispatched its first agents to Fortress Monroe, Virginia, in September 1861, and by mid-1865, the association employed more than 200 teachers and missionaries throughout the South. Although these men and women were mainly preoccupied with the physical and spiritual wants of former slaves, Union occupation also presented a golden opportunity for other Northerners to demonstrate the veracity of their belief that free labor was morally and economically superior to slave labor. The 53 men and women who arrived at Port Royal in the South Carolina Sea Islands in March 1862 included not only educators and preachers but also ambitious young men like Edward S. Philbrick, who, as plantation superintendents, aimed to show that cotton could be successfully cultivated under conditions of freedom. Philbrick and his colleagues hoped to stimulate the newly freed slaves to provide labor on what some disdainfully regarded as the "slave crop" by offering regular wages and providing access to Northern-made goods in recently established plantation stores. This approach, it was argued, would enable plantation superintendents to improve freed slaves' living standards and provide an education in the ways of the market parallel to the skills of literacy and religious instruction being taught in the schools.

Closely watched by the press and consciously publicized by its participants, the wartime "Port Royal experiment" was widely seen in the North as a vindication of free black labor and at the same time highlighted the combination of philanthropy and self-interest that typified the attitude of many Northerners toward the rebuilding of the South. Some of the missionaries expressed reservations about what teacher Laura M. Towne described as her colleagues' obsession with making the former slaves show "what they can do in the way of cotton, unwhipped," but others argued that teaching the freedpeople that hard work was now in their own interest was a vital part of the "civilizing" process (Holland 1969, 55). For men like Edward Philbrick, the future success of black labor hinged on its profitability, and as Northerners began to invest in these lands, booming cotton prices ensured that the former slaves were not the only ones with the potential to reap the benefits of the new labor system. Willie Lee Rose estimates that Philbrick and his group of Boston-based investors netted a profit of at least $80,000 from their 1863 operations of the cotton lands, which they had purchased from the government for a mere $7,000 earlier that year. The lure of such profits drew other Northerners southward after the fall of Vicksburg in the spring of 1863, as the Union military began to offer year-long leases of abandoned and confiscated lands in the Mississippi Valley. A $2,000 investment would, promised the publicity agents of commanding general Lorenzo Thomas, be sure to net a return of at least $15,000, while military regulations setting low wage rates for plantation labor provided an additional attraction for those not concerned with the welfare of the freedpeople. A small minority of the lessees, such as New England philanthropist George L. Stearns, hoped to replicate the fusion between philanthropy and profit that had been pioneered in the Sea Islands, but the vast majority were motivated purely by the latter. Even though pay rates were scandalously low, Northern lessees frequently swindled their employees out of their wages at the end of the season. According to James Yeatman, who compiled a report on the situation for the U.S. Sanitary Commission, most were speculators who cared little whether their profits came "out of the blood of those they employ or from the soil" (Yeatman 1864, 8).

In fact, very few of these lessees made any money at all from their planting efforts, and most had returned to the North by the end of 1864. Lack of security from Confederate raiders paralyzed their operations (one superintendent claimed to have been captured by guerillas four times in the space of a year), while the ravages of the army worm decimated their crops. The rather poetic fate of those Northerners who approached the wartime South only as a matter of dollars and cents was not, however, the only instance in which Northerners faced disappointment, or indeed exhibited a darker side to their professed idealism. In their published and private correspondence, Northern teachers and labor superintendents frequently praised the thirst for learning and the aptitude for hard work exhibited by the freedpeople. Much of this sentiment was genuinely felt, and yet lurking beneath the positive veneer were attitudes toward the former slaves that were more ambiguous. Most teachers proclaimed that their black students

SEA-ISLAND SCHOOL, No. 1.—ST. HELENA ISLAND. ESTABLISHED APRIL, 1862.

TEACHERS { MISS LAURA M. TOWNE,
" ELLEN MURRAY,
MRS. HARRIOT W. RUGGLES.

Supported by the Pennsylvania Branch.

EDUCATION AMONG THE FREEDMEN.

Pennsylvania Branch of the American Freedman's Union Commission.

PENNSYLVANIA FREEDMEN'S RELIEF ASSOCIATION,

No. 711 Sansom Street.

To the Friends of Education among the Freedmen.

As we enter upon our work for another year, we wish to present a statement of our plans and wants to the people.

The various organizations throughout the country having the education of the Freedmen in charge, have provided schools for 150,000 persons, in care of fourteen hundred teachers. The expense of supporting these schools has been borne by voluntary contributions.

It is frequently asked, Does not the Government accomplish this work through the "Freedmen's Bureau?" The simple answer is, No! The "Bureau" has no authority to employ teachers. The representatives of the "Bureau," from the honored Commissioner

The Port Royal Experiment was an effort to demonstrate that freedmen could be converted from slave labor to free labor. It was also a way to prepare for the upcoming emancipation of the slaves and to deal with the numerous slaves who had attached themselves to advancing Union forces. (Library of Congress) showed a similar aptitude for learning as whites, but some were also fond of predicting that racial differences would become more pronounced at the higher stages of education—to the detriment of African Americans. A few complained in private that the "vices of slavery"—lying and theft—remained rife among the emancipated, a belief that led Superintendent Charles P. Ware to declare that freedom had been "too easy" for his charges at Port Royal. "They have not had a hard enough time of it," Ware wrote, and went on to claim that in many cases the former slaves in his employ were "fair spoiled" (Pearson 1969, 287). Both black and white Northerners also tended to find the freedpeople's religious practices particularly perplexing, and even the most sympathetic among them could not help but regard the characteristic dancing and clapping as a "savage" and "barbarous" remnant of the African past. Neither did things work out entirely as planned for those who had attained some success in executing their grand plans of schooling the freedpeople in the ways of free labor. In spite of his early profits, as the war drew to a close, Edward Philbrick found himself increasingly mired in disputes with his workforce. From the viewpoint of the freedpeople, Philbrick paid exploitatively low wages and had broken his promise to sell them plots of land at cost price, an issue that was far more central to the former slaves' view of freedom than was the ability to work for wages under Northern management. According to Philbrick, his workers were as yet ill prepared for such independence and were also manifestly ungrateful for all that he had done for them. By no means did all of those who had come to the wartime South as evangels of Northern values become as embittered or disillusioned, but the sum of their experiences did seem to indicate that the road toward the Northernization of that section would be neither as smooth nor as direct as many had anticipated.

Northerners in the Postwar South

Historians have found it very difficult to ascertain precisely how many Northerners went South after April 1865, for many had come and gone before a census would be taken at the end of the decade. One Northern editor claimed that almost 10,000 demobilized Union soldiers had settled in Mississippi alone. Such figures are difficult to verify, but Lawrence N. Powell has estimated that up to 50,000 Northern men attempted to establish themselves as cotton planters in the immediate aftermath of the war (Powell 1980, xii). With land cheap and cotton prices high, the South appealed to the Northern entrepreneurial spirit as a land of opportunity, and the vast majority of these Yankee planters were motivated mainly by the prospect of financial success in this "new West." They also came with the active encouragement of prominent white Southerners, whose decimated fortunes and war-torn lands cried out for the capital that only Northerners could provide. At least initially, many Southern landowners adopted a pragmatic attitude toward the idea of detested Yankees settling among them, and by the end of 1865, a land agency established by Massachusetts governor John A. Andrew, to facilitate Northern investment and migration, was offering more than 3 million acres of Southern land for sale.

Writing to Republican radical Charles Sumner in November 1865, Andrew declared that the presence of Northern men in the South was absolutely vital to the success of political and economic Reconstruction. Andrew, in common with many Northerners, believed that the men of his section would prove to be more effective managers of black free labor than their white Southern compatriots, who continued to maintain that former slaves simply would not work in the absence of coercion. Not only would cotton cultivation become more productive and more profitable in Northern hands, but such a practical demonstration of the workings of free labor would serve to benefit Southerners of all races as well. This fusion of philanthropic and materialistic aspirations that had animated men like Edward Philbrick during the war continued to persist, in varying degrees, among most Northerners who tried their luck at planting. For a small minority of Yankee planters, assisting the former slaves was a far greater priority than either their own pecuniary success or the impulse to "prove" the superiority of Northern modes of production. In May 1866, Charles Stearns, a veteran Garrisonian abolitionist, purchased a 1,500-acre plantation near Augusta, Georgia and set about establishing a cooperative labor system among his employees. Not only did Stearns anticipate that his operations would provide the freedpeople with an education and the opportunity ultimately to purchase small sections of his land, he also hoped that his cooperative farm might point toward a solution to the "vast discrepancy" in wealth that he believed existed between labor and capital throughout the United States (Stearns 1969, 31).

Most Northern planters were not animated by such lofty aspirations, and indeed, very few were more than marginally concerned with the welfare and elevation of their laborers. Yet most established schools on their plantations and, in contrast with the dominant attitude of Southern whites, believed that African Americans were to some degree the equals of whites, if only in their ability to respond to the incentives of wage labor. Nevertheless, this Northern mania for cotton planting turned out to be short lived.

By early 1867, the secretary of John Andrew's land agency despondently reported that of those who had secured land through his offices, every single one had lost his entire investment. Drought, flooding, and the continued presence of the dreaded army worm had combined to ensure crop failures throughout the South in the two years following the end of the war. To make matters worse, the high cotton prices that had served as a cushion to some of these problems became a thing of the past in 1867. For many would-be planters, the sale of the meager quantities of cotton that they had managed to salvage from nature's ravages did not even cover the cost of its production. Mississippi carpetbagger Henry W. Warren doubted whether any "considerable number" of his fellow Northerners had made a success of their operations in these years. They had, Warren stated rather baldly, simply "planted their money" (Warren 1914, 22).

This agricultural depression did more than ruin many Northerners. With Southern anger already aroused by the coming of congressional Reconstruction in March 1867, economic problems combined with this political hostility to produce a significant deterioration in Northerners' relationships with white Southerners. Despite the mutual self-interest that led many Southerners to initially accept their Northern "guests," there had always been a strain of antagonism which was rarely far from the surface. Reports of growing Southern belligerence had, as early as late 1865, succeeded in deterring many potential investors from venturing southward at all, and the individual experiences of those who did often served to confirm this growing reticence. Northerners regularly suffered insults, experienced attacks on their property, and faced threats such as that issued to Albert T. Morgan in Mississippi. Morgan was told in no uncertain terms by his Yazoo County neighbors that "no Yankee radical could ever come into that county, make a crop and get away with it" (Powell 1980, 59). Not all Northerners abandoned the South as a result of these trying circumstances—Morgan himself survived both death threats and economic failure to embark on a career in local politics. Yet the rapid collapse of the Yankee planter movement clearly served as a stern corrective to Northern ambitions and also ensured that the predicted flood of Northern migrants to the postwar South would remain a dream rather than a reality.

Aside from their rather poor luck, Northerners who came south to engage in business shared a common social profile: frequently veterans of the Union army, they often came from a professional background, and all were white males (though sometimes accompanied by their wives). In contrast, those who worked as missionaries and teachers came from similarly educated backgrounds but exhibited much more diversity of both race and gender. The image of the "Yankee schoolmarm" was a ubiquitous one in the postwar South, and historians have long noted the preponderance of women among those who taught in the freedmen's schools. Although some estimates of female participation have run as high as 85 percent, recent research conducted by the Freedmen's Teachers Project at the University of Georgia suggests that women accounted for around 60 percent of the teachers employed by the various benevolent organizations. Like their male counterparts, Northern women teachers were motivated by a sense of religious and patriotic duty, and most possessed a genuine desire to assist the freedpeople. Some were perhaps more concerned with their own personal salvation, yet a significant minority held strong antislavery convictions. Those with a background in the antebellum abolitionist movement often tended to have the greatest staying power, as was the case with Sallie Holley and Caroline Putnam, who established a school in Lottsburgh, Virginia, in 1868 and remained in the South for 25 and 49 years, respectively. Women teachers already predominated in the common schools of the North, and from the viewpoint of cash-strapped benevolent associations, they could usually be paid less than men. Teaching in the South was not without its benefits for the women themselves, however. It provided many with a unique means of fulfilling their personal and moral aspirations and, as Jacqueline Jones has argued, offered an opportunity to escape the limitations of a middle-class existence at home (Jones 1980). Cordelia Hancock, writing to her fellow Quaker and friend Emily Howland in 1869, declared that she was "so impressed" with the feeling of "usefulness" that teaching former slaves in South Carolina engendered. "I wish to demonstrate two things by the undertaking," she continued, "that women [and] colored persons are capable of managing for themselves" (Howland, reel 2). The prospect of working as teachers and missionaries among former slaves also attracted significant numbers of Northern black men and women to the Reconstruction South. Boston-born carpenter John Oliver had arrived in Virginia in May 1862 and was the first black teacher to be employed by the American Missionary Association. Others followed suit, both during and after the war. Pennsylvania native Jonathan J. Wright came to South Carolina in 1865, initially to teach, and subsequently worked as a legal adviser for the Freedmen's Bureau, while Wright's AMA colleague Francis L. Cardozo was instrumental in the establishment of Charleston, South Carolina's Avery Normal Institute, a training college for black teachers, in 1866. Although born in South Carolina, Cardozo had lived in the North and had studied at the University of Glasgow in Scotland, and many of the Northern black women who served as teachers came from similarly well-educated backgrounds. Louisa L. Alexander and Sara G. Stanley, both also Southern born, had attended biracial Oberlin College in Ohio and went on to teach in a number of Southern states after the war. While Stanley appears to have returned to the North by 1870, Alexander remained in the South for 25 years. As Ronald E. Butchart has noted, African American participation in the freedmen's education movement was actually proportionally greater than that of Northern whites, because blacks constituted only 2 percent of the Northern population but accounted for approximately 20 percent of all teachers (Butchart and Rolleri 2003, 4). Undoubtedly, black teachers shared many of the same motives as their white colleagues, but they frequently expressed a particular desire to aid their race and saw their activities as a practical demonstration against claims of racial inferiority. In their dealings with white-dominated benevolent societies, some also argued that as African Americans they were better positioned to gain the confidence of former slaves and to assume positions of leadership within their communities. According to Virginia-based teacher Sallie L. Daffin, "none can so fully experience the strength of their needs, nor understand the means necessary to relieve them as we who are identified with them" (Richardson 1986, 192).

Carpetbagger Politics

In the opinion of many Southern whites, the Northern educators in their midst were not only encouraging notions of "social equality" and fostering hostility toward former masters among the freed slaves but were also deliberately propagandizing on behalf of Radical Republicanism. In reality most teachers did endeavor to provide their students with the basics of a civic education, but the majority did not become formally involved in politics. Some did run for office as a way of furthering the cause of freedmen's education. For example, AMA teacher Samuel S. Ashley was elected delegate to the North Carolina Constitutional Convention of 1868 and subsequently became the state's superintendent of public instruction, a position that was occupied in Florida by C. Thurston Chase, another AMA veteran. Political activism was probably more widespread among Northern blacks who had originally come South as teachers but became involved in grassroots Republican politics with the advent of black suffrage in 1867. Southerners who had been slaves until the outbreak of the war constituted the majority of black officeholders, but at least 137 blacks who had lived outside the South prior to 1861 held political positions during Reconstruction. Black carpetbaggers achieved particular prominence in South Carolina politics.

Former educators Francis Cardozo and Jonathan Wright were both active participants in their adopted state's constitutional convention, where they were joined by others, including Union army veterans William J. Whipper and Langdon S. Langley, and Richard Harvey Cain, who had been born in Virginia but was raised in Ohio. Along with yet another Northern transplant, Robert B. Elliott, Cain served as a member of Congress for two terms during the 1870s, while Cardozo was elected as South Carolina's secretary of state in 1868 and Wright became the only black member of a state supreme court during this period.

However, the largest number of carpetbagger politicians came from the ranks of those who had moved south initially to pursue economic ambitions and, in many cases turned to politics as an alternative career when their business activities floundered. In the constitutional conventions held across the former Confederacy between 1867 and 1869, Northern delegates played a major role in every state except Texas. Although on average carpetbaggers made up less than 20 percent of the delegates (native white Republicans were the largest group), they compensated for their numerical weakness by holding important committee positions and, in five cases, the presidencies of the conventions. White carpetbaggers tended to represent constituencies with large black populations, and, indeed, throughout Reconstruction their power continued to be the greatest in states such as Mississippi, where native white Republicans were relatively insignificant and African Americans were numerically preponderant. Eight out of ten Northerners who sat in the conventions went on to hold political office of some sort, and by the end of Reconstruction, six Southern states had had at least one carpetbagger governor and a total of 60 Northerners had represented the region in the U.S. Congress.

Contrary to the traditional stereotype, few of these men had originally intended to seek political office, and they also tended to be both young and relatively well educated. In spite of the financial vicissitudes that many had experienced since the end of the war, the median wealth of Northern-born delegates to the constitutional conventions was, at $3,500, higher than that of Southern Republicans of either race. If carpetbagger politicians were neither ignorant nor completely penniless, they were nevertheless singled out by their political opponents as particularly responsible for the corruption that was allegedly endemic in the Reconstruction South. As Eric Foner points out, the massive expansion in state activities and spending undertaken by Republican state governments did create new opportunities for graft, although it was often difficult to pinpoint exactly where legitimate spending on schools and railroads ended and the lining of individual pockets began (Foner 1988, 384–385). Indeed, the "extravagance" about which white conservatives complained incessantly was directed as much against honest expenditure as against fraud and corruption. In a few cases, the cry of corruption was more than warranted. Louisiana governor and carpetbagger Henry Clay Warmouth got rich through dealing in state bonds and accepting payments from railroad companies, while his counterpart in South Carolina, Robert K. Scott, also speculated in state bonds and benefited from unethical land dealings. Personal enrichment via politics was, of course, hardly unique, either to the South or to the Republican Party, and it is probably fair to conclude that the average Southern Republican (Northern or native born) was no more corrupt than the average 19th-century American politician at large. What may have distinguished carpetbaggers from other groups was the fact that the livelihoods of many came to depend almost exclusively on politics. Even those who had not been ruined financially by the postwar crop failures saw their businesses deliberately boycotted by Southern whites, so office holding became increasingly central to their survival. Yankee politicians in the Reconstruction South were not, as Lawrence N. Powell points out, greedier than the norm—they were simply needier, and this need in turn fueled a level of factionalism and infighting over patronage among Southern Republicans that ultimately contributed to the Republican Party's inability to stay in power (Powell 1982).

The air of desperation that this struggle for office conjures up should not be understood to mean that carpetbaggers were immune to the more idealistic aspects of politics. Most supported economic development as a means to modernize the South, but saw this development as intrinsically linked to a reformist spirit in politics. As well as championing state aid to internal improvements, Northern-born Republicans tended to support civil rights, public education, and the creation of more equitable systems of local taxation. In the Southern constitutional conventions, they played an active role in securing the inclusion of provisions that promoted democracy and guaranteed equality before the law, and a number of these provisions were taken directly from Northern state constitutions. Indeed, after African Americans, carpetbaggers were the most consistently radical faction in the conventions, although this radicalism, of course, had its limits. Northerners generally opposed measures to redistribute Southern lands to former slaves, and in the South Carolina convention, black carpetbaggers were among those delegates most strongly opposed to discussions of confiscation. Mississippi carpetbaggers also adopted a kind of "moderate radicalism," supporting public schools but at the same time evading the issue of racial integration and exhibiting a growing reluctance toward any further legislation to protect black rights. Black support in Mississippi had been instrumental to the success of Adelbert Ames's gubernatorial candidacy in 1873, but elsewhere the alliance between African Americans and white carpetbaggers proved to be more fragile. The 1874–1877 governorship of Ames's fellow Northerner Daniel H. Chamberlain proved to be the final straw for black Republicans in South Carolina. Many favored his efforts to root out corruption, but his attempts to reduce spending on education and to consolidate white control of the party by wooing former Democrats alienated his former allies. Originally an abolitionist, Chamberlain left the state in 1877 and would go on to voice criticisms of Reconstruction which would not have been out of place among his erstwhile Democratic allies.

A Fool's Errand?

Republican factionalism was not the only problem that beset Northerners who became involved in Southern politics. Although carpetbaggers were by no means the only target of the endemic violence that plagued the Reconstruction South, political activism certainly put at risk the personal safety of those who engaged in it. A few paid the ultimate price for their politics, including Arkansas congressman and carpetbagger James M. Hinds, who was assassinated by the Ku Klux Klan in 1868. Others were less unfortunate but found their careers overshadowed by persistent threats. Having been forced to go into hiding during the 1868 state election campaign, Mississippi Republican Albert Morgan nonetheless went on to serve in the state legislature and as sheriff of Yazoo County. Ultimately, Morgan would suffer the consequences of the support that he had given to local education and to African Americans who sought to buy land; in 1875, he was driven out of the state along with other Republican officials by a band of armed whites. Morgan was not the only Northerner to fall victim to the violent campaigns that overthrew the Reconstruction governments of the Deep South during the mid-1870s. Marshall H. Twitchell, a former Union soldier who had become the Republicans' political chieftain in Louisiana's Red River Parish, saw three of his relatives murdered in the 1874 election campaign, and two years later he was himself shot and lost both of his arms as a result of his injuries. For some Northerners, the threat to life and limb was sufficient to prompt the abandonment of any further aspirations to office holding. After suffering numerous threats and acts of intimidation for holding political meetings on his plantation in 1868, the abolitionist Charles Stearns journeyed to Apling, Georgia, to take up the position of judge-in-ordinary. On his arrival, Stearns was promptly beaten by a white mob and as a result decided to resign his office in order to save his own life and that of his driver.

Northerners who worked as teachers and missionaries among the former slaves were also frequently the targets of Southern white intimidation. Edmonia G. Highgate, a Northern black woman who had been a school principal in Binghamton, New York, was shot at twice in Louisiana, while one of Highgate's AMA colleagues was beaten almost to death by an armed gang in North Carolina. Such instances of actual assault were far less common, however, than the all-pervasive climate of rumor and intimidation that almost all teachers experienced to some degree. Educators became familiar with the derogatory epithet "Nigger teacher," were refused credit by local merchants, saw their mail interfered with, and were usually completely ostracized from local white society. White women in particular found themselves the favorite targets of malicious gossip, which usually involved the circulation of stories accusing them of having sexual relations with their students and bearing illegitimate children to African American fathers. Ultimately, white Southerners feared that black education, and particularly black education in Northern hands, would destroy their control over the laboring population, and this was the source of much of the antagonism directed toward the freedmen's schools. The irony of this conflict has not, however, escaped the notice of historians. In a summary of the objects of freedmen's education, AMA teacher Samuel Ashley described an ethos that was shared by many of his fellow Northern educators. Aside from basic literacy, the main purpose of schooling would be to inculcate former slaves with the values of "obedience to law and respect for the rights and property of others, [and] reverence for those in authority" and to caution them against "fostering animosities and prejudices . . . and all unjust and indecorous assumptions" (Richardson 1986, 149). Had they taken the time to listen, Southern whites would have understood that this was a rather conservative message, and one which they themselves would not necessarily have disapproved.

Whites were not the only Southerners who acted in ways that frustrated Northern ambitions and expectations. After emancipation, black Southerners sought to define the terms of their own freedom, above all by maximizing their independence from white control. It was this desire for autonomy that would often clash with the impulse to impose Northern ideas about work, domesticity, and religious practices. Former slaves thus tended to accept the assistance of teachers and missionaries when it suited them and to reject their interference when it did not, and the latter was often the case when it came to attempts at "reforming" the emotional style of worship that many Northerners had found so troubling. Those who had purchased plantations had similarly assumed that blacks would accept their day-to-day supervision and interference, and it was not long before many Northerners began to complain about the stubborn and obstructive behavior of their labor force. Henry Warren claimed to have been largely satisfied with the efficiency of his hands, but many of his fellow Yankee planters increasingly indulged in racialized explanations of their own labor problems. Because Northern styles of management and the system of free labor itself were seen as beyond rebuke, many reasoned that the fatal flaw must be located in the African American character. As early as 1867, an English visitor to the South reported having encountered large numbers of Northerners who had "a strong sense of the inferiority of the negro, and of the necessity of his being coerced into obedience and industry" (Powell 1980, 117). Even those who were ideologically committed to the cause of racial equality were not immune to the pressures exerted by daily conflicts on the plantation. Charles Stearns incessantly bemoaned his laborers' propensity for theft, their attachment to "heathenish" forms of worship, their rampant vices, and the "systematic disobedience" to orders that he and his wife encountered "at every step of our intercourse with the blacks" (Stearns 1969, 45–46). Financial difficulties ultimately forced Stearns to abandon his Georgia project in 1872, although by that time some of his workers had at least managed to purchase small plots of the land.

On reading *A Fool's Errand* in 1880, freedmen's teacher Sallie Holley observed that Albion W. Tourgée's fictionalized account of his experiences in postwar North Carolina "must be my own story of my life here in Virginia. How hopeless it seems ever to educate the Southerner up to Northern civilization" (Chadwick 1969, 234). The challenges of being a Northerner in the Reconstruction South were clearly enough to try the patience of even the most dedicated veterans of the antislavery cause. Yet it would be misleading to conclude that all Northern activity in the former Confederacy ended in failure, or that all Northerners became embittered by their experiences and succumbed to the lure of scientific racism. Holley herself remained in the South for the rest of her life, as did a number of her fellow teachers and missionaries. Although most carpetbaggers eventually returned to the North, some held onto the hope expressed by Henry Warren in his 1914 autobiography that racial justice would one day come to the South. Louis S. Post, a native of New Jersey who had spent only two years working as a stenographer in South Carolina, went on to publicize the work of W. E. B. Du Bois and penned newspaper articles condemning lynching. Some black carpetbaggers

Albion Winegar Tourgée: Carpetbagger in Fact and Fiction

After serving in the Union army during the Civil War, Ohio-born Albion W. Tourgée (1838–1905) settled in Greensboro, North Carolina, in 1865. Tourgée had not been an active opponent of slavery prior to the war, yet his experiences in the Reconstruction South shaped what would become a lifelong commitment to democratic reform and racial justice. Although the pursuit of economic opportunity had been his initial motive for moving south, Tourgée's concern for the plight of both African Americans and Southern Unionists during presidential Reconstruction propelled him into local Republican politics, and he soon became a prominent figure among North Carolina Radicals. In the 1868 state constitutional convention, he was an active proponent of public education, fairer taxation, and a more democratic system of local government, and for the following six years he served as a superior court judge. In spite of the fact that he regularly received death threats, Judge Tourgée persisted in his efforts to bring the perpetrators of Ku Klux Klan violence to justice, and the combination of his political and judicial activities made him a familiar hate figure for Conservative whites. In response to the North's growing indifference toward Reconstruction during the 1870s, Tourgée penned a fictionalized account of his own experiences, which he hoped would educate Northerners on the realities of Southern life and demonstrate the flaws of the postwar settlement. Published in 1879, *A Fool's Errand* became a best seller during the following decade, and although it failed to transform national policy, its success nevertheless ensured that Tourgée himself would not be forgotten. Although he had returned to live in the North that same year, Tourgée's reformist commitments did not cease. He continued to campaign for a federally funded system of education, and during the 1890s he served as legal counsel for Homer Plessy, the African American man whose ultimately unsuccessful challenge to Louisiana's "separate but equal" railroad laws led to the landmark Supreme Court case *Plessy v. Ferguson,* which gave constitutional sanction to segregation.

were able to maintain their Southern careers, even after the Democratic Party–engineered redemption took place (see the Introduction to this book). Former congressman Richard H. Cain became president of a Texas college, while William Whipper, Cain's fellow delegate to the 1868 South Carolina Constitutional Convention, was one of the few voices to defend black voting rights at that state's convention in 1895. Nevertheless, many Northerners had seen their Southern aspirations largely frustrated, not merely by circumstances but also by the sheer magnitude of those very same ambitions. "Oh for a thousand Yankees to enter and make a paradise of this magnificent region" had been the cry of one Northerner in wartime Louisiana (Smith 1944, 256–257). Yet it would take many more than a thousand Northerners to transform the South, and with their visions of postwar society competing with those of white and black Southerners, what would have constituted a "paradise" depended very much on the eye of the beholder.

References and Further Reading

Abbott, Richard H. 1991. *Cotton & Capital: Boston Businessmen and Antislavery Reform, 1854–1868.* Amherst: University of Massachusetts Press.

Butchart, Ronald E., and Amy F. Rolleri. 2003. "Reconsidering the 'Soldiers of Light and Love': Color, Gender, Authority, and Other Problems in the History of Teaching the Freedpeople." In *The Freedmen's Teachers Project.* (Online article; retrieved 4/29/08.) http://www.coe.uga.edu/ftp/docs/ReconsiderSoldiers.pdf.

Candeloro, Dominic. 1975. "Louis Post as a Carpetbagger in South Carolina: Reconstruction as a Forerunner of the Progressive Movement." *American Journal of Economics and Sociology* 34:423–432.

Chadwick, John White, ed. 1969 [1899]. *A Life for Liberty: Anti-Slavery and Other Letters of Sallie Holley.* Reprint. New York: Negro Universities Press.

Current, Richard N. 1988. *Those Terrible Carpetbaggers: A Reinterpretation.* New York: Oxford University Press.

Foner, Eric. 1988. *Reconstruction: America's Unfinished Revolution, 1863–1877.* New York: Harper and Row.

Foner, Eric. 1996. *Freedom's Lawmakers: A Directory of Black Officeholders during Reconstruction.* Baton Rouge: Louisiana State University Press.

Harris, William C. 1974. "The Creed of the Carpetbaggers: The Case of Mississippi." *Journal of Southern History* 40:199–224.

Harris, William C. 1979. *The Day of the Carpetbagger: Republican Reconstruction in Mississippi.* Baton Rouge: Louisiana State University Press.

Holland, Rupert Sargent. 1969 [1912]. *Letters and Diary of Laura M. Towne.* Reprint. New York: Negro Universities Press.

Howland, Emily. 1797–1938. Emily Howland Papers, Division of Rare and Manuscript Collections, Cornell University Library, Ithaca, New York.

Hume, Richard L. 1977. "Carpetbaggers in the Reconstruction South: A Group Portrait of Outside Whites in the 'Black and Tan' Constitutional Conventions." *Journal of American History* 64:313–330.

Jones, Jacqueline. 1980. *Soldiers of Light and Love: Northern Teachers and Georgia Blacks, 1865–1873.* Chapel Hill: University of North Carolina Press.

McPherson, James M. 1975. *The Abolitionist Legacy: From Reconstruction to the NAACP.* Princeton, NJ: Princeton University Press.

Morris, Robert C. 1981. *Reading, 'Riting, and Reconstruction: The Education of the Freedmen in the South, 1861–1870.* Chicago: University of Chicago Press.

New York Times. 1865. "Negro Suffrage an Uncertain Remedy—The True Reliance." *New York Times,* July 26, 4.

Olsen, Otto H. 1965. *Carpetbagger's Crusade: The Life of Albion Winegar Tourgée.* Baltimore: Johns Hopkins University Press.

Pearson, Elizabeth Ware. 1969 [1906]. *Letters from Port Royal: Written at the Time of the Civil War.* Reprint. New York: Arno Press.

Powell, Lawrence N. 1975. "The American Land Company and Agency: John A. Andrew and the Northernization of the South." *Civil War History* 21:293–308.

Powell, Lawrence N. 1980. *New Masters: Northern Planters during the Civil War and Reconstruction.* New Haven, CT: Yale University Press.

Powell, Lawrence N. 1982. "The Politics of Livelihood: Carpetbaggers in the Deep South." In *Region, Race, and Reconstruction: Essays in Honor of C. Vann Woodward,* ed. James M. McPherson and J. Morgan Kousser. New York: Oxford University Press.

Richardson, Joe M. 1986. *Christian Reconstruction: The American Missionary Association and Southern Blacks, 1861–1890.* Athens: University of Georgia Press.

Rose, Willie Lee. 1999 [1964]. *Rehearsal for Reconstruction: The Port Royal Experiment.* Reprint. Athens: University of Georgia Press.

Scroggs, Jack B. 1961. "Carpetbagger Constitutional Reform in the South Atlantic States, 1867–1868." *Journal of Southern History* 27:475–493.

Small, Sandra E. 1979. "The Yankee Schoolmarm in Freedmen's Schools: An Analysis of Attitudes." *Journal of Southern History* 45:381–402.

Smith, George Winston. 1944. "Some Northern Attitudes toward the Post–Civil War South." *Journal of Southern History* 10:253–274.

Stearns, Charles. 1969 [1872]. *The Black Man of the South and the Rebels; or, the Characteristics of the Former, and the Recent Outrages of the Latter.* Reprint. New York: Negro Universities Press.

Tourgée, Albion W. 1966 [1879]. *A Fool's Errand: A Novel of the South during Reconstruction.* Introduction by George M. Frederickson. Reprint. New York: Harper and Row.

Tunnell, Ted. 2000. *Edge of the Sword: The Ordeal of Carpetbagger Marshall H. Twitchell in the Civil War and Reconstruction.* Baton Rouge: Louisiana State University Press.

Warren, Henry W. 1914. *Reminiscences of a Mississippi Carpet-Bagger.* Holden, MA: S. N.

Williams, Heather Andrea. 2002. " 'Clothing Themselves in Intelligence': The Freedpeople, Schooling, and Northern Teachers, 1861–1871." *Journal of African-American History* 87:372–389.

Yeatman, James E. 1864. *A Report on the Condition of the Freedmen of the Mississippi, Presented to the Western Sanitary Commission, December 17th, 1863.* St. Louis: The Commission.

American Indian Issues during Reconstruction | 5

Gabriella Treglia

The experiences of American Indians during the Reconstruction era tend to be overlooked in general histories of the period. Reconstruction is viewed primarily as a white-black/North-South phenomenon, with little room for minorities of other ethnic/racial identities. The Indian Territory (present-day Oklahoma) was, however, the scene of both Civil War conflict and Reconstruction legislation, and the experiences of the resident American Indian nations provide an insight into how the federal government pursued its political and racial Reconstruction aims. This chapter provides a brief, general overview of the imposition of Reconstruction upon the nations of the Indian Territory and looks in greater detail at the experiences of the Muskogee-Creek and Cherokee nations and their freedpersons during the period 1865–1877.

Indian Territory before 1861

The 1830s was a time of major upheaval for the southeastern American Indian nations: the Cherokees, Choctaws, Chickasaws, Muskogee-Creeks, and Seminoles. Prompted by the demands of the non-Native residents of the states of Georgia and Alabama, presidents Andrew Jackson and Martin Van Buren notoriously forced the southeastern Indian tribes to relocate westward to an area of land designated "Indian Territory," where they supposedly would be safe from any further non-Native settlement and would be permitted to conduct their affairs in peace. The nations in question were known collectively as the Five Civilized Tribes, as they had developed largely nonnomadic lifestyles, created multihouse governments, and excelled at agriculture. In other words, their lifestyles seemed, in American eyes, to have more in common with Euro-American culture than with the "savage" cultures that they believed other Native groups practiced. Significantly, this supposedly civilized lifestyle did nothing to protect the tribes from forced removal: racism and the desire for fertile Indian lands and gold deposits effectively overrode the rights of nations such as the Cherokees and Choctaws to remain on the land that they had farmed and developed and on which their ancestors were buried. Indeed, even the intervention of the U.S. Supreme Court against removal (*Worcester v. Georgia*, 1832) was merely dismissed by Jackson.

Once settled on Indian Territory, the Five Civilized Tribes worked hard to reestablish their societies, economies, and schools. By the onset of the American Civil War, they had largely succeeded. One feature of their societies was the institution of African American slavery. Slaveholders, and many nonslaveholders, existed in each of the five nations. Approximately 12 percent of Cherokees owned slaves, while 18 percent of Chickasaws and 10 percent of Creeks were slaveholders. The numbers of slaves had indeed increased in the period since removal: in 1860, the Cherokee Nation owned the highest number of black slaves (2,511), while at the other end of the scale, the smaller Chickasaw Nation owned 975. The treatment of the slaves in the individual tribal nations has been the subject of much debate. Although it is generally agreed that the slaves were largely treated more leniently than those owned by Euro-Americans, they still endured significant hardships and in many cases were not permitted education or the right to marry tribal members. Abolitionist activity did occur and was generated both by missionaries and by intratribal groups such as the secret Cherokee Keetoowah Society. However, for the greater part, abolitionists were not welcome in Indian Territory: as early as 1836, the Choctaw General Council banned all proabolition missionaries from the Choctaw Nation. Views on slavery were, nonetheless, divided in each nation and so cannot alone explain the Confederate or Unionist allegiances of the Five Tribes during the Civil War.

Indian Territory and the Civil War

The geographical location of Indian Territory made its inhabitants unavoidable participants in the burgeoning conflict between the Union and the

Confederacy. As historian William Loren Katz has observed, Indian Territory in 1861 was "surrounded by the Confederacy and flooded with its agents and sympathizers" (Katz 1986, 141). In such a situation, neutrality was not a viable option. As one Cherokee recalled:

> My father was neutral and did not want to go away; he did not believe in fighting. Also, he did not believe in slavery, and long before the war he freed the one Negro slave whom he had inherited from his father's estate.
>
> In 1861, a company of Southern soldiers led by Captain Charley Holt came to our place. Captain Holt called to father and said, "Get ready, Watt, and let's go. You will have to fight." Consequently, father was forced into the Southern Army (Perdue 1980, 7).

Personal sympathies of Native Americans were therefore often disregarded by Confederates in the conscripting of troops.

Shrewd tactics were sometimes employed by Confederate officials to win Indian support against the Union. For example, Cherokees were informed that the United States no longer existed and that consequently their treaties with the federal government were obsolete. The only way to secure peace with neighboring whites and state governments was to join the Confederacy against the Union. It should therefore have come as no surprise that the Chickasaw and Choctaw nations had signed treaties with the Confederacy by April 1861 and that the Cherokees, Creeks, and Seminoles had followed suit by November. Confederate forces were able to occupy Native land and use Native resources, and soldiers from the Five Civilized Tribes engaged in active duty against the Union. Indeed, Cherokee leader Stand Watie served as a Confederate colonel, and later as a brigadier general, and distinguished himself as the last Confederate military commander to surrender to the Union in 1865.

Given the presence of the peculiar institution (see Chapter 1) amongst these Indian nations, their decision to support the Confederacy might appear obvious. In reality, however, the situation was far from simple and the vote of allegiance scarcely unanimous. The Creek, Seminole, and Cherokee nations in particular experienced divided sympathies. Loyalist factions rejected the Confederate alliance and reaffirmed their treaty relationship with the federal government. Various factors influenced this tribal factionalism, in particular long-standing tension between persons of mixed blood and full-blood descent and between so-called progressives and traditionalists. Such tensions had their roots in the Indian removal era (1820s and 1830s) and would continue throughout the Civil War and the Reconstruction period. The loyalist groups soon realized that they could not remain on their lands, encircled by Confederate sympathizers, without Union protection. On August 15, 1861, the leader of the loyalist Creeks, Opothleyahola, wrote to President Abraham Lincoln, urgently requesting his protection and reminding the government of its treaty obligations to the Creeks. As Opothleyahola noted:

> I write to the President our Great Father who removed us to our present homes, and made a treaty . . . you said that in our new homes we should be defended from all interference from any person and that no white people in the whole world should ever molest us . . . . Now the wolf has come. Men who are strangers tread our soil. Our children are frightened and the mothers cannot sleep for fear. This is our situation now. When we made our Treaty at Washington you assured us that our children should laugh around our houses without fear and we believed you. We . . . want it to be so again and we want you to send us word what to do . . . . It was at Washington when you treated with us, and now white people are trying to take our people away to fight against us and you (Abel 1915, 245–246).

Unfortunately for Opothleyahola and the loyalist Creeks, no help ever came. A similar response met loyalist Cherokees, who rejected the Confederacy and proclaimed allegiance to the federal government in 1863. Confederate parties repeatedly raided loyalist communities, looting, destroying crops, and brutally murdering Cherokee boys and men, the prime agriculturalists. Contemporary reports indicate that these raiders were never subjected to pursuit or harassment by the U.S. Army, despite the close proximity of Union forces at Fort Gibson and the acknowledged Unionist status of the victims. The loyalist Creeks, together with many loyalist Seminoles and their African American former slaves, were forced to flee to Kansas, suffering horrifying losses due to Confederate attacks, starvation, and freezing conditions en route. Many, especially children and the elderly, perished or lost limbs to frostbite. The Creek, and in particular the Cherokee, land bases experienced the full brunt of wartime devastation: schoolhouses and homesteads were burned to the ground, crops were destroyed, livestock was plundered by both Confederate and Union forces, and surviving buildings were severely damaged through use as military stables and stores. Indeed, the period 1861–1864 witnessed six major battles waged on or near Cherokee territory, notably the Battle of Cabin Creek (July 1863). Native casualties were high. A census taken in 1863 indicated that one-third of the loyal Cherokee adult women were widows, and a quarter of the children were orphans.

By comparison the Choctaw and Chickasaw nations did not suffer so greatly during the war, as they were occupied by Confederate forces

Portrait of Opothleyahola, ca. 1830. (Oklahoma Historical Society)

throughout its duration and thus were spared wide-scale punitive destruction. However, they, too, were significantly disadvantaged by Confederate requisitioning of livestock and homes, with the result that by 1865 at least one-third of Choctaws and Chickasaws were without a viable means of subsistence. The war ultimately held few benefits for any occupants of Indian Territory, irrespective of their allegiance. Even the freedpersons suffered greatly from wartime-induced deprivation, and many were forced to adopt refugee status alongside their former masters. The plight of Native Americans and freedpersons alike received little attention in the Union during the war: as historian Christine Bolt has noted, "for most northerners Indian policy remained an unimportant sideshow while the nation fought the first modern war" (Bolt 1987, 72).

The Reconstruction Settlement

With the Union victory in June 1865, the process of reconstruction was implemented in the secessionist states. Indian Territory was also included in the federal government's vision of a new South. The government was determined to reconstruct its relationship with the Five Civilized Tribes and to fundamentally alter their governments and land base. At the Southern Treaty Commission held at Fort Smith, Arkansas, on October 30, 1865, Commissioner of Indian Affairs Dennis Cooley acknowledged the loyalty of certain intratribal groups yet also noted that "a portion of the several tribes had united with wicked white men who have engaged in war" (Prucha 1975, 96). Although these rebel Indians had "rightfully forfeited all annuities and interests in the lands of the Indian Territory," the Commission assured the tribal nations that "the President is willing to hear his erring children in extenuation of their great crime . . . . The President has been deeply pained by the course of those who have violated their plighted faith and treaty obligations by engaging in war with those in rebellion against the United States" (Prucha 1975, 97).

The language employed by Cooley is very revealing: references to the Indian nations as "red children" and to the United States as their "great father" indicate the federal government's desire to continue the paternalistic relationship between Washington and the American Indians. The decision by some Indians to support the Confederacy was dismissed as solely the result of manipulation by "wicked white men." This tendency to reduce Native Americans to a childlike and vulnerable intellectual state, incapable of independent action, was typical of the federal government's attitude in the later 19th century and actually became government policy in 1871 with the Indian Appropriations Act, which officially ended the era of treaty making. According to Ely S. Parker, commissioner of Indian Affairs in 1869, the Indians were to be regarded as mere wards of the government rather than sovereign nations; in his words, treaties were a "cruel farce" that gave these "helpless and ignorant wards" the illusion of national independence (Prucha 1984, 164).

Perhaps of more concern to the Five Tribes in 1865, Cooley's report concluded that, irrespective of any loyalist factions, all the tribal nations had forfeited their existing treaty rights by allying with the Confederacy. Despite the reassurance that the president "[did] not wish to take advantage of or enforce the penalties for the unwise actions of these nations", the report stated that new treaties must be established with the tribal governments—treaties that sought to change dramatically the way the tribes conducted their affairs (Prucha 1975, 98). The formal Reconstruction treaties signed with each of the Five Tribes in 1866 reveal that the U.S. government pursued five key objectives. First, the treaties each specified the emancipation of all African American slaves and their transformation into tribal citizens. Slavery was prohibited throughout the Indian Territory. Second, the tribes had to agree to government terms for compensation for the loyal Indians and the freedpersons. These two provisions related specifically to the Civil War and can be seen as logical outcomes of the Union victory. However, the Reconstruction treaties each contained three further conditions that had little to do with Native defection to the Confederacy. The tribes had to cede large portions of their territories—the same territories that had been granted to them by President Jackson "for as long as the Grass grows or water runs" (Zinn 2003, 134). These new land cessions were to be used for the resettlement of some of the southern Plains tribal nations and those from eastern Kansas whose lands were desired by non-Native settlers. Indian Territory was therefore halved as a result of the Reconstruction treaties.

In addition to land gains, the federal government also wanted unrestricted transportation access through Indian Territory. The tribes had to agree to allow the transcontinental railroad companies access through their lands and use of their timber resources. This caused great alarm amongst the tribal nations, for they correctly anticipated that the railroads would bring an onslaught of non-Natives onto their lands. Yet even less popular than the railroad was the final treaty condition: the consent to a general council to govern the Indian Territory. The federal government intended to dissolve the individual tribal governments of the Five Tribes and replace them with a consolidated territorial government. Although the tribes had to agree to consider this as part of the 1866 treaties, in practice the majority resisted government consolidation as long as possible, for it represented a threat to their cultures and political systems and their identities as individual nations.

The Reconstruction treaties can therefore tell us much about the federal government's aims for the Indian Territory. The tribes paid heavily for

The Okmulgee General Council of Indian Territory

The Reconstruction treaties signed by the United States and the Five Tribes in 1866 required the tribal nations to give consent to the future formation of a single consolidated territorial government for the Indian Territory that would be known as a general council. This condition aroused significant opposition from the existing national councils on the basis that tribal consolidation could weaken national identity and the individual political autonomy of the Five Tribes. However, during this period, railway companies were seeking to influence Congress to make government land grant subsidies effective in Indian Territory, and it was this threat to Indian landownership that convinced some leaders that benefits might be gained by presenting a united front.

The first full session of the General Council was held at Okmulgee, the Muskogee-Creek capital, on December 6, 1870, but divisions arose over a proposed constitution. A key stumbling block was the heavy-handed control that the federal government sought to exercise over the General Council. President Ulysses S. Grant recommended to Congress that the proposed constitution be amended to grant congressional veto power over all the Council's legislation and give executive and judicial appointment power to the president alone. In response to this blatant attempt to seize control of the political administration of Indian Territory, the tribes, with the exception of the Creek Nation, refused to ratify the amended constitution, and the proposal never resurfaced. Consequently,

their support of the Confederacy. Land loss and increased threats to their political autonomy, independence, and cultural identity were the unfortunate results of participation in the Civil War. The remainder of this chapter examines the impact of Reconstruction upon some of the inhabitants of Indian Territory—the Muskogee-Creek and Cherokee nations and the freedpersons—and discusses the general impact of the railways that, following the 1866 treaties, gained coveted access through the tribal lands.

Railways Arrive in the Indian Territory

Railways were perhaps not the most immediate concern for the Five Tribes at the end of the Civil War, for the transcontinental railroads had not yet reached the borders of Indian Territory. Yet, given the go-ahead by the 1866 treaties, construction proceeded at a rapid pace. The privacy and seclusion of Indian Territory was threatened by two rail lines: the

the General Council never attained the status of a lawmaking entity.

Yet this was not the end of the Okmulgee General Council. It still functioned as a united protest body, particularly against the railroad companies. From 1871 to 1875, the Council presented the federal government with a series of petitions that protested the policy of changing Indian land tenure to benefit the railroads. Unfortunately, it was this continued determination to lobby the government against opportunist non-Native corporations that led directly to the General Council's downfall. The federal government had envisaged that a united council would create a consolidated territorial government that would be amenable to U.S. demands, but the Okmulgee General Council was simply too independent for the federal government's liking, and in 1876, it slashed the Council's funding.

Federal government interference in Native affairs continued to irk the Five Tribes. According to treaty guarantees, the Cherokee courts possessed full jurisdiction in cases that involved all Cherokee citizens, including non-Natives who had been adopted into the nation, yet U.S. marshals sometimes violated Cherokee authority by arresting tribal members to be tried in U.S. district courts. The resentment generated by these incursions led to the growth of sympathy to Cherokee outlaws who thwarted the marshals; by refusing to submit to U.S. authority, such men were seen as striking a blow for Cherokee autonomy.

southern branch of the Union Pacific, known as the Missouri, Kansas, and Texas railroad (the "Katy"), and the Atlantic and Pacific railroad (the "Frisco"). These routes sliced across the Cherokee Nation in 1870 and 1872, dissecting the land from north to south and from east to west. The Katy crossed the Creek Nation in 1871–1872 and reached the Choctaw Nation in the spring of 1872. Similar events and strategies followed in each nation. The Choctaw and Creek tribal councils attempted to make the best of the situation by passing laws designed to protect national timber and stone resources. The Choctaw Council attempted to maintain tribal, as opposed to individual, control over resources by decreeing that timber could only be bought from the Choctaw Nation, and not from enterprising individuals. The Creek Council adopted a slightly more flexible approach in the bid to retain timber profits: from October 1870, only Creek citizens were freely permitted to cut and sell timber to the railroad company. Non-Creek citizens who wished to profit from Creek timber would have to purchase a permit and pay a royalty to the Creek Nation.

However, both of these safeguards were circumvented by unscrupulous non-Native entrepreneurs. The Choctaws found that the railroad company was content to buy timber directly from individual Choctaw citizens, in flagrant violation of the tribal law, and the Creeks discovered that the railroad preferred to buy from white contractors who did not possess Creek permits or pay royalties. The end result was therefore the uncompensated plundering of the lucrative natural resources of Indian Territory by the railroad companies.

In addition to taking valuable resources, the railways damaged the Indian Territory *after* construction was completed. Trains killed livestock, for example the semi-wild hogs tended by the Choctaws. Despite government promises to limit and monitor the influx of non-Natives into Indian Territory, in practice, unregulated "tent towns" soon sprang up around the rail stations, and traders and others set up home and work on the tribal lands. This veritable invasion had been predicted by many Indians. According to one Chickasaw-Creek reminiscing in the 1930s, the schoolchildren had been warned of the dangers of the railroads in 1882: they were told that "people would come in here from everywhere, and if we were not prepared to care for ourselves they would knock the dirt from under our feet" (Perdue 1980, 156). In addition to the problem posed by non-Native settlers, a further concern was that not all of these interlopers were honest, industrious persons—the railroads brought trouble in the form of bootleggers and whiskey peddlers who, despite the efforts of tribal councils and the federal government, managed to ply their trade with relative ease. There were even Choctaw reports of illegal whiskey cargoes being transported in funeral caskets on the trains. Although his conclusion may have been exaggerated, in 1886, one government official estimated that 90 percent of Cherokee crime stemmed from the liquor sellers. In a final irony, very few Indians could enjoy the benefits of rail travel in the later 19th century: tickets for destinations within Indian Territory were simply too expensive for the majority of inhabitants.

Given the exploitative nature of the railroad enterprise in Indian Territory, it is hardly surprising that some Indians protested. Indeed, such was the volume of Choctaw complaints that in 1876, President Ulysses S. Grant allowed them to file claims against the railroad company. Unfortunately for the claimants, the claims were dismissed on the grounds that the 1866 treaty had granted the railroad company right of way and that individual Choctaws had been paid for their timber. The story of the railroads in Indian Territory in the Reconstruction era was therefore one of exploitation and invasion, rather than of mutual benefit for both the railroad companies and the Indians.

Reconstruction and the Muskogee-Creek Nation

The Reconstruction treaty of 1866 certainly altered the physical geography of the Muskogee-Creek Nation. Echoing the punitive land cessions that followed their involvement in the War of 1812, the Creeks once again had to relinquish a large portion of their territory—an estimated 3,250,000 acres—to the United States. This time, however, the ceded land was to be used to resettle other Native tribes. As specified in the Creek Reconstruction Treaty of 1866, the western half of the tribal land was "to be sold to and used as homes for such other civilized Indians as the United States may choose to settle thereon" (Prucha 1975, 100). Consequently, the Creeks gained new neighbors chosen by the federal government, notably the Seminoles, who had accepted resettlement as a condition of their own Reconstruction treaty. Land transfer was an initially turbulent ride for several of the communities involved, both financially and logistically. Creeks and Seminoles were the victims of a small-scale government swindle over land prices: whereas the Seminoles had to pay 50 cents an acre for the former Creek land, the federal government paid the Creeks a mere 30 cents an acre for the land cession. The Seminole Nation suffered especially, as the government only paid 15 cents an acre for the lands that they ceded, leaving the Seminoles considerably disadvantaged, as they had paid the higher price for the Creek land. Yet the problems did not end with the financial cost. Five years after the Seminoles had moved onto their new land base, it was discovered that the territorial boundaries had been incorrectly drawn. The Seminoles were in fact too far east and were settled on Creek land that had not been ceded. The border dispute was not settled until 1881. A similar error occurred with the relocated Sac and Fox Nation, who were mistakenly moved onto Creek land in 1870. When the Creeks refused to sell the disputed land, despite government pressure, the Sac and Fox tribe was relocated yet again.

The Creek lands had suffered much destruction during the war, so a key Reconstruction priority for the Creek Nation was to restore agricultural self-sufficiency. This was no small task, and for the three years immediately following the conclusion of hostilities, it appeared that fortune had turned against the Creeks. Drought and repeated plagues of grasshoppers resulted in successive crop failures and heightened malnutrition amongst the population. To make matters worse, the federal government rations that had been instituted were stopped on July 1, 1866. The Creeks, however, remained determined to rebuild their economy, and by 1869 they were once again agriculturally self-sustaining. In 1871, they established an agricultural society, to facilitate discussion and development of improved cultivation methods, and they requested that the federal government share agricultural techniques with them through the establishment and operation of a model farm. In 1875, the Indian International Fair Association was established in Muskogee to promote Indian agriculture. The annual fair was fondly remembered by many as an opportunity for dances and as a "reunion of friends and relatives that perhaps saw each other at no other time" (Perdue 1980, 74). Grasshoppers attacked again in 1874, but by this stage, the Creeks were in a stronger economic position, and poverty-stricken individuals received relief payments directly from the Muskogee-Creek Nation. In addition, the blind, the disabled, and the impoverished elderly were granted $30 per year for their support. Indeed, by 1870, the only federal financial assistance required by the Muskogee-Creek Nation was for school reform.

Education was a key reform embarked upon by Creeks in the Reconstruction era. Schools had been seriously damaged during the war; some were burned, while in others, the brick walls had been dismantled by federal forces seeking building materials for, among other uses, ovens at Fort Gibson (in present-day Oklahoma). Missions had not escaped the plunder and desecration. Tullahassee Presbyterian Mission lost all its windows and doors, and residents returned to find the dining room unfit for use after its stint as a military stable. However, by 1868, the two major mission schools for boys, Asbury (Methodist) and Tullahassee Manual Labor School had resumed operation and boasted an intake of approximately 80 students apiece who were receiving instruction in agriculture and morality. In addition, by 1876, the Creek Nation operated 33 public schools (including 6 for African American tribal members) and was spending an estimated $30,000 on education, including teachers' salaries. The public schools were relatively small institutions, attracting an average daily attendance of approximately 20 to 25 students, but the increasing number of schools testified to a burgeoning demand for a formal (school-based) education amongst Creeks. Indeed, in 1873, an all-girl mission boarding school, the Muskogee Female Institute, was established, and four years later the Creek Council sought new funds for the opening of two additional mission boarding schools.

Yet if Creeks broadly agreed on educational reform, political reform was another matter entirely. Creek society had been divided long before the Civil War into the Upper and Lower Creek groups. At the outbreak of the Civil War, slavery was not a key divisive issue, as slaveholders and nonslaveholders were present in both camps. However, by the time of the Reconstruction meetings at Fort Smith, Arkansas, in 1865, divisions had developed over the future status of the freedpersons. Whereas the Upper Creek delegation favored emancipation of the slaves, and indeed relied upon an African American interpreter, the Lower Creek delegation resolutely opposed the bestowal of Creek citizenship upon the freedpersons. Yet the issue of the freedpersons was not the only bone of contention between the two factions. The Lower Creeks were largely of mixed-blood descent and favored political change: members of this group called themselves the Government Party and pressed for a new Muskogee-Creek constitution. Their opponents, many of them Upper Creeks, were dubbed the Anti-Government Party and were less inclined to changes in government. Despite their differences, the two groups vowed to unite as one nation in February 1867, and a new constitution was decreed in October of that year. A high court was established, and the office of principal chief of the Muskogee Nation was created as a four-year elected post. A council of two houses, the House of Kings and the House of Warriors, was inaugurated and consisted of elected representatives from the six districts of the Creek Nation. Local government was also altered to feature district judges, attorneys, and 12 man juries. To guard against outsider manipulation of individuals, the constitution decreed that the National Council alone had the power to ratify treaties and that, once ratified, treaties would function as the law of the Nation.

The Euro-American elements of the new constitution did not satisfy everyone. The traditionalist Anti-Government Party favored a return to established Creek political systems and soon refused to participate in the new council. Political dissent, exacerbated by claims that the Government Party had not distributed certain funds to its opponents, sparked grassroots lawlessness, with violent skirmishes and murders littering the years 1867–1868. The council elections of October 1871 witnessed particular problems: the Anti-Government Party, headed by Oktarsars-Harjo (also called Sands) forcibly took possession of the council house at Okmulgee and declared its own representative, Cotochochee, to be principal chief, rather than the established leader, Samuel Checote. Although the situation was diffused peacefully and civil war was never a realistic concern, tensions persisted until the dissolution of the Creek National Government in 1907. For its part in the proceedings, the U.S. government openly favored Checote's administration, which had officially won the 1871 election, albeit amid accusations of vote rigging and unfair practice. On the other hand, the Anti-Government Party, composed of Upper Creeks who had largely supported black citizenship of the Creek Nation, successfully courted the freedperson vote. Despite the continued dissent, however, the new constitution remained in place for four decades.

Reconstruction for the Creeks heralded major changes, both political and geographical. Not only did they lose half of their land base and experience bitter boundary disputes, but the need to rebuild the Nation economically and reestablish its autonomy paved the way for political change as well. However, the Muskogee-Creek Nation was able to function adequately despite dissent and environmental disasters, and by the time of tribal dissolution in 1907, it had achieved stability and economic self-sufficiency.

Reconstruction and the Cherokee Nation

Of all the nations of Indian Territory, the Cherokee Nation suffered the worst physical effects of the Civil War. Military campaigns, such as the Battle of Cabin Creek, were fought on Cherokee land, and Confederate raiders terrorized the inhabitants. The large-scale devastation wreaked by the war had a disastrous impact upon agricultural production. A Cherokee interviewed in the early 1930s recalled that, upon returning home at the war's end, the family found only a chair and "our old black mottled-face cow who had escaped being eaten by the soldiers . . . . That is all we had to start our home on again" (Perdue 1980, 8). This experience was not atypical. Unsurprisingly, the Cherokees depended largely on federal government aid for the year following the war's end. It is therefore remarkable that, by 1869, the Cherokee economy had largely recovered: tobacco factories, coal mines, and sawmills were in operation, and cattle ranching and agriculture flourished. Families rebuilt their log cabins and replanted their fields. Cattle ranching proved a lucrative industry for some. In the words of a former Cherokee rancher, "Indian Territory was a splendid area for the ranching industry, considering the climate, soil, and land system"—indeed, "Everything was a free cattle range with no fences." Other, less affluent Cherokees lived a subsistence lifestyle and "simply lived at home with what we had" (Perdue 1980, 53–54, 149).

Aside from economic recovery and the discovery of new economic resources such as coal deposits, the Cherokee Nation experienced other significant changes during the Reconstruction period. Land cessions formed part of the 1866 treaty, and new neighbors were brought in by the federal government. Shawnees and Delawares were transferred from Kansas to former Cherokee land, as were members of the Osage Nation. Yet new arrivals also materialized at the invitation of the Cherokee National Council. In 1869, the Cherokee Council invited the Eastern Cherokees of North Carolina to join them in Indian Territory. The Eastern Cherokees had also suffered during the Civil War and had endured epidemics and poverty in the postwar period. Following the relocation invitation, 130 Cherokees emigrated from North Carolina to join their western brethren in 1871. This was followed by a second migration in 1881. Together with the adoption of the freedpersons, the influx of new tribal members swelled Cherokee ranks. Indeed, by 1877, the Nation comprised approximately 19,000 members.

Yet, despite these successes, the Cherokee Nation was not immune from the seemingly endemic problems that plagued Indian Territory during the early Reconstruction period. Lawlessness was a particular concern. Aside from the usual influx of thieves and bootleggers attracted by the confusion over legal jurisdiction that existed between the U.S. government and the national councils, some Cherokee criminals wrought havoc of their own. Feuds erupted between those who had fought on opposing sides in the war, and tension mounted over perceived U.S. interference in Cherokee legal affairs, leading to violent reactions such as the shoot-out at the Going Snake Court House in 1872. Resentment at U.S. involvement led to much sympathy for those outlaws who defied it, such as the notorious Ned Christie. Christie, whose criminal activities began with the fatal shooting of a government officer and purportedly extended to 10 additional murders, was pursued by U.S. marshals for seven years before being shot dead in a final gun battle. As a result of his confrontations with the unpopular U.S. authority, Christie was regarded sympathetically by some Cherokees who perceived him to be "an honourable Cherokee citizen" (Perdue 1980, 25).

A further problem that beset the Cherokee Nation in the Reconstruction era was political factionalism. Described by one historian as "a political schism of long standing" (Bailey 1972, 78), Cherokee political division was exacerbated by the wartime experience. Indeed, the extent of the disagreement between the main parties resulted in two Cherokee delegations attending the Washington treaty talks in 1866. The origins of the conflict lay in the removal crisis of the 1830s. The Ross Party, originally headed by John Ross, principal chief of the Cherokee Nation, had opposed removal, whereas the Ridge Party had supported removal as the best option for Cherokees and had illicitly negotiated the removal treaty, the Treaty of New Echota (1835), with the federal government. Divisions continued after the forced removal of 1838. The Ridge Party, under Stand Watie, had chosen to ally with the Confederacy in 1861, whereas the ruling Ross Party claimed it had been forced to support the Confederacy in the absence of

John Ross (1790–1866) was one of the greatest leaders of the Cherokee Nation during the 19th century. He campaigned vigorously against removal in the 1830s and left a legacy of determined Cherokee cultural preservation. (Cirker, Hayward and Blanche Cirker, eds. *Dictionary of American Portraits*, 1967)

federal assistance. The Ross Party denounced the Confederate alliance in 1863 and declared the abolition of Cherokee slavery as well as proclaiming support for the Union. Given the established animosity between these two factions, and also the eventual outcome of the war, it is unsurprising that the Ridge Party wished to be separated from its opponents. However, under the 1866 treaty, both sides were able to reach a compromise that saved the Nation from dividing into two political entities; the Cherokee Nation was to be united under one constitution, but the Ridge faction was granted the option of living in an area apart from its opponents. The Cherokee Nation in Indian Territory therefore continued as a single political entity. The political factionalism continued, however, through the 1870s, and at times erupted into violent confrontation. Despite such unrest, the Nation was able to function effectively and experienced various improvements, notably in the education sphere.

The Freedpersons of Indian Territory

Like their counterparts from the Southern plantations, the freedpersons in the Indian Territory emerged from the Civil War with one key benefit: freedom. The emancipation of all slaves was a stipulation of each Reconstruction treaty. The implementation of emancipation, however, was varied at the grassroots level. The Cherokee National Council had already passed an emancipation law in 1863, whereas some Chickasaws resisted the full abolition of forced servitude until the 1890s. In addition, emancipation itself did not automatically signify full equality or tribal citizenship—and it was the demand that these latter stipulations be met that caused particular tensions in certain nations.

The future of the freedpersons in Indian Territory depended partly upon the attitudes of the individual tribal nations. In the Seminole Nation, a relatively rapid progression to full citizenship was in place. Six African Americans were elected to the 42-seat Seminole National Council, thereby giving black tribal members representation in tribal government. Indeed, by 1869, it was reported that Seminole freedpersons held "equal rights in the soils and the annuities" of the Nation (Bolt 1987, 169). Individual freedpersons, most notably Coody Johnson, rose to prominence within the Nation. Johnson served as an interpreter and lawyer and was secretary to Chief Hulputta Micco. This equanimity was shaped by many factors, including perhaps the relatively small size of the Seminole Nation in 1865 (2,000 to 3,000 tribal members), the large proportion of freedpersons (approximately

800), and the desperate need to rebuild the Nation onto a new reservation land base as rapidly as possible.

The implementation of citizenship rights in the Creek Nation took a less smooth turn. A government report issued in 1866 returned an optimistic assessment of Creek attitudes toward the freedpersons. According to Gen. John Sanborn, commissioner for regulating relations between the freedpersons and the Indian Nations, "The Creek Nation look upon the freedmen as their equals in rights, and have, or are in favour of, incorporating them into their tribes, with all the rights and privileges of native Indians" (Bailey, 1972, 48).

Yet, in practice, limitations were placed on this equality. The Creek National Council conferred citizenship upon all individual freedpersons legally residing on Creek soil provided they had returned to Creek land within one year of the ratification of the 1866 Reconstruction treaty. This provision excluded refugee freedpersons who had been displaced during the Civil War and who could not return home in time. The situation was more extreme for displaced Cherokee freedpersons, who were scattered across Kansas, Arkansas, and as far as Mexico by the war's end. They had a mere six months in which to return to Cherokee land; those who returned after the deadline were regarded as intruders and risked being expelled from the Nation. The inflexibility of the law meant that many Cherokee freedperson families were separated, for relatives were not allowed to return even if a family representative met the deadline and qualified for Cherokee citizenship. A key concern held by the National Council was the risk of large-scale invasion of Indian Territory by emancipated slaves from the former Confederate States, seeking land and a new life away from the scene of their former servitude.

The attitude of the U.S. government toward the freedpersons of Indian Territory was initially one of support. It was clearly in the government's interest to see the freedpersons settled and self-supporting, and given the severe strain already placed upon the Freedmen's Bureau, if the former tribal slaves could remain the responsibility of the tribal nations, so much the better. General Sanborn was dispatched to Indian Territory to ensure that citizenship was conferred as agreed in the treaties. Of particular concern was the situation experienced by the Choctaw and Chickasaw nations where a de facto form of slave labor code persisted after abolition. Harsh vagrancy laws that appeared to target freedpersons disproportionately and that effectively supplied forced labor were also enacted. The Choctaw and Chickasaw nations both requested the removal of freedpersons from their territory—a choice that was allowed by their treaty provided that the freedpersons received a compensation payment. However, the removal could only be carried out with the approval of Congress, and no response from Congress to their request ever came. Realizing that the only viable option open to them was to adopt the freedpersons, the Choctaw Nation granted citizenship to the former slaves in 1883.

The government reacted in a similar fashion to Cherokee attempts to limit the number of freedpersons admitted to the tribal rolls. After December 1869, the Cherokee Supreme Court decided the citizenship claims of persons arriving after the six-month deadline. A report issued in 1871 indicated that while 47 of these claimants received Cherokee citizenship, 130 were rejected as intruders and were scheduled for removal from the Nation. The Office of Indian Affairs, however, instructed the Cherokee agent (the representative of the federal government to the Cherokees) to allow intruders to remain. The federal government therefore demonstrated both contempt for the authority of the Cherokee Supreme Court and support for the plight of the freedperson claimants.

The freedpersons themselves were often divided as to their choice of homeland. Some Choctaw freedpersons did choose to accept the $100 compensation payment and remove from the Choctaw Nation. However, it appears that the majority did not want to leave the nations in which they had been raised. As Sanborn reported in 1866, "They all desire to remain in that territory upon lands set apart for their own exclusive use" (Katz 1986, 45). The black Cherokees expressed similar sentiments in 1879 when they issued a petition for equal civil rights:

> The Cherokee nation is our country; there we were born and reared; there are our homes made by the sweat of our brows . . . . There we intend to live and defend our natural rights, as guaranteed by the treaties and laws of the United States, by every legitimate and lawful means. (Katz 1986, 147)

A black Chickasaw delegation went even further by reaffirming their attachment not just to the Chickasaw land base but also to the Chickasaws themselves. In 1884, they issued a statement declaring that "As natives, we are attached to the people among whom we have been born and bred. We like the Chickasaws as friends and we know by the experiences of the past that we can live with them in the future in a close union" (Katz 1986, 147–148).

In practice, the majority of freedpersons opted to stay within their tribal nations in the Reconstruction era. Although the granting of full political and civil rights in some cases took much time and lobbying, by the 1880s, the situation had improved for many African American tribal citizens. Creek

The Cherokee Seminaries

Long before Reconstruction, the Cherokee Nation devoted considerable funds and effort to the provision of education facilities soon after removal to Indian Territory. Indeed, the national legislature set aside funds for the building of two seminaries in 1846, but soon after opening in 1851, the funds dried up and both seminaries were forced to close after just five years of service. The enthusiasm for revitalization that characterized Cherokee Reconstruction, however, gave the seminaries a new lease of life. The Female Seminary reopened in 1871, followed by the war-damaged Male Seminary in 1875. The schools taught similar subjects, although the boys' curriculum was apparently more varied. Unlike many mission and federal government Indian schools of the time, academic subjects featured prominently and included algebra, logic, Latin, astronomy, and German.

The Female Seminary was unfortunately destroyed by fire but reopened in 1889 to an enthusiastic reception. According to one Cherokee, it was a "beautiful high-class institution of learning" and "the pride of the Cherokee Nation" (Perdue 1980, 134). Featuring running water, steam heat, and inside toilet facilities, the New Female Seminary attracted

freedpersons could stand for election to the National Council and could also serve as judges and attorneys. They also demonstrated an interest in tribal affairs: in the 1870s, Creek freedpersons attended intertribal councils formed to challenge illegal settlements on Native lands. Freedpersons were successful agriculturalists and also found work in the towns that flourished in Indian Territory in the later 19th century. Some worked in manual vocations, and some owned their own businesses, such as barber shops and restaurants. Significantly, the racial segregation that swept across the South in the postwar era also characterized Indian Territory. Freedpersons tended to congregate in their own towns and communities—in the Reconstruction era, more than 20 freedperson towns were founded in Indian Territory and what became Oklahoma Territory. In addition, black-Native intermarriage was discouraged by Creek, Cherokee, and Choctaw laws, although it did sometimes occur in practice. Although the Cherokees in particular provided schools for freedpersons, educational establishments in Indian Territory were segregated, and black Cherokees were not permitted to attend the Cherokee higher education seminaries.

The freedpersons therefore gained a mixed blessing from Reconstruction. On the positive side, they gained freedom from enslavement, eventual political equality, and access to education. Simultaneously, they endured

250 Cherokee students. The tastes of its first superintendent, Spencer Stephens, apparently verged on the opulent: although very dedicated, he was rumored to have used money appropriated for new teaching appointments to purchase linen tablecloths and napkins, silver cutlery, and dishes for the school dining room. When criticized for squandering the Nation's money, Stephens replied that "young ladies of the best families demanded the best" (Perdue 1980, 135). Unfortunately for Stephens, the voters were unimpressed with this defense, and he was replaced as superintendent after his first term. Resentment of Stephens's extrav-agance was understandable given the far tighter budgets of some of the smaller rural Cherokee schools. Such schools were based in log cabins that often had dirt floors and no windows. However, by 1874, the Cherokee Nation operated 65 public schools with a total enrollment of 800 boys and 933 girls. In addition, of the 60 teachers employed at the schools, 48 were themselves Cherokees. Although mission schools still functioned, formal schooling became a tribal enterprise in the Reconstruction era.

racial prejudice and inferior facilities. Overall, however, freedperson communities flourished in Indian Territory and, despite segregation, did not suffer the extreme violence endured by African Americans in the rest of the American South during this period.

Conclusion

The period 1865–1877 saw many changes imposed upon Indian Territory and its residents. Severe poverty and upheaval generated by a war that was not of the Indians' making and major land cessions forced by the federal government meant that the postwar era was a traumatic one. However, it is a testament to the resilience of the Five Tribes, and their determination to retain national autonomy and cultural identity for as long as possible, that each tribal nation was able to survive the Reconstruction period intact. Unfortunately, the swelling population of the United States in the early 20th century ensured that demands for Indian land only intensified. The continued influx of Americans onto Indian Territory did just what many Indians had feared: non-Native citizens, in increasing numbers, demanded a government of their own that would benefit them and not the Five Tribes. In

1898, the federal government passed the Curtis Act, which dissolved the tribal governments of Indian Territory and thus paved the way for the fractionalization of tribal land bases into individual land allotments. In 1901, Native residents of Indian Territory were granted U.S. citizenship, and in 1907, 41 years after the signing of the Reconstruction treaties, Indian Territory was absorbed into the new state of Oklahoma and, in the words of historian Angie Debo, "the concept of an Indian state was abandoned forever" within the United States (Debo 1970, 309). It is a testament to the determination and persistence of the Cherokee, Creek, Seminole, Chickasaw and Choctaw nations that they have continued to flourish as political and cultural entities into the 21st century.

References and Further Reading

Abel, Annie Heloise. 1915. *The American Indian as Slaveholder and Secessionist.* Cleveland: Arthur H. Clark.

Abel, Annie Heloise. 1919. *The American Indian as Participant in the Civil War.* Cleveland: Arthur H. Clark.

Abel, Annie Heloise. 1925. *The American Indian under Reconstruction.* Cleveland: Arthur H. Clark.

Bailey, M. Thomas. 1972. *Reconstruction in Indian Territory: A Story of Avarice, Discrimination, and Opportunism.* New York: Kennikat Press.

Bolt, Christine. 1987. *American Indian Policy and American Reform: Case Studies of the Campaign to Assimilate the Indians.* London: Allen and Unwin.

Burton, Geoffrey. 1995. *Indian Territory and the United States, 1866–1906.* Norman: University of Oklahoma Press.

Debo, Angie. 1970. *A History of the Indians of the United States.* Norman: University of Oklahoma Press.

Finger, John R. 1984. *The Eastern Band of Cherokees, 1819–1900.* Knoxville: University of Tennessee Press.

Katz, William Loren. 1986. *Black Indians: A Hidden Heritage.* Baltimore: Ethrac Publications.

La Vere, David. 2000. *Contrary Neighbors: Southern Plains and Removed Indians in Indian Territory.* Norman: University of Oklahoma Press.

Perdue, Theda. 1980. *Nations Remembered: An Oral History of the Five Civilized Tribes, 1865–1907.* Westport, CT: Greenwood Press.

Prucha, Francis Paul, ed. 1975. *Documents of United States Indian Policy.* Lincoln: University of Nebraska Press.

Prucha, Francis Paul. 1984. *The Great Father: The United States Government and the American Indians.* Lincoln: University of Nebraska Press.

Reese, Linda. 2002. "Cherokee Freedwomen in Indian Territory: 1863–1890." *Western Historical Quarterly* 33 (3): 273-296.

Zinn, Howard. 2003. *A People's History of the United States: 1492–Present.* London: Pearson.

Former Slaveholders and the Planter Class | 6

David Deverick

For African Americans, the abolition of slavery meant freedom; for former slaveholders, it brought the loss of valuable property and represented a profound challenge to their established way of life, social and political dominance, and racist ideology. During Reconstruction, former slaveholders of diverse backgrounds and identities worked to adjust to these new circumstances within the confines of tumultuous national- and state-level political developments and the context of Confederate defeat. They fought, sometimes violently, to maintain their political power, struggled to secure a cheap and subservient labor force to work their farms and plantations in place of slaves, and resisted movements toward increased African American political influence and social and legal standing. Yet, while clinging to the social structures and race relations of the past, many former slaveholders, and especially their descendants, also strived to come to terms with the rapidly changing economic world of the New South as the agricultural sector fell upon hard times and the region slowly began to embrace industry and manufacturing and became more influenced than ever before by global markets and cultures.

Slaveholders in the Antebellum South and Civil War

In the years immediately preceding the Civil War, one-third of all white Southern families owned at least one slave. Yet slaveholders were a geographically, economically, and socially disparate group of men and women. Just as the umbrella term "the South" falsely implies a consensus of belief, culture, or society that never actually existed, so it is misleading to assume that all slaveholders and their experiences were the same. At the top of the social structure, 10 percent of slaveholders, numbering around 40,000 men and women, were classified as "planters," meaning that they owned more than 20 slaves. These were the wealthiest and most powerful individuals in the South. Together, they owned more than half of the 4 million African Americans who were enslaved in 1860 and dominated Southern politics, society, and culture. But these slaveholders were the exception to the rule. Nearly half of all slaveholders owned five slaves or fewer, and the reality was that few could aspire to planter status and most were more likely to live out their days in a log cabin than a mansion. Frederick Law Olmsted recounted, with a degree of incredulity, white Southerners' desire for slave labor despite their apparent poverty. While touring the turpentine plantations of North Carolina in 1853, he observed a log cabin with furnishings, as he described, "[more] scanty and rude than I ever saw before in any house, with women living in it, in the United States." The two inhabitants were not so poor, however, as "they had a negro woman cutting and bringing wood for their fire" (Olmsted 2001, 330).

When the Civil War broke out in 1861, an overwhelming majority of even the poorest slaveholders supported secession. By this reaction, it can be seen that the peculiar institution (see Chapter 1) had permeated the South and had influenced the region's white population beyond considerations of wealth and profit. United by their common faith in the inherent inferiority of people of African descent, the interests of both large- and small-scale slaveholders were bound together by a common political cause. Proslavery and often virulently antiblack propaganda was fomented and encouraged by slaveholders and ensured that class differences between whites in the Southern states remained secondary to the racial basis of the region's society that could always be played upon and used to bolster white cohesion. Even so, the strength of white racial solidarity in the South had been tested in the 1850s by growing class divisions among whites and the rising costs of slaveownership, which served to bar entry to the highest echelons of society to all but the wealthiest individuals. Right up until the eve of the Civil War, and despite widespread fears that President Abraham Lincoln's opposition to the expansion of slavery into the West would fatally compromise Southern economic and political interests, the white South was far from solid in its support of secession, and public meetings were held across the region in the winter of 1860 to debate the impending crisis.

A series of speeches delivered in Milledgeville, the antebellum capital of Georgia, in mid-November 1860, illustrates the diversity of slaveholders' opinions on secession and Unionism. All of the main speakers in Milledgeville owned at least a dozen slaves and included among their number two of the state's most prominent figures, Alexander H. Stephens and Robert A. Toombs. Toombs, a charismatic lawyer, politician, and planter, was one of the largest slaveholders in the country and boasted enormous tracts of land and hundreds of slaves. He spoke passionately for secession, but not all men of his standing concurred with his views. Indeed, his friend Stephens, a congressional representative for Georgia and the owner of approximately 20 slaves, gave an impressive speech in favor of remaining in the Union. Although even among the planter elite opinion in support of breaking up the Union was not unanimous, ultimately men like Stephens proved to be in the minority and after the first shots were fired on Fort Sumter, South Carolina, in April 1861, little planter-class opposition to Confederate independence could be found.

War and Confederate Defeat

As in the 1850s, discord among Southern whites continued during the Civil War to the extent that some analysts have sought to explain Confederate defeat in terms of internal divisions and weaknesses. During the Civil War, acts such as the implementation of the draft and the "Twenty Negro Law," which enabled planters who owned more than 20 slaves to avoid conscription, proved controversial and compromised lower-class white support. Little wonder that the move was disliked, and a few disgruntled shouts were heard of the conflict being a rich man's war but a poor man's fight. A number of slaveholders did fight in the war, however, including Toombs, who served briefly and inadequately in charge of a command until returning home to Georgia, bitter at failing to win a promotion. Other slaveholders served their new nation in different ways. For example, Stephens, despite his Unionist inclinations, became vice president to Jefferson Davis, although he proved to be a thorn in the side of the Confederate administration.

As the strains of supporting the war effort placed an increasingly heavy burden on the Southern civilian population during 1863 and 1864, opposition to the continuation of the war began to surface even among the Confederate planter class, albeit most often only in private conversations and correspondence. These doubts were voiced loudest by women who had been left to run plantations while their male relatives signed up to the

Robert Toombs, one of the nation's largest slaveowners, served as the first secretary of state of the Confederate States of America and later became a brigadier general in the Confederate Army. Toombs fled to Paris after the war but returned to Georgia and once again became an influential political figure. (Library of Congress)

Alexander Hamilton Stephens (1812–1883) was the vice president of the Confederate States of America and a major slave owner. At the end of Reconstruction in 1877, he was elected to the U.S. Congress and later served as governor of Georgia. (Ridpath, John Clark, *Ridpath's History of the World,* 1901)

ranks of the Confederate Army. As one Confederate woman wistfully commented, on watching the men from her community ready themselves for war, "We who stay behind may find it harder than they who go" (Faust 1990, 1204). As the Southern landscape became ever more unrecognizable due to the devastation of the war, Confederate women faced a growing struggle to provide for themselves and their families, and many penned letters to Confederate officials seeking assistance in return for their continued support of the war effort. Harriet Stephenson of North Carolina, whose five sons had enlisted in the army, informed Secretary of War James Seddon that "I think I have did enough to you for you to take sum interest in what I so mutch desire of you" (Faust 1990, 1223). Several slaveholding women warned that they would convince their menfolk to desert if support was not forthcoming. Others wrote to their enlisted loved ones directly, instructing them to desert the ranks, return home, and try to salvage what they could from the economic and social ruins of the conflict. One woman wrote to her son, a Confederate captain who had been taken as a prisoner of war, "I hope, when you get exchanged, you will think, the time past has sufficed for *public* service, and that your own family require yr protection and help—as others are deciding" (Faust 1990, 1224).

The surrender of the Confederate armies and the emancipation of the enslaved in 1865 threatened the status and property of the white elite more than that of any other class of Southerners. President Andrew Johnson's Reconstruction Proclamations, issued in May 1865, specifically excluded the wealthiest planters from the blanket pardons that were extended to most Confederates. Of more immediate concern, rumors were widespread of former slaves planning violent revenge against their one-time masters and of Radical Republicans planning to divest former slaveholders of their land and redistribute it to the freedpeople. Despite these alarming possibilities, a minority among the old Southern elite bore the defeat of the Confederacy with stoicism. One delegate to Mississippi's Constitutional Convention in September 1865 who had once been a wealthy slaveholder concluded that the South, having fought for the right both to keep slaves and to secede from the Union, now had to accept that both were a thing of the past. With illuminating acquiesence, he told his fellow delegates that "having assisted at the internment of slavery, I am anxious to assist at the funeral of his twin brother secession" (Carter 1985, 63). Likewise, Dolly Burge, a Georgia slaveholder, had expressed doubts over the rights and wrongs of slavery prior to the Civil War. At the start of the conflict, she confided that she believed the war would provide the test of whether or not God thought slavery a fair and just practice. If the South was right,

Dolly had faith that God would grant the Confederacy victory on the battlefield, but if slavery was wrong, "I trust that He will show it unto us"
(Roark 1977, 97).

Notwithstanding the attitude of women like Dolly Burge, for most former slaveholders, the shock of defeat and abolition was a heavy burden to
bear. As Laura Edwards has shown, the extreme transformations that were
required of former slaveholding men seemed to many completely overwhelming: "Faced with ruined fields, dilapidated buildings, confiscated
stock, an emancipated labor force, and scattered fortunes, few could escape
the unsettling feeling that they had failed as men." In one illustrative case,
James H. Horner, a former slaveholder in Granville County, North Carolina,
and an ardent secessionist and organizer of one of the county's first Confederate companies, suffered an emotional breakdown at the end of the
war, the severity of which led to his incarceration in the state's insane asylum (Edwards 1997, 113). Although few Southern men were institutional-
ized like Horner, many would likely have sympathized with his fate.

Southern Landowners and the Postwar Economy

Historians have disputed the economic impact that the Civil War and Reconstruction had on the Southern planter class. Some depict the era as a
time of revolution in which the plantation owners who had dominated the
antebellum era and led the movement for secession were surpassed in political influence and social and economic standing by a new class of property holders whose wealth and status were as often rooted in commercial
interests as in land. By contrast, others argue that large numbers of slaveholders survived the war and even the most radical stages of Reconstruction with their antebellum fortunes and landholdings largely intact (Wiener
1976, 236–237; Wayne 1983, 76–105).

The experiences of former slaveholders in the late 1860s and 1870s were
sufficiently diverse that both of these interpretations contain an element of
truth. Some former slaveholders were ruined by the war and forced to sell
their property, often to Northern investors. Others made a pragmatic decision
to uproot their families and restart their lives in new and cheap lands opening up in the western territories. However, most remained on their antebellum lands and sought either to persevere with a modified version of the old
plantation system or else adjust their working practices or diversify their occupations to meet the economic challenges of the New South. In extreme
cases, once-powerful planters were reduced to working at menial labor,

sometimes side-by-side with their former slaves in a desperate effort to turn a profit from their land. One 63-year-old former secretary of the Commonwealth of Virginia took to the fields to work, and a former mayor of Savannah, Georgia, was reported by his wife to be "hard at work" with "his hands hard and burnt like a common laborer's" (Roark 1977, 149).

After Reconstruction, the toils of the Southern elite during the era of Republican Party rule were reinterpreted in almost mythical terms as evidence of the honor and fortitude that characterized the white South even after military defeat. Writing in 1887, Susan Dabney Smedes recalled with pride how her father, Thomas Dabney, once a wealthy planter, adapted to very different economic circumstances in the late 1860s than he had ever known before. Dabney lost his fortune when a series of writs was served against him for repayment of bad debts on which he had acted as security before the war. Notwithstanding that he was nearly 70 years old at the time, Dabney refused to accept bankruptcy or offers of assistance from his creditors. As a man of honor, he determined to repay everything he owed by turning his hand to manual labor for the first time in his life. Susan Dabney Smedes recalled her father's actions as "heroic." As well as "cultivating a garden that was the best ordered that we had ever seen," Thomas "planted vegetables in such quantities that it was impossible to consume all on the table, and he sold barrels of vegetables of different kinds in New Orleans." Although his hands "were much bent with age and gout," Dabney also "persisted in cutting wood in the most painful manner, often till he was exhausted." Thomas Dabney had largely brought about his own financial downfall, but even so, his daughter interpreted the whole episode as a forceful retort to Northern aggression. Dabney had heard it reported that General William T. Sherman wanted "to bring every Southern woman to the wash-tub," but through his unstinting hard labor, he successfully protected his daughters from such humiliation (Smedes 1998, 235–236).

Not all former slaveholders who turned to new occupations after the war faced such hardship as Thomas Dabney. Although generalizing for the South as a whole is difficult, in most regions, a majority of the landed aristocracy of the 1850s continued to own real estate in the 1870s, albeit with their property usually much devalued. In a study of the Natchez region of Misssissippi, for example, Michael Wayne concluded that at least 60 percent of planters who owned more than 1,000 acres of land in 1880 were descended from the prewar elite. Moreover, despite the political upheavals of the late 1860s, these wealthiest of landowners continued to dominate positions of social and political prominence in their local communities even though their influence at the federal level remained weak (Wayne 1983, 88, 99).

Yet, even as they clung to their land, the Southern white elite struggled to produce profitable harvests amidst the changing economic circumstances of the postwar world around them. Even the most prominent planters, such as Milledge Luke Bonham, one-time governor of South Carolina, bemoaned that "Although the owner of two of the best and largest cotton plantations in . . . South Carolina, my life has been absorbed in trying to keep my head above water" (Foner 1988, 400). Compared with the antebellum era, the average Southern planter in the 1870s was more heavily in debt, paid far higher taxes to both state and county governments, and was able to farm land at only a fraction of former rates of productivity. Moreover, as railroad construction proceded at a rapid pace and Southern banks and financiers faced financial ruin after the war, landowners in the South were increasingly drawn into national and international markets and became dependent on Northern investors and manufacturers. Even men who had been among the most committed Confederates, such as Robert Toombs, John C. Breckinridge, and former general Jubal A. Early, ended up working for Northern business interests in order to recoup the fortunes they had lost when their once-valuable slaves were freed (Camejo 1976, 51).

A common response of Southern planters and farmers to economic hardship was to dedicate ever more of their land to the production of cotton, but as a conservative convention in South Carolina warned in 1867, this course left landowners exposed in the event of bad harvests or overproduction and falling prices. The convention advised the Southern people instead to pursue diversity in their farming, "cultivate less cotton and more breadstuffs; raise for their own use and for sale, horses, mules and stock of all kinds; cure their own hay, make their own butter and sell the surplus" (*New York Times* 1867). With few landowners heeding this advice, however, the Southern economy remained highly susceptible to the fluctuations of the commercial market economy, which contributed to the disastrous impact of the 1870s depression on Southern agriculture.

By the 1880s, the plantation system was in decline, and as Southern lands passed to a new generation, old estates were frequently broken up and the descendants of the slaveholding class sought new careers and investments beyond the agricultural economy (Ayers 1995, 18). Medicine, law, and mercantile trades were common career paths, especially for elite Southerners who came to maturity during the 1860s. The experiences of the Hart family in Greene County, Georgia, were typical. During the antebellum era, James B. Hart was a successful planter, but after the Civil War, his two sons pursued occupations away from the family farm, James F. Hart opening a dry goods store and John C. Hart practicing law.

A slaveholder from Kentucky, John C. Breckinridge was U.S. vice president from 1856 to 1860 and a leading Confederate military and political figure during the Civil War. After the war, Breckinridge fled abroad but returned to Kentucky in 1869 where, until his death six years later, he practiced law and worked in the railroad industry. (Library of Congress)

A former slaveholder and lieutenant general in the Confederate Army, Jubal Early became president of the Southern Historical Society during Reconstruction and played an important role in establishing the ideology of the Lost Cause. (Library of Congress)

Although the brothers kept their father's plantation lands in the family, they did so only as a secondary source of income (Bryant 1996, 173).

The Planter Class, Black Labor, and Racial Violence

While increasing numbers of white Southerners embarked on professional careers, for the majority of landowners who continued to derive their principle income from agricultural production, the most pressing economic question after the war was how to adjust labor practices in the wake of the abolition of slavery. Few African Americans were willing to work under the old conditions of white domination, yet slaveholders were equally unwilling to countenance the idea that an independent black landowning class might develop within the region, or even, in some cases, that African Americans could be employed as wage laborers to work the fields. A white delegate to the Georgia State Convention in 1866 expressed to a *New York Times* reporter commonly held white fears about the consequences that would result from permitting former slaves to own property and become citizens. In a short time, the delegate believed, poor whites would become envious of African Americans and "would seek to share their prosperity by intermarriage, and the result would be that in fifty years the people of Georgia would be ashamed of themselves" (*New York Times* 1866). Freedmen's Bureau agents in the South reported similarly hostile attitudes held by former slaveholders to the prospect of black wage labor. After spending six months in Savannah "among planters of every grade, from the interior, as well as the city," A. P. Ketchum reported that "ex-slaveholders will take no interest whatever in the free labor system except to find fault with it, and subject it to ridicule." Irrespective of how African American wage earners actually worked, Ketchum heard only "continual complaints, that the negroes 'won't work,' 'won't fulfill their agreements,' '[and] are worthless as free laborers'" (Ketchum 1865). Such comments were in keeping with proslavery characterizations of black men and women as inherently childlike and in need of paternalistic white guidance and care, views that were so deeply ingrained in the collective mind of the white South that the diaries and letters of many educated white Southerners revealed surprise on occasions when they witnessed demonstrations of competence from black free laborers. One Virginia planter hoped to "get good white labor before long" but did admit that the black workers were "doing quite well." A Florida man likewise felt moved to confess that his former slaves had "gone to work rather better than [he] had hoped" (Roark 1977, 160).

Apart from their strongly held racist beliefs, many former slaveholders simply did not have the financial resources to pay wages during Reconstruction, and instead, they sought to establish alternative forms of labor relations. In certain conditions, such as those found in the tobacco regions of Virginia and North Carolina, as well as the Cotton Belt, these relations often, though far from always, took the form of sharecropping, whereby landowners permitted tenants to work a piece of their land in return for a share of the crops that they produced. Sharecropping had advantages for those who worked the land as well as for those who owned it. From the perspective of former slaves, sharecropping offered an opportunity to labor with a degree of independence that compared favorably with conditions under the slave regime. Yet all too often, postemancipation labor relations also retained characteristics of the master-slave relationship, including the widespread threat and reality of violence to enforce black subservience. Reporting from Demopolis, Alabama, in 1868, Freedmen's Bureau agent R.A. Wilson explained that, due to "financial embarassments" brought about by the war, many local planters would be unable "to sustain their present position in society if they deal[t] justly with their colored laborers." White employers therefore regularly violated contracts with black workers and Wilson argued that only a detachment of federal soldiers could stop the practice. The courts, Wilson believed, were powerless to act and he cited as evidence the fact that local whites facing legal proceedings for indebtedness had recently burned the Court House to the ground, destroying in the process the papers relating to the cases against them (Wilson 1868).

The control that former slaveholders sought to exercise over African Americans during Reconstruction was motivated not only by economic considerations but also by a pronounced fear that freedpeople would seek violent revenge for slavery upon their former owners. A prominent streak of paranoia within the slaveholding class had always been evident in the extreme violence with which even rumors of slave rebellions were met during the colonial and antebellum eras. Slaveholders' letters indicate that they were mindful of the successful slave insurrection in Saint-Domingue (now Haiti) in the 1790s, and in the uncertain climate of Reconstruction, whites who stuck to the racist assumptions on which they had been weened since their youth were firmly of the opinion that the 4 million former black slaves could do untold damage if left to their own devices after emancipation (Rable 1984, 16). These fears were heightened at the end of the Civil War by the fact that the Union forces had armed approximately 180,000 black troops and incorporated them into the U.S.

Army in regiments such as the 54th Massachussetts Volunteer Infantry, which had stormed Fort Wagner, South Carolina, in July 1863.

In spite of the overwhelming evidence that free black workers provided a profitable and mostly peaceful labor force, suspicions and paranoia persisted among whites. A newspaper correspondent in South Carolina in late 1865 reported that large numbers of whites were calling for federal protection from what they believed would be an "imminent rising" of African Americans (Carter 1985, 193). Similarly, a rice planter in South Carolina admitted in 1868 that "the negroes on the plantation are orderly enough just now," but nevertheless he mistrusted them, adding, "they are treacherous and only await their opportunity" (Roark 1977, 160). In order to maintain the status quo as much as possible and allay their fears of a violent black uprising, many white Southerners held over formerly enslaved African Americans' heads a viable threat of force and violence in order to keep them under control. To this end, a number of paramilitary organizations were formed across the region, usually with the stated brief to defend "honest white folk" against the perceived "menace" of the unchained former slave. White supremacist groups with names like the Knights of the White Camelia, the Pale Faces, the White Brotherhood, the Men of Justice, and the Ku Klux Klan became synonymous with the wave of racial terror that swept across the former slave states after emancipation.

Planters often tried to distance themselves from the worst excesses of racist violence, and some historians have concluded that the elite had little incentive to participate in or endorse terrorist activites against the freedpeople. Michael Fitzgerald has explained how white terrorism could disrupt local economies and drive away much-needed black laborers (Fitzgerald 2001, 164, 168). However, white violence was not only motivated by economic considerations; it was also intended more generally to limit black advancement and political freedom in the interests of preserving white supremacy. In pursuit of such objectives, countless planters throughout the South played a leading part in the activities of the Klan and related organizations and committed less ritualized homicides that targeted grassroots political leaders from the black community, statesmen and so-called carpetbaggers from the North, black-run farms and businesses, and schools for freedpeople. Among the most prominent members of the Ku Klux Klan was Nathan Bedford Forrest, a wealthy plantation owner and Confederate war hero who had made his fortune as a slave trader in the 1850s and became the Klan's first leader, or grand wizard, in 1866.

Analyzing the class basis of white murderers, one study of more than 500 white men who were involved in killing African Americans in

Nathan Bedford Forrest, 1821–1877

Born into poverty in Tennessee, Nathan Bedford Forrest entered the planter class in the 1850s as a result of his business acumen and involvement in the slave trade. At the start of the Civil War, Forrest was one of the richest men in the South, with a personal fortune believed to amount to more than $1 million. Unsurprisingly, Forrest fought for the Confederacy's right to keep the financially beneficial institution of slavery as it was. He quickly rose through the ranks of the Confederate Army as a cavalry commander of considerable skill and daring, utilizing guerrilla tactics with some success and reaching the rank of lieutenant general by the end of the war. Despite considerable military success, Forrest's reputation was blighted by his involvement in the Fort Pillow massacre, when more than two-thirds of the African Americans defending the fort were killed, many of them as they tried to surrender. Lingering rumors remained over the extent to which Forrest was responsible for this atrocity. Following the Confederacy's surrender, Forrest could no longer profit from the slave trade, but he remained among the economic elite thanks to income from his plantation and his role as president of a Tennessee railroad company.

In 1866, Forrest was involved in the founding of the most infamous antiblack organization in the United States, the Ku Klux Klan, and was named the organization's first grand wizard, or overall leader. He denied involvement in the secret society, though he also boasted that it had more than a half million members in the Southern states. Ironically, in light of his role in the Fort Pillow massacre and estimates that he personally had killed 31 men during the war, Forrest called for the Klan to disband due to its propensity to commit acts of horrific violence, although the localized structure of the organization made this edict virtually worthless, and the Klan continued without Forrest's leadership.

Louisiana in the decade after the Civil War found that 33 percent were planters and an additional 27 percent were farmers on a smaller scale. Some of these men were among the wealthiest individuals in the state, with three owning property valued at more than $30,000 (Vandal 1991, 28, 378, 385). Widespread planter involvement in Klan violence was also evident in South Carolina, where federal authorities specifically targeted Klansmen of social prominence in their attempts to clamp down on the organization in the early 1870s. Among the men convicted in the first set of South Carolina Klan trials in 1871 was John W. Mitchell, a prominent individual in York County who was shown to have conspired to restrict black voting rights (Williams 1993, 62). Even when planters did not commit murders themselves, they were at the very least complicit in creating the conditions within which attacks on freedpeople could flourish. As historian George

Racial Violence in York County, South Carolina

Upcountry South Carolina experienced some of the worst racial violence of the Reconstruction era and was subject to more intensive federal intervention than anywhere else in the South during Reconstruction. Fueled by the strength of local black politics and Republican Party success in state and national elections in 1868, York County became a hotbed of Ku Klux Klan activity. Assaults, whippings, and murders were commonplace, and the violence only escalated when the Republican state governor, Robert Scott, appointed three all-black militias in the county in the spring of 1870. The pres-ence of the militias helped protect black voters sufficiently to secure a Republican victory in the 1870 elections, but when Klan atrocities subsequently increased once more, the federal government intervened.

In March 1871, Col. Lewis Merrill arrived in York County with a company of about 90 men to investigate the violence and found evidence of at least seven murders and 300 whippings perpetrated by the Klan since the previous fall. Additionally, by July 1871, several black homes, schools, and churches had been destroyed and, in response, African Americans had

Rable has argued, the white Southern elite "condoned if they did not participate in attacks on the freedmen. The pulpit, the press, and the upper echelons of southern society occasionally issued mild condemnations of the outrages but took no effective action to stop them . . . the outrages persisted because the dominant elements of white society at least tacitly approved them" (Rable 1984, 30).

In addition to extralegal violence, white dominance over the freedpeople was abetted by formal mechanisms of law enforcement that were mostly drawn up by legislatures dominated by former slaveholders. In 1865, during the era of presidential Reconstruction when Southern governments remained firmly under white control, state legislatures instituted the Black Codes, which addressed the question of labor control explicitly. For example, vagrancy was made a crime punishable by a fine, which often had to be worked off on a plantation or at some other job until the "debt to society" had been paid. This system of "debt bondage" was one way of keeping formerly enslaved laborers tied to the plantations. Other methods included the introduction of restrictive contracts in which formerly enslaved laborers were derogatively referred to as servants and their employers termed masters. Frequently, employers did not honor contracts and refused to pay wages once the year's harvest was in, and although the started at least 22 fires targeting white property. Interpreting events in South Carolina as constituting a rebellion against the United States, Congress passed the Third Enforcement Act, and on October 17, 1871, President Ulysses S. Grant used the act to suspend the writ of habeas corpus and introduce martial law across nine Piedmont counties. Within two weeks, more than 100 white men had been arrested in York County alone under the provisions of what became known as the Ku Klux Klan Act. In total, more than 1,300 indictments were made for Klan activities in South Carolina, and although the overwhelming majority never came to court, at least 40 men from York County were convicted of various offenses and sentenced to between 18 months' and eight years' imprisonment at the New York state penitentiary in Albany. Most of the convicts were farmers and laborers, because wealthier participants in Klan atrocities were able to flee the region before federal troops arrived. Arrests continued sporadically through 1873, but racial violence persisted in York County, and by 1876, President Grant had pardoned all convicted Klansmen. (West 2002, 83–116)

Freedmen's Bureau sought to resolve disputes that arose between freedpeople and white employers in such situations, its influence was limited and, in at least some regions, evidence shows that Bureau agents acted in ways consistent with the interests of local whites.

The dissolution of the Freedmen's Bureau and the election of a succession of "redeemer" governments (see the Introduction to this book) across the South during the first half of the 1870s once again left African Americans with minimal recourse to legal remedies in labor disputes and more susceptible than ever to extralegal violence. As whites strengthened their grip on political power, the criminal law emerged as an effective vehicle for bolstering the dominance of the white elite. The introduction of chain gangs and convict leasing heralded the onset of a penal system that bore striking similarities to slavery and provided a source of forced labor for white employers to exploit. Yet these new forms of punishment were also indicative of social and economic developments that were changing the South and that in subtle ways steadily eroded the traditional foundations upon which the region's ruling classes had based their power. Most convicts worked not in agricultural pursuits but on railroad construction projects and later in mines, occupations that reflected the gradual transformation of the Southern economy and the slow, long-term decline of the agricultural sector.

"Colonel" Frederick Dent, 1786–1873

Hailing from Maryland, Frederick Dent trained as a lawyer and worked as a business-man before moving west, where he established himself as a plantation owner and master of 30 slaves in the 1850s. In the process, he acquired the honorific title of "colonel," even though he had no military background. Dent owned approximately 1,000 acres of land just southwest of St. Louis and named the property White Haven. Although Dent was not a plantation owner on the grand scale of some men in the Deep South, such as Robert Toombs of Georgia, he was a big plantation owner in Missouri terms. He was also a stout defender of slavery and arrogantly held to the belief that the North would not go to war to abolish the institution, as the financial consequences would damage the Northern economy. In 1848, Frederick Dent's eldest daughter, Julia Boggs Dent, married Ulysses S. Grant, a West Point graduate and veteran of the Mexican War. After resigning his commission in 1854, Grant moved to Missouri to live with Julia and her

Conclusion

Recent historiography has rightly condemned the violence and racist ideol-ogy of the Southern white elite that persisted both during and long after Re-construction and that contributed greatly to denying African Americans in the South full civil rights and equal social, economic, and political opportuni-ties for a century after the abolition of slavery. There can be little doubt, however, that regardless of how they are viewed today, most former slave-holders genuinely believed that their actions and their cause were just. With-out this misplaced conviction existing on a grand scale throughout the South, it is unlikely that the antebellum elite would have been so successful in maintaining their social, economic, and political dominance for so long. It is, after all, difficult to view the Reconstruction period as anything other than a success for former slaveholders or, indeed, as a tragic failure for the United States. On the whole, former slaveholders were successful in their aims, in-cluding staving off the challenge of racial equality and justice for the freed-people. For the most part, they also kept their land. Despite the passage of wide-ranging federal legislation intended to guarantee the civil rights of African Americans, in practice, these laws were at best sporadically adhered to in the South, and more often than not, they were entirely ignored and cir-cumvented by a combination of fraud, gerrymandering, and violence. As evi-dence of the planters' persistent political influence, Redeemer governments also pursued taxation policies that explicitly favored the property-holding family, and until 1859, he often worked side-by-side with the Dent family's slaves.

The Civil War divided Frederick Dent and Ulysses Grant, and Dent never truly forgave his son-in-law for his role in bringing about the abolition of slavery. Even so, in 1869, at the age of 83, Frederick Dent moved with his daughter Julia and her husband into the White House following Grant's election as president of the United States, but Dent's pro-Conferderate opinions did not change. He continued to defend the South and the institution of slavery, even at the executive dinner table, and the First Lady was often required to sit next to her father during mealtimes in order to try and quell his unreconstructed ardor and prevent diplomatic incidents. Frederick Dent died in 1873 at the age of 87. As a result of his close personal ties to the president, Dent stands as an emblematic figure of Southern white intransigence on issues of race and reunion during Reconstruction.

classes. Taxes were levied more heavily on tools than on land and consequently fell disproportionately on the shoulders of the poor and the laboring classes. In Eric Foner's assessment, Redeemer governments "in effect restor[ed] the oligarchic antebellum system of local government," a system dominated by the landholding elite (Foner 1988, 591).

Throughout much of the 20th century, the elite white Southerners of the Reconstruction era were commonly portrayed as the victims of oppressive federal policies enforced by racially inferior people and their white supporters, many of them derisively depicted as Northern carpetbaggers or Southern scalawags. The period was referred to pejoratively as "Black Reconstruction," and tales were spread of black miscreants trying to force themselves on God-fearing white women. These images and beliefs endured, serving as justification for race riots and lynchings well into the 20th century, as former slaveholders made efficient use of propaganda, including speeches, pamphlets, and novels, in a largely successful effort to win the peace even though they had lost the Civil War. In 1915, D. W. Griffith turned the most famous example of this propaganda, Thomas Dixon's novel *The Clansman*, into *The Birth of a Nation*, one of the most important and influential films in American cinema. *The Birth of a Nation* represented black people as not just inferior to whites but also as marauding, godless rapists, and the film featured an entirely erroneous depiction of heroic members of the Ku Klux Klan fighting *bravely* to save the honor of their

D. W. Griffith's 1915 film *The Birth of a Nation* perpetuated a view of Reconstruction as a time when the Ku Klux Klan saved the white South from Republican Party corruption and African American ignorance and brutality. (Library of Congress)

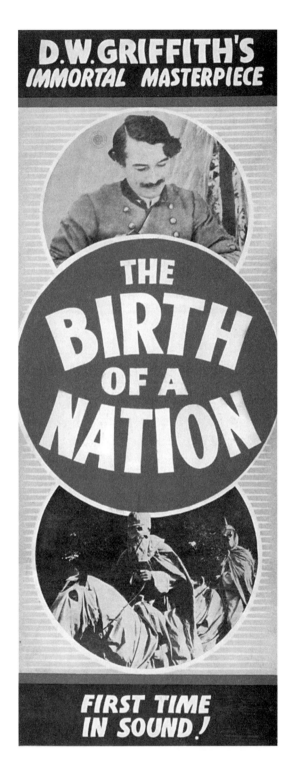

womenfolk. The film's release and widespread popularity clearly indicate the persistence of both pro-Confederate propaganda and belief in a decidedly inaccurate interpretation of Reconstruction even 50 years after the end of the Civil War. Though the slaveholding generation had long since died out, its deeds cast a long shadow over the course of American history.

References and Further Reading

Ayers, Edward L. 1995. *Southern Crossing: A History of the American South, 1877–1906.* New York: Oxford University Press.

Bryant, Jonathan B. 1996. *How Curious a Land: Conflict and Change in Greene County, Georgia, 1850–1885.* Chapel Hill: University of North Carolina Press.

Camejo, Peter. 1976. *Racism, Revolution, Reaction, 1861–1877: The Rise and Fall of Radical Reconstruction.* New York: Monad Press.

Carter, Dan T. 1985. *When the War Was Over: The Failure of Self-Reconstruction in the South, 1865–1867.* Baton Rouge: Louisiana State University Press.

Edwards, Laura F. 1997. *Gendered Strife and Confusion: The Political Culture of Reconstruction.* Urbana: University of Illinois Press.

Faust, Drew Gilpin. 1990. "Altars of Sacrifice: Confederate Women and the Narratives of War." *Journal of American History* 76 (4): 1200–1228.

Fitzgerald, Michael. 2001. "Extralegal Violence and the Planter Class: The Ku Klux Klan in the Alabama Black Belt during Reconstruction." In *Local Matters: Race, Crime, and Justice in the Nineteenth-Century South,* ed. Christopher Waldrep and Donald G. Nieman. Athens: University of Georgia Press.

Foner, Eric. 1988. *Reconstruction: America's Unfinished Revolution, 1863–1977.* New York: Harper and Row.

Ketchum, A. P. 1865. "Reports of Conditions and Operations." Report to Bvt. Maj. Genl. R. Saxton, September 1. Records of the Assistant Commissioner for the State of South Carolina, Bureau of Refugees, Freedmen and Abandoned Lands, 1865–1870. National Archives microfilm publication M869, roll 34. (Online information; retrieved 4/30/08.) http://freedmensbureau.com/southcarolina/scoperations4.htm.

New York Times. 1866. "Georgia." *New York Times,* January 27.

New York Times. 1867. "Southern Industry—Views of Planters." *New York Times,* November 15.

Olmsted, Frederick Law. 2001 [1856]. *A Journey in the Seaboard Slave States: With Remarks on their Economy.* Documenting the American South. University Library, University of North Carolina at Chapel Hill. (Online information; retrieved 4/30/08.) http://docsouth.unc.edu/nc/olmsted/olmsted.html.

Rable, George C. 1984. *But There Was No Peace: The Role of Violence in the Politics of Reconstruction.* Athens: University of Georgia Press.

Roark, James L. 1977. *Masters without Slaves: Southern Planters in the Civil War and Reconstruction.* New York: W. W. Norton.

Smedes, Susan Dabney. 1998 [1887]. *Memoirs of a Southern Planter.* Documenting the American South. University Library, University of North Carolina at Chapel Hill. (Online information; retrieved 4/30/08.) http://docsouth.unc.edu/fpn/smedes/smedes.html#smedes223.

Vandal, Gilles. 1991. "'Bloody Caddo': White Violence against Blacks in a Louisiana Parish, 1865–1876." *Journal of Social History* 25 (2): 373–388.

Wayne, Michael. 1983. *The Reshaping of Plantation Society: The Natchez District, 1860–1880.* Baton Rouge: Louisiana State University Press.

West, Jerry Lee. 2002. *The Reconstruction Ku Klux Klan in York County, South Carolina, 1865–1877.* Jefferson, NC: McFarland.

Wiener, Jonathan M. 1976. "Planter Persistence and Social Change: Alabama, 1850–1870." *Journal of Interdisciplinary History* 7 (2): 235–260.

Williams, Lou Falkner. 1993. "The South Carolina Ku Klux Klan Trials and Enforcement of Federal Rights, 1871–1872." *Civil War History* 39 (1): 47–66.

Whites, LeeAnn. 2005. *Gender Matters: Civil War, Reconstruction and the Making of the New South.* New York: Palgrave Macmillan.

Wilson, R. A. to T. H. Rugon. Report for August 1868, Demopolis, Alabama, August 31, 1868. Records of the Assistant Commissioner for the State of Alabama, 1865–1870, Bureau of Refugees, Freedmen, and Abandoned Lands.

Wood, Kirsten E. 2004. *Masterful Women: Slaveholding Widows from the American Revolution through the Civil War.* Chapel Hill: University of North Carolina Press.

Black Women, Work, and Freedom | 7

Kate Dossett

The meaning of Reconstruction to freedwomen and freedmen was determined not only by how African Americans experienced and shaped their freedom in the years immediately following the Civil War but also how they continued to redefine their freedom after Northern troops withdrew from the South in 1877 and left Southerners to manage their "race problem." Central to African Americans' experiences of Reconstruction was their attempt to make their freedom as different as possible from their experiences as slaves. As slaves, African Americans' working lives were almost always dominated, although never entirely dictated, by the demands of a white master, mistress, or overseer; as free men and women, African Americans would struggle to negotiate the terms and conditions under which they would offer their labor. By exploring the working lives of black women in the aftermath of emancipation, through Reconstruction and the entrenchment of Jim Crow laws, this chapter examines how black women interpreted and molded their lives as free women. Work is important in helping us understand the social history of Reconstruction, because, as Jacqueline Jones explains, "The work that people did, and the terms and conditions under which they did it, revealed both their place and their possibilities within American society" (Jones 1998, 13).

During Reconstruction, African American women continued to perform those jobs they had been forced to do during slavery. Between 1865 and 1890, the majority of African American women continued to work as either agricultural laborers or domestic servants. Angela Davis argues that by 1890, the economic position of black women was so bad that "freedom must have appeared to be even more remote in the future than it had been at the end of the Civil War" (Davis 1983, 88). Certainly the census figures support the pessimistic view that women continued to be severely confined in terms of their economic opportunities. Similarly, the wording of labor contracts, which bound many women and men to the new system of sharecropping, suggests that black women were severely restricted in their work roles as agricultural labors. However, exclusive focus on how the activities of Reconstruction-era Northern legislators, Freedmen's Bureau agents, and former planters affected African American women can obscure the ways in which black women in freedom also exercised agency and challenged the boundaries of traditional jobs like domestic service. In the years that followed the end of the Civil War, African American women exploited their status as free laborers to develop new methods for resisting exploitation in the workplace.

In addition to redefining and contesting their work identities as domestic servants and agricultural laborers, African American women claimed new areas such as beauty salons and savings banks as legitimate black women's work. Some of these new areas opened up to black women's entrepreneurial skills precisely because of the gradual but increasingly rigid application of Jim Crow customs and laws, which, ironically, fostered black businesses and communities. Black women took advantage of Jim Crow to develop businesses that both benefited from black-only clientele and provided community services and racial uplift in order to alleviate some of the worst excesses of the segregated South. The story of Reconstruction is not just one of northern and white intervention in black communities; it is also the story of how ordinary black women workers shaped their new freedoms and were actors in their own lives. Black women workers drew on strategies of resistance developed during slavery and used them to adapt to and continue to try to shape their lives and identities as free women in a society that would try to circumscribe that freedom in various, and ever changing, ways.

Black Women and Work during Slavery

As slaves, African American females had been defined primarily in relation to their roles as workers and breeders rather than as women. By contrast, white females were women, and only sometimes women who worked, whether at home as contributors toward the household economy or as (and sometimes in addition to) participants in the wage labor force. An idealized vision of gender relations and work in the 19th century that applied to few women but nevertheless shaped attitudes toward women and work rested upon what Barbara Welter has called the "cult of domesticity." This ideology saw men and women as belonging to separate spheres. Women undertook duties in the private sphere such as child rearing and running of the household. Men occupied the public sphere: they went out to work, earned a wage to support their family and participatied in the life of the body politic. Prominent advocates of the cult of domesticity included Lydia Maria Child (author of *The Mother's Book*) and Catherine Beecher (author of *A Treatise on Domestic Economy*). In the 1830s and 1840s, Beecher and others celebrated the status of white women as homemakers and child rearers, arguing that these roles were different from but equal to white men's work. Although all women were believed to be "naturally" suited to a life of domesticity, in practice this idealized vision was distinctly white and middle or upper class. Similarly, ideas of manhood and work in the 19th century were built around whiteness, middle-class status, separate spheres, and the ideology of free labor. White women as well as slaves were excluded from this ideal because none of them could hold property in their own labor, which belonged instead to their owners, husbands, and fathers.

Although both black and white women were excluded from the ideology of free labor, their relationship to work was defined very differently. Whereas white femininity was defined in opposition to work—hard work was something done by men—by contrast, black women were valued for their labor. Black female slaves frequently worked in the fields alongside their men, picking cotton and cultivating rice. They were also valued as breeders of slaves. The private sphere and family life of black slaves were deemed inconsequential: marriage was not legally recognized, work practices and hours made no allowance for women's own family responsibilities, and families were often split up and children sold off.

The Reconstruction of Work

One of the first choices that African Americans made in freedom concerned their relationship to work and their status as laborers. Freedwomen and freedmen exerted their freedom to make choices about how, when, and where they worked that would distinguish their new laboring lives from their previous condition of servitude. Just as black women and men understood the ability to choose what sort of work they would engage in as the defining battleground upon which they would defend their new freedoms,

African American woman doing laundry with children on the ground watching and helping, 1900.
(Library of Congress)

so did those whites who sought to limit the work roles African Americans
would be allowed to perform. Many accounts of black women's work after
the Civil War emphasize these limitations and the continuing exploitation of
black women during Reconstruction. Between 1865 and 1890, the majority
of black women still occupied the same types of jobs they had held during
slavery. The 1890 census showed that 38.7 percent of working black women
were employed in agriculture, 30.8 percent in household domestic service,
and 15.6 percent in laundry work, with only 2.8 percent in manufacturing
(Davis 1983, 88). Yet historians of women's work have demonstrated that
black women were not simply passive victims of racial, sexual, and class oppression after emancipation. While white Southerners during Reconstruction and beyond sought to recreate the racial hierarchies and reconstruct the
work identities that African Americans had endured as slaves, black women
drew on previous strategies of resistance to slavery and on new methods of
resistance developed in freedom to challenge whites' expectations of black
women workers. In the process, they created new work opportunities and

identities for themselves that could be adapted to help them deal with the worst excesses of overt racism embedded in the policies and practices of local and state governments in the New South.

Agricultural Labor

During the Civil War, a considerable amount of Southern land had been abandoned, seized, or confiscated. At the war's end, it was unclear what would happen to land that had been worked and cultivated under forced labor and owned by Confederate planters and that was now under the control of the Freedmen's Bureau. General William T. Sherman had settled 40,000 African Americans on plantations in Georgia and South Carolina in early 1865, but President Andrew Johnson ordered restoration of confiscated and abandoned lands in the summer and fall of the same year. Throughout late 1865 and early 1866, as Republicans in Congress battled with President Johnson to implement their competing visions of Reconstruction, many freedwomen and freedmen continued to cultivate the plantations they had worked during slavery in anticipation that they would be given rights to the land. Freedwomen played an active role in resisting restoration of lands to their former owners and were willing to use violence when necessary. For example, freedwomen and freedmen on the Keithfield plantation in South Carolina drove their white overseer off the plantation in March 1865 and cultivated their own crop of rice. When the absentee owner recruited local officials, including a former Confederate provost marshal and plantation slave driver as well as two soldiers, to restore her lands, the former slaves, led by the freedwomen, attacked and drove the men off. Reports of the incident describe the officials' appeals to freedmen to "exert themselves" and call off the "maddened women." The freedwomen who had led the defense of the plantation repeatedly struck the officials until they limped away in fear for their lives. Five of the women were charged and served sentences for their role in defending what they believed to be their property. The incident at the Keithfield plantation reflected a broader and ongoing pattern of African American resistance to attempts to restore former planter-slave relationships in the aftermath of the Civil War. Even after many plantations had been restored to their former owners, planters often found it extremely difficult to gather a workforce. Freedwomen and freedmen refused to sign labor contracts and ignored threatened evictions or sometimes moved to unrestored plantations where they squatted and cleared the land to cultivate their own crop (Schwalm 1997, 193–194).

As a result of the institution of the notorious Black Codes across the Southern states in late 1865 and early 1866, as well as military intervention and the actions of Freedmen's Bureau agents, many freedwomen and freedmen eventually joined the contract labor system. But planters soon learned that taking away freedpeople's land and making them sign labor contracts did not mean they were able to control how, when, and where the new laborers worked. As one rice planter complained of his former slaves, "they will only work in their own way & at such times as they see fit" (Schwalm 1997, 334). One of the ways in which agricultural laborers insisted on working on their own terms was by refusing to work under or for white overseers. They also asserted their freedom by making their own decisions about which family members would work. Indeed, accounts of Reconstruction have placed major emphasis on black women's apparent departure from the cotton fields of the South following emancipation. Certainly, white employers in the South were vocal in their condemnation of formerly enslaved women who "played the lady" and rejected their former slave roles as cotton pickers for whites. For example, John De Forest, a Freedmen's Bureau agent in South Carolina, wrote that "myriads of women who once earned their own living now have aspirations to be like white ladies and, instead of using the hoe, pass the days in dawdling over their trivial housework, or gossiping among their neighbors" (Jones 1998, 59).

Both contemporaries and some historians, such as Leon Litwack (1979), have interpreted black women's withdrawal from the fields as evidence of African Americans' desire to conform to white family and gender roles. But women's work patterns during Reconstruction were shaped by a number of factors. For black women, withdrawing from white supervised agricultural work was more about survival and family needs than any notion of aping white womanhood. As Jacqueline Jones has demonstrated, some black women may have stopped working for white slave owners or overseers, but they often did so in order to pick cotton and cultivate rice for their families. Freedwomen and freedmen were exerting their freedom to shape their work priorities according to the needs of their own families rather than those of their white employers. Nor did these choices reflect a straightforward desire to assimilate to white, middle-class, gendered and work norms about private and public spheres. Rather, both black men and women wanted black women to be able to work in environments where they were not exposed to the risk of sexual exploitation at the hands of white men, as they had been under slavery (Jones 1995, 59). Reconstruction records show numerous instances of black freedmen attempting to protect their women from rape and other forms of sexual assault. They petitioned state constitutional conventions, complained to Freedmen's Bureau agents, protested against military authorities who arrested women and raped them in jail, and made speeches condemning white men's exploitation of black women (Hunter 1997, 34). Others, like freedman Sam Neal, intervened directly against the continued assaults on his daughter by the Tennessee planter for whom the family worked. The planter ordered Neal to be beaten and denied his wages for his efforts. The Freedmen's Bureau ruled that Neal be compensated by the landowner and allowed to keep his share of the crop (Gutman 1976, 393).

Domestic Service

The desire on the part of black women to resist white control and oversight and to manage their families' work patterns according to their own needs was also reflected in their attitudes toward domestic service roles. The largest category of work for women outside agriculture, domestic service also carried strong reminders of women's enforced labor for other people's families during slavery. Although the tasks performed and conditions of household service varied over time and place from Reconstruction through to the early 20th century, the low status and low wages paid domestic workers remained constant. Most worked seven days a week, and wages typically ranged from four to eight dollars a month (Hunter 1997, 52–53). The responsibilities of a domestic worker varied according to the family size and means of her or his employer, but an average day could last from 14 to 16 hours and could include any aspect of household labor from cleaning, cooking, and hauling water to child care, shopping, and waiting on a table (Aptheker 1990, 47).

Although exploitation and poor wages remained a feature of domestic service, black women's entry into paid household service was not simply a continuation of the domestic slave roles black women held during slavery. Prior to emancipation, the role of the paid, live-in servant belonged almost exclusively to young, white, and usually single girls and women. Growing job opportunities for white women in factories, clerical work, and sales industries meant that household service was no longer performed predominantly by white girls. By the end of the 19th century, domestic service had become *the* occupation associated with black female labor. As one contemporary writer noted, "household service now drew the despised race to the despised calling" (Eaton 1899, cited in Clark-Lewis 1987, 197). Of the 2.7 million black women and girls engaged in paid labor in 1890, almost half worked in either domestic service (30.8 percent) or as washerwomen (15.6

percent). In the first half of the 20th century, the number of black women household workers continued to grow (Davis 1983, 88, 98). Black women and girls became increasingly associated with domestic service, partly because native-born white women were able to move into other occupations, but also because African American women were barred from 86 percent of employment categories (Clark-Lewis 1987, 198). Even opportunities for migration to urban centers with thriving black populations like Washington, D.C., did not necessarily provide escape from laboring in the homes of others. Domestic service was the principal occupation for black men as well as women in 32 out of the 48 states in 1890 (Davis 1983, 93). Established black communities in urban centers like Washington did not, as Campbell argued in Chapter 3 of this volume, readily open themselves to the large influx of newcomers or employ them in their businesses. Class-based prejudices within the race as well as discrimination by whites could limit black women's occupational mobility.

Although black females had limited access to jobs outside domestic service, they were able to shape the parameters of their daily work. As with agricultural labor, freedwomen fought to distinguish their labor as free domestic workers from their former status as household slaves. Many chose to leave the house and plantation where they had been at the beck and call of the mistress of the house and vulnerable to sexual exploitation by men of the house. Others chose to stay and redefine their work roles. One of the ways in which they did this was by insisting that they work around their own family needs and consequently refusing to live in their employers' home. One white employer in Atlanta complained about black domestic workers after the Civil War: "Very few of them, cooks or servants, will consent to sleep on the premises where they work as servants. They seem to think that it is something against their freedom if they sleep where they are employed" (Hunter 1997, 59). White employers not only did not understand this urge for freedom but also resisted it. Clark-Lewis has shown the importance of women's collective action in helping black workers to set their own conditions for domestic service. Black domestic workers organized penny-saving clubs in order to help make this transition from live-in servant to daily household worker economically viable. Penny-saving clubs offered live-in servants the financial security that could help them leave a live-in job and set up a new job as a dayworker. Becoming a dayworker held many advantages: domestic servants were more likely to be able to dictate the pace and time of their work, take off Sundays to go to church, and join clubs such as the National Association of Colored Women, thereby ending the total isolation of live-in domestic work. Daywork also meant that black domestics were less likely to be directly supervised by whites, and domestic workers also believed that it gave them greater control over their body and work conditions. For example, domestic workers who went home at the end of the day redefined their work roles by dividing their work into tasks to be performed rather than serving the every waking need of an individual or family. Domestic tasks were separated out, with some workers insisting they would cook, but could not be asked to manage laundry or child-care arrangements. Similarly, dayworkers exercised greater control over what they wore. For example, many domestic workers regarded wearing a uniform as something to which only a live-in servant would consent. As one domestic servant, Virginia Lacey, put it, "Wearing your own clothes—that's like you being your own boss! You was on your own job for a day and pay, then go home" (Clark-Lewis 1987, 207).

Domestic household workers also resisted bad working conditions by leaving particularly exploitative employers. Spreading the word about bad employers in order to get them blacklisted could be done both informally through word of mouth and formally through networks such as secret societies. These networks could also help a domestic worker secure another position. Understandably, records of these societies are often untraceable, yet the complaints of white Southerners on the difficulties of finding and keeping good domestic workers testify to the networks' organizational effectiveness. For example, George Brown, a white doctor who ran for the office of mayor of Atlanta in 1912, recognized the power of domestic workers' collective action and ran on a platform that determined to put an end to this resistance: "Today, if you discharge your cook, every one of that number belong to a negro secret society. . . . They immediately go to the next meeting of that society and black list you and what is the result? You will find in a month that your wife will be possibly unable to secure a servant under any consideration" (Hunter 1997, 210).

In addition to taking advantage of organized resistance and seeking out jobs that offered minimum contact with white supervision, African American domestic workers and washerwomen utilized what James Scott has called "infrapolitics." *Infrapolitics* refers to "the circumspect struggle waged daily by subordinate groups . . . like infrared rays, beyond the visible end of the spectrum" (Scott 1990, 183). African American domestic workers struggled against racial hierarchies of the job market as well as the injustices of individual employers by engaging in daily acts of resistance. These acts included insisting on taking leave or pretending to be ill in order to attend a family or community celebration or to look after a sick family member, taking unscheduled breaks, and performing work tasks badly and sabotaging their employer's possessions. One employer recognized this form of resistance: "Tell them to wipe up the floor, and they will splash away from one end of the room to the other; and if you tell them that is not the way to do, they will either be insolent or perhaps give you a vacant stare as if they were very much astonished that you thought that was not the way to do it, and they will keep right on" (Hunter 1997, 61). Domestic workers also sought to shape the conditions of their work and resist exploitative wage agreements through pan toting. Pan toting was the practice of taking leftover food (the service pan), or sometimes clothing materials, in order to compensate for the various wage abuses to which domestic servants were vulnerable, including low wages and the withholding of wages on the grounds of apparent misdemeanors, such as being late or slovenly with work or breaking a household item. As one domestic servant explained, "The service pan is the mainstay in many a home. . . .We don't steal; we just 'take' things—they are a part of the oral contract, expressed or implied" (Aptheker 1990, 51).

Older and married women, especially those with children, were much more likely to find employment as washerwomen (Gutman 1976, 630–631). Laundry work, while laborious and often endless, held considerable advantages over a life of domestic service. Washerwomen tended to view the white families whose washing they took in as clients rather than employers. Washerwomen would pick up laundry at the beginning of the week and take it back to their own neighborhood, where they would wash it free from white supervision. Moreover, washerwomen often worked together to create networks of interdependence and facilitate communal child care. Indeed, domestic servants frequently held up washerwomen as the ideal of autonomous working to which they might aspire (Hunter 1997, 62–63). This aspiration is not to suggest that African American washerwomen were entirely autonomous agents who could set the terms and conditions of their work. Rather, as Hunter has shown, washerwomen worked hard to organize resistance and employed tactics that ranged from the blacklisting of harsh employers to instituting formal strikes in order to protest the unreasonable demands and low wages that white men and women tried to impose on them.

Like domestic household workers, washerwomen engaged in acts of everyday resistance when employers tried to exploit them. One white Southerner complained about the "servant problem" in the South: "the washerwomen . . . badly damaged clothes they work on, iron-rusting them, tearing them, breaking off buttons, and burning them brown" (Kelley 1996, 21). The everyday struggles of domestic workers and washerwomen help us

African American woman hanging laundry, ca. 1900. (Library of Congress)

Washerwomen's Strike in Atlanta (1881)

The 1881 strike by washerwomen in Atlanta was part of a series of strikes by washerwomen and other Southern black workers who articulated their economic and political grievances during Reconstruction. At the beginning of July 1881, a group of 20 women and some men came together to establish the Washing Society. A secret organization, the group agreed on a minimum uniform rate at which the washerwomen of Atlanta would offer their services. The washerwomen called a strike to achieve this goal of higher wages on July 18, 1881. Through door-to-door canvassing as well as threatening women who refused to participate, the Washing Society gathered as many as 3,000 "strikers and sympathizers" within the first three weeks of its campaign, including a very small number of white women. The white community and city officials responded to the washerwomen's growing power and political intervention by threatening to put them out of business. Local capitalists built an industrial steam laundry and undercut the washerwomen's prices. At

to understand both the place and possibilities of black women as workers after emancipation. We should, as Kelley has argued, see these acts of everyday resistance not simply as individual examples of heroism but rather as "diagnostic" of power. That is, they help us understand how power operates and how it is shaped from below as well as above (Kelley 1996, 8). In spite of the limited job opportunities open to them, black women workers were able to shape how and when they did their jobs and to create spaces in which they could both contribute to and draw strength from black community life.

Industry and Factory Work

Black women were keen to find other avenues of work that would challenge the occupational hierarchies that kept them bound to domestic service and agricultural labor. The gradual industrialization that characterized the New South might have offered an opening for black women ambitious to find more profitable work in urban areas. Jacqueline Jones and others have suggested that black women played only a limited role in the industrial New South and were never integrated into the industrial workforce. Indeed, technological innovation in Southern industries such as iron and tobacco was to a large extent delayed by the racialized hierarchies of the Southern the same time, the city council threatened to introduce a resolution to regulate laundry workers by insisting that members of washerwomen's organizations pay a license fee of $25.00.

The washerwomen's reaction to these developments revealed that they were far from novices in the game of politics. They called the city's bluff, agreeing to pay the business tax but insisting it should serve as a protective fee; in return, the city had to respect their right to self-regulation. Ultimately, the Atlanta City Council abandoned the license fee proposal in August 1881. Tera Hunter argues that the strike is revealing of the contested nature of gender and work relations in the New South. White employers and the state might have been able to determine which jobs black women could perform, but they were not able to control how and when they did those jobs (Hunter 1997, 97). Even as blacks' civil rights were curtailed, domestic servants and washerwomen continued to resist the control of individual whites and white state authorities.

industrial workforce. The ready supply of cheap black labor and the exclusionary racial practices of unions meant that the most grueling and backbreaking jobs could be performed at low costs by segregated groups of black men and women. Segmented workforces were preserved both between and within different industries. For example, in the Southern textile industry, which lay at the heart of Southern industrial development, black women were almost entirely excluded, in spite of their long years of enforced textile production on Southern plantations. By privileging whiteness as a requirement for work in more preferential industrial jobs such as cotton mills, Southerners helped to block any interracial alliance between poor white and black farmers who had been hard hit by a fall in cotton prices and helped to establish the racialized and gendered hierarchies that would come to define the Jim Crow South (Jones 1995, 135–136).

In accordance with their position at the very bottom of this hierarchy, when African American women were employed in factories, it was to perform the least desirable of tasks. For example, one of the few industries in which black women were able to find employment was in the tobacco factories, where they were employed, as they had been during slavery, as "rehandlers." Rehandling involved stripping, stemming, and hanging raw tobacco leaves. White women, on the other hand, were employed in tobacco factories as skilled workers responsible for rolling cigarettes.

African American women sorting tobacco at the T. B. Williams Tobacco Company in Richmond, Virginia, ca. 1899. (Library of Congress)

Although black women were employed almost exclusively in the hazardous manufacture of raw tobacco, many seemingly preferred rehandling to the personal interactions of domestic service. By 1910, nearly 8,500 black women were employed in the Southern tobacco industry. Although this number represented less than 2 percent of Southern black women in nonagricultural jobs, it seems high when compared with the mere 883 black women employed—usually as scrubwomen—in cotton mills. As with domestic workers, the wages and conditions of tobacco workers hardly changed over time: in 1880, the average daily wage of tobacco workers in North Carolina was between 40 and 80 cents, and by 1915 it was rarely more than one dollar. Workers typically toiled for five and a half days a week for as much as 12 hours a day with almost no prospect of career progression (Jones 1995, 137–138).

Another area where black women could find factory employment was in oyster processing. While oyster gathering was performed by black men, women and children often formed more than half the workforce employed in oyster factories, where in season women could earn an average of five to six dollars a week for oyster shucking. Steaming or forcing open oysters was unpleasant and hard work, but in coastal regions of Georgia, many women preferred it to domestic service, as they could work at their own pace, receive payment according to work completed, and avoid extensive white supervision (Jones 1995, 141).

Few other industries were prepared or able to open their doors to black women workers, and this dearth of factory jobs had an impact on black factory workers' place and career possibilities. The limited number of factory jobs open to black women and the desire of black women to move out of domestic service meant that, unlike household workers, those women who had gained factory work could not easily afford to walk out of their jobs when treated badly. This made it easier for employers to dismiss them for minor infractions in the knowledge that they would have little difficulty finding replacements. In spite of this set of circumstances, factory workers did resist being treated poorly by taking unauthorized holidays, refusing to respond to the factory bell, and constructing "networks of solidarity" to resist sexual harassment at work (Kelley 1996, 27–28). Other strategies included communal singing to combat the tedium and unpleasantness of their jobs. Although, like many black workers, female factory workers were wary of unions, with their long tradition of racial hostility toward black workers, they took part in both their own spontaneous and sometimes successful strikes as well as in formal strikes organized by the National Tobacco Workers Union at the end of the 19th century.

Women who worked in factories also resisted by refusing to accept the low-status work identities that industrial employers imposed on them through poor wages and disrespectful treatment. For example, in some factories, workers were not allowed to sit down and had nowhere to hang their coats or put their belongings. Even so, many tobacco workers recognized that, despite such treatment, they were skilled laborers. As one worker, Elviry Maggee, explained: "I know tobacco. I knows all de grades an' blends. . . . You 'members Old Man Hughes what built all dese here schools an' horspitals in town? Well, I learnt Mister John how to grade tobacco when he first come in de factory. Yes, Jesus, I give Mister John his start. I'm po' now an' I was po' den but he come to be a rich man. But it didn't do him no good. De Lawd called him away with Bright's misery" (Jones 1995, 140). In her testimony, Maggee asserts her value and identity as a skilled worker who believes her knowledge and skills could not easily be replaced. At the same time, however, she reveals that she, unlike her boss, was able to find meaning and identity outside work and money through her own sense of self-respect and religious faith. Such evidence demonstrates that the ability of female slaves to find identity outside work, through family, motherhood, community, and religious faith, continued to mark black women's work experiences through Reconstruction and into the late 19th and early 20th centuries.

The Work of Reconstruction: Building Black Businesses and Communities

Freedwomen and freedmen reshaped their work patterns as domestic and agricultural laborers not just to spend more time with their families but also to build a black community. That many freedwomen and freedmen labored quietly for their own is, inadvertently, reflected in the official records of Reconstruction, which show that white Southerners believed that African Americans were incapable of working unless forced to do so. If African Americans, particularly women and children, were insisting on working half shifts or not at all, then what happened to all this "missing" labor? According to white Southerners, African Americans spent it idling. Many white landowners would have shared the views of South Carolina planter E. B. Haywood, who in 1867 complained: "The women appear most lazy, merely because they are allowed the opportunity. They wish to stay in the house, or in the garden all the time—If you chide them, they say 'Eh ch! Massa, aint I mus' mind de fowl, and look a' me young orn aint I mus wach um' " (Schwalm 1997, 205). Conversely, census records concerning black property ownership, as well as oral histories, suggest that black men and women saw labor for their household economies as equally important as the labor they performed for whites.

Sharon Holt has argued that small-scale household production was central to the maintenance of freedwomen and freedmen's families both during and beyond Reconstruction. Labor withdrawn from white-owned fields and households was invested in looking after chickens, growing vegetables for household consumption or sale, and making clothing for the family or for sale. Households that were able to feed themselves and save up money to buy or make warm clothes for winter would be able to produce more and for a longer duration. But household production was not simply a matter of building a household's health and well-being. The additional labor for the household economy, which the readjustment of work priorities during Reconstruction allowed, must also be understood as central to the creation of black-controlled communities: "Household production soaked up the labor that former masters longed to see in the fields, and it provided the fuel to develop and fulfill the individual and community aspirations of the emancipated slaves" (Holt 1994, 236). It was this extra household production that Holt believes allowed the development of black-controlled community life during Reconstruction, a community life that would prove essential to survival in the years that followed the ending of Reconstruction and the onset of Jim Crow customs.

Even during slavery, black businesses, churches, and secret schools existed in Southern cities such as Richmond, Virginia and Augusta, Georgia. During the Civil War and the early years of emancipation, the efforts of African Americans to educate themselves and establish churches and business grew dramatically. Northern benevolent societies and missionary groups such as the American Missionary Association as well as the Freedmen's Bureau played an important role in establishing black schools, but the initiative often began with freedwomen and freedmen (Gutman 2000, 6–57). When John W. Alvord, the superintendent of education for the Freedmen's Bureau, toured the South in 1865, he was struck by the fact that everywhere he went, freedwomen and freedmen seemed to lack "the patience to wait for the coming of white teachers." Instead, he found "a class of schools got up and taught by colored people, rude and imperfect, but still groups of persons, old and young, *trying* to learn" (Gutman 2000, 59). The first schools established by freedwomen and freedmen were often Sabbath schools. Attached to the new church structure built to facilitate black-controlled worship, Sabbath schools were often led by a preacher and taught both adults and children. Many of these and other black schools were financially dependent on both the Freedmen's Bureau and local parents for survival. By the late 19th century, when even most Southern states assumed some financial responsibility for public schools, many black schools continued to rely on local parents contributing to teachers' wages and contributing small items from their household economy such as food or clothing to help maintain the school. When, by the late 1870s, Northern benevolent societies lost interest and white violence made the presence of missionaries too dangerous, African Americans had developed a tradition of contributing toward and often running their own schools and other community welfare services. This tradition would be important to African American survival and progress in the 1880s and 1890s.

Jim Crow and New Work Opportunities

Just as the building of black community institutions was intimately connected to the household economy of families during Reconstruction, from the 1880s onward the success of black business and the growth of community institutions became closely entwined. The limited availability of state funds for the upkeep of segregated black institutions in the New South, as well as the growing levels of segregation in all areas, left an opening for black business and the development of black institutions. Indeed, the growth of black businesses, churches, and schools often went together, as black business was a potential source of funding for black churches, schools, and welfare projects. For example, black-controlled business premises might become sites of socializing or community congregation, or companies might compete with each other in presenting themselves as race proud and interested in putting something back into the community.

Although African Americans have a rich business history that dates back to the late 18th century and continued through slavery, prior to the 1880s, black businesses mainly served a white clientele (Schweninger 1989, 28–29). The decline of federal efforts at Reconstruction after 1877 and the entrenchment of Jim Crow laws in the 1880s and 1890s encouraged a range of entrepreneurs and black businesses dedicated to providing services for African Americans. Not only did black businesses offer services and products that African Americans might not be able to secure through other means (or only at the risk of racial insult due to segregation), but they could also offer funding for community projects, thereby avoiding the requirement for white supervision that often accompanied the money of white philanthropists or the state. The relationship worked both ways: just as communities relied on blacks with property and wealth to put money into the community, black businesses were often dependent on an expanding and increasingly prosperous community to purchase their products and services. Areas of growth in the late 19th century included real estate, financial services, funeral services, and barbers and beauty shops.

The extent to which the onset of formal segregation facilitated the expansion of black-owned businesses was variable. As Jacqueline Jones has demonstrated, it depended in large part on time and place. For example, in the far West, black communities were frequently too small to support local black business. Meanwhile, in the South, black businesspeople could become victims of their own success, as was the case with Ida B. Wells's friends Thomas Moss, Calvin McDowell, and Henry Steward, who were lynched for trying to defend their successful grocery store in Memphis in 1892. In the North, assaults on black business tended to be economic: the rise of department stores that could offer lower prices undermined local black grocers, particularly during times of depression when black customers faced unemployment and low wages. Segregation, then, could both foster and destroy black businesses (Jones 1998, 333).

Photo of Maggie Lena Walker, African American businesswoman, teacher, and banker. (The Library of Virginia)

Black women played a crucial role in creating new business opportunities in the 1880s and 1890s. Perhaps one of the reasons for this success was that black women often used preexisting community, and particularly women's, networks, which they had developed during slavery and Reconstruction. But they were also skilful in creating new networks to attract customers. Black female–owned businesses tended to offer a service or product designed especially for black Americans with an element of community uplift. For example, Maggie Walker, who grew up in Richmond during Reconstruction, founded a women's insurance company and became the first black female bank president of the Saint Luke Penny Savings Bank. These business ventures grew out of and were sponsored by the Independent Order of Saint Luke (IOSL), one of many African American mutual benefit societies that had helped sustain free black communities since the 18th century. The IOSL had originated as a women's sickness and death mutual society after the Civil War. When Walker took over as grand worthy secretary in 1899, she drew around her a group of capable women who helped her transform the IOSL into a force for political mobilization and community uplift and a provider of new work opportunities for black women. For example, IOSL women led a streetcar boycott in 1904, and they used the organization's newspaper, the *St. Luke's Herald,* to protest against lynching and segregation. IOSL women would later lead voter registration drives and citizenship education following the women's suffrage amendment in 1920 (Brown 1989, 616–618).

Maggie Walker and the women of the IOSL believed that racial solidarity, self-help, and cooperation between black men and women were crucial survival strategies in an era when African Americans were increasingly barred from political office, limited in job opportunities, and segregated in education, travel, and other public accommodations. Toward this end, the IOSL sought to develop the work opportunities available to black women. The Penny Savings Bank itself was one means of creating new opportunities. By welcoming "the small depositor," the Penny Savings Bank attracted a large number of washerwomen whose ability to save a little money for hard times was, as we have seen, crucial to maintaining a level of autonomy in their relationship with clients. But Maggie Walker was also concerned that black women's exclusion from the job market would condemn them to a life of serving whites. In order to expand women's job opportunities, 22 black women from the IOSL opened a department store with the purpose of offering goods at more affordable rates to the black community and providing jobs as sales clerks for black women. The Saint Luke Emporium lasted just seven years due to the efforts of local white merchants who were determined not to lose black dollars to a black-owned business. Local white merchants set up the Retail Dealers Association and wrote to wholesalers in Richmond and as far afield as New York threatening to withdraw their customer base if they supplied the black department store. The IOSL and its associated businesses serve as a good example of the ways in which black women successfully responded to, and at others times were defeated by, white racism in the years following the end of Reconstruction.

White businessmen were prepared to take on and work together to defeat a local black store that sold products they were prepared to sell themselves to black men and women. However there were certain services that white businesses were less willing to offer, or less able to sell to black customers. One of the curious by-products of segregation was that black women achieved more success in selling products and services that dealt with intimate aspects of black lives, in particular, the black body. In hair dressing and beauty culture black women entrepreneurs were particularly successful in combining the business opportunities of the black-only market with community uplift. A considerable white manufacturing base already existed for hair and beauty products for black women. White pharmaceutical companies manufactured products such as Wonderful Face Bleach, designed to "whiten you up," and Kink-No-More, which promised to "take the kink out of your hair." But the lack of race pride associated with these products (many black newspapers refused to advertise them) left a gap in the market for products made by and for black women.

Black women have a long history as hair dressers. During slavery, black women sometimes looked after and dressed the hair of their mistress as well as helped each other look after their own hair. However, female slaves often wore a bandana to protect their hair from the unrelenting sun in the cotton fields. By contrast, from Reconstruction onward, growing hair, taking time over it, and displaying it with pride became a signifier of black women's status as free people. The growth in the black women's hair industry also coincided with the development of commercial beauty culture across many American towns and cities in the late 19th and early 20th centuries, a process in which women were to play a vital role. As Kathy Peiss has shown, women entrepreneurs developed American beauty culture outside the networks of national advertising and distribution that were coming to characterize mass consumption. Rather, they made beauty culture personal and social by developing techniques of mail-order and door-to-door selling to circumvent the male-dominated distribution networks that ensured large manufacturers got their products into pharmacies and that often denied women credit (Peiss 1998, 72–73). But whereas white beauty

Madam C. J. Walker: Businesswoman and Entrepreneur

Mythologized as black America's first female millionaire and founder of the Madam Walker Manufacturing Company, black businesswoman Madam Walker and her daughter A'Lelia Walker built up a million-dollar hair and beauty company in the late 19th and early 20th centuries. Born to former slaves on a plantation in Delta, Louisiana, at the height of Radical Reconstruction in 1867, Walker escaped the cotton fields of the South and moved to St. Louis, where she worked as a washerwoman to support herself and her young daughter. Desperate to escape the drudgery of laundry work, Walker began work as a sales agent for Annie Turnbo, another black entrepreneur and businesswoman who manufactured and sold black hair and beauty products. Walker soon developed her own hair products, which she claimed alleviated scalp conditions and other symptoms of poor diet and hygiene that prevented black women from growing healthy hair. Like Avon, and later Turnbo, Walker relied on sales agents to buy her products and sell them door-to-door as well as use them in her chain of beauty salons.

By 1916, Walker's sales figures had reached the $100,000 mark and she could claim more than 10,000 agents. Walker's success lay in her ability to link individual economic incentive and community building. Walker not only of-

culture developed in line with individual white women's increased work opportunities and focused on enhancing women's individual beauty, African American beauty culture was embedded in and grew out of black community and political activities. There is no better illustration of this culture than the life and career of the most well-known African American beauty culturalist, Madam C. J. Walker.

Conclusion

How, when, and for whom African Americans worked shaped every aspect of black life during Reconstruction and the decades that followed. Between 1865 and 1890, the majority of black women continued to work in domestic service as cleaners, cooks, nurses, and washerwomen, or as agricultural laborers. But their work was no longer shaped only by the demands and desires of whites. Black women workers used the strategies they had developed in slavery as well as the rights of freedom to reconstruct their working lives in ways that reflected their families' priorities and needs. They reorganized their work patterns and conditions to enable them to devote fered women a job with good wages and free from white supervision but also encouraged her agents to follow her example and engage in racial uplift. Walker herself was a leading donor and member of a range of women's clubs and race organizations, including the National Association of Colored Women and the National Association for the Advancement of Colored People, as well as a founding member of the International League of Peoples of the Darker Races. For her agents, she founded the Madam Walker Benevolent Association. The Association was designed to bring together agents to discuss their common problems and as a forum to promote and engage in charity work. Madam Walker challenged the occupational hierarchies that condemned black women to a life of domestic or agricultural labor. In the process, she offered women the opportunity to shape their own work identities and to celebrate the ways in which they could use work to transform their status as black women. At the same time, Walker's investment in black communities, churches, and racial uplift groups helped sustain important institutions that gave black women workers the space to find identities outside their work for whites, as well as the strength to carry on that work. (Dossett, 107–149)

more labor not only to their families but also toward the building of black-controlled churches, schools, and communities. Some were able to find openings in new fields of labor that developed along with the industrialization of the South, such as factory work. However, most were denied access to many of the new jobs, and in the early 20th century, black women grasped opportunities to move north. In Northern cities, black women refused to work as live-in servants and formed community networks and clubs to help each other survive and sometimes escape jobs as daily domestic workers. A few, like Maggie Walker and Madam C. J. Walker, searched out new avenues of employment: they set up businesses that took advantage of the segregated market and that were intimately connected to community improvement. Although the success of both Walkers was unusual, their businesses were made possible because they continued the traditions and invested in the community institutions that black Americans, and black American women in particular, had developed to protect themselves. These entrepreneurs shared the values and drew on the aspirations of washerwomen and agricultural workers from the eras of slavery and Reconstruction: their economic future lay in escaping white supervision where possible, resisting white devaluation of black worth through community networks, and sharing cultures of survival and struggle to shape their own work identities and opportunities.

References and Further Reading

Aptheker, Herbert. 1990 [1912]."More Slavery at the South." *The Independent* 72:196–200. Reprinted in *A Documentary History of the Negro People in the United States,* vol. 3, *From the NAACP to the New Deal.* New York: Carol.

Brown, Elsa Barkley. 1989. "Womanist Consciousness: Maggie Lena Walker and the Independent Order of Saint Luke." *Signs* 14:610–633.

Clark-Lewis, Elizabeth. 1987. "'This Work Had a End': African-American Domestic Workers in Washington D.C., 1910–1940." In *"To Toil the Livelong Day": America's Women at Work, 1790–1980,* ed. Carol Groneman and Mary Beth Norton. Ithaca, NY: Cornell University Press.

Davis, Angela. 1983. *Women, Race and Class.* New York: Vintage.

Dossett, Kate. 2008. *Bridging Race Divides: Black Nationalism, Feminism, and Integration in the United States, 1896–1935.* Gainesville: University Press of Florida.

Eaton, Isabel. 1899. "Special Report on Negro Domestic Service." In *The Philadelphia Negro,* ed. W. E. B. Du Bois. Philadelphia: Publications of the University of Pennsylvania.

Gutman, Herbert. 1976. *The Black Family in Slavery and Freedom, 1750–1925.* Oxford: Basil Blackwell.

Gutman, Herbert. 2000. "Schools for Freedom: The Post-Emancipation Origins of Afro-American Education." In *Major Problems in African-American History,* vol. 2, ed. Thomas C. Holt and Elsa Barclay Brown. New York: Houghton Mifflin.

Holt, Sharon Ann. 1994. "Making Freedom Pay: Freedpeople Working for Themselves, North Carolina, 1865–1900." *Journal of Southern History* 60 (2): 229–262.

Hunter, Tera. 1997. *To 'Joy My Freedom: Southern Black Women's Lives and Labors After the Civil War.* Cambridge, MA: Harvard University Press.

Jones, Jacqueline. 1995. *Labor of Love, Labor of Sorrow: Black Women, Work and the Family, From Slavery to the Present.* New York: Vintage.

Jones, Jacqueline. 1998. *American Work: Four Centuries of Black and White Labor.* New York: W. W. Norton.

Kelley, Robin D.G. 1996. *Race Rebels: Culture, Politics and the Black Working Class*. New York: Free Press.

Litwack, Leon. 1979. *Been in the Storm So Long: The Aftermath of Slavery*. New York: Alfred A. Knopf.

Peiss, Kathy. 1998. *Hope in a Jar: The Making of America's Beauty Culture*. New York: Henry Holt.

Schwalm, Leslie A. 1997. *A Hard Fight for We: Women's Transition from Slavery to Freedom in South Carolina*. Urbana: University of Illinois Press.

Schweninger, Loren. 1989. "Black Owned Businesses in the South, 1790–1880." *Business History Review* 63 (1): 22–60.

Scott, James C. 1990. *Domination and the Arts of Resistance: Hidden Transcripts*. New Haven, CT: Yale University Press.

Former Confederate and Union Soldiers in Reconstruction

8

Susan-Mary Grant

Oliver Wendell Homes, Jr. was a Civil War Union veteran who, after the war, would become one of the most famous justices of the U.S. Supreme Court. An officer in the 20th Massachusetts Volunteers, he was wounded in that regiment's first major engagement—at Ball's Bluff—and again at Antietam, when he was left for dead behind enemy lines. On Memorial Day, 1885, Holmes gave an address that became popularly known as "The Soldier's Faith" because of its advice to former comrades "to pray, not for comfort, but for combat; to keep the soldier's faith against the doubts of civil life." By the time that Holmes delivered his address, the American Civil War was already a distant memory; the guns had been silent for 20 years—for almost a generation—and who, apart from those who shared Holmes's memories, understood what he was saying, or why that war had been so central for his contemporaries? Holmes saw this as inevitable, and he welcomed it in a way. "We do not save traditions, in our country," he observed. "The regiments whose battle-flags were not large enough to hold the names of the battles they had fought vanished with the surrender of Lee, although their memories inherited would have made heroes for a century" (Posner 1992, 92). Union general Daniel Sickles, who received the Medal of Honor for his part in the Battle of Gettysburg—and lost a leg there—reached the same conclusion some five years later. Sickles took an active part in the transformation of Gettysburg from battlefield to national shrine, but he accepted the limitations of this marker for those too young to remember the war. Although fresh in the minds of those who had fought it, to "the new generation," Sickles observed, "the battle of Gettysburg is an historical event, like the battle of Marathon" (Sickles 1891, 258).

In fact, as both Holmes and Sickles reflected on the lack of awareness of the war among the rising generations, interest in the Civil War was on the increase. That it had taken two decades to reinsert itself into general consciousness was not surprising. The war had exerted a terrible physical and emotional toll, and Americans at first simply wanted to forget. As lawyer and civil rights activist Albion Tourgée noted:

> Immediately upon the conclusion of any great conflict, but more especially of a civil war, there always comes a period when public interest in the causes and incidents of the strife may be said to lag. The soldier is glad to be at home and rest from war's alarms, and the non-combatant has heard more than enough about the struggle in which he had no part. So when the returning heroes have been fairly welcomed home . . . the people turn away from the agony of strife and seek relief in lighter themes. The conqueror palls of triumph and the conquered shun whatever reminds them of defeat. (Tourgée 1887, 1)

By 1887, however, when Tourgée was writing, the American public could not get enough of the war. As Tourgée observed, the younger generation had "awakened to a positive and active interest in the events in which their fathers participated or witnessed, animated by that pride which always exalts the exploits of an ancestor, while the survivors of those who fought have passed the period of satiety and are fast approaching the reminiscent stage which occupies itself in reviewing the rear" (Tourgée 1887, 2–4).

Therefore, two decades after the conflict the Civil War was refought in the pages of publications such as *Century Magazine*. Its "Battles and Leaders" series, begun in 1884, offered the Civil War generation, North and South, the opportunity to tell their side of the story of a specific battle, engagement, or campaign or just recall their memories of the war generally. If, for many Americans in the later 19th century, the Civil War was already history, for its participants it was still very much living history, and for some it was not even over yet. In the North, the veterans' organization, the Grand Army of the Republic (GAR), established in 1866, was reaching its zenith by the time Holmes spoke in 1885. From relatively modest beginnings after the war, by 1890 it had attracted some 400,000 members, organized in more than 7,000 posts across the United States, mainly in the North but, by that point, several in the South as well. The GAR took upon itself the conjoined tasks of providing a focal point for former Union soldiers—offering practical help in the form of providing soldiers' homes,

Civil War veteran and U.S. Supreme Court Justice Oliver Wendell Holmes. (Library of Congress)

Meeting of the Grand Army of the Republic in Philadelphia, 1879. (Library of Congress)

building orphanages, and seeking Civil War pensions on behalf of soldiers—and constructing the foundations on which the yet to be reconstructed nation would rise and through which parts of it, at least, would find expression. Both a social and a political force, the GAR confirmed the Union veteran's place in American society during Reconstruction and long after, but, for obvious reasons, it was the battle to win the war and not to secure the peace that took center stage in GAR ceremonies.

What was absent from the late 19th century Civil War heritage industry was any obvious or overt acknowledgment of the war's immediate aftermath, that awkward period when the armies were demobilized and the soldier became, once again, a civilian. Particularly in the South, the period of Reconstruction was one of an uneasy peace, imposed by federal occupation, sometimes in the form of African American troops, who had not been officially accepted into the Union armies until 1863, and consequently whose three-year term of enlistment had a further year or more to run after Appomattox. The bitterness of defeat stung the South, and the presence of federal troops ensured that the wound remained a raw one. Writing from the outermost edges of the Confederacy in Texas, Kate Stone looked with dismay on the ending of Southern hopes for independence:

"Our glorious struggle of the last four years, our hardships, our sacrifices, and worst of all, the torrents of noble blood that have been shed for our loved Country," she mourned, "all, all in vain. The best and the bravest of the South sacrificed—and for nothing" (Anderson 1995, 340). Southern veterans, unlike their Northern counterparts, were unable to push the war from their minds, let alone shun any reminders of defeat. The visible evidence of that defeat surrounded them. Many returned to a physical landscape that showed too clearly the destructive power of war and to a civilian population worn down and dislocated by the conflict and, above all, struggling to come to terms with the new status of their former slaves. Slaves no longer, but equal to the white population, the South's African American population served as perhaps the starkest reminder—more so even than the obvious and unwelcome presence of federal troops—that the South had gambled, and lost, everything in its bid for independence and the retention of slavery.

Coming Home

Robert E. Lee's surrender of the Army of Northern Virginia to Ulysses S. Grant at Appomattox Courthouse on April 9, 1865, officially terminated a war that Southern determination and unwillingness to accept defeat had dragged out to a very costly end. In the closing months of the conflict, in some of the last battles fought during the icy winter of 1864–1865, the Confederate armies in the West had been, one survivor recalled:

> pinched by hunger and cold. The rains, and sleet, and snow never ceased falling from the winter sky, while the winds pierced the old, ragged, gray-back Rebel soldier to his very marrow. The clothing of many were hanging around them in shreds of rags and tatters, while an old slouched hat covered their frozen ears. Some were on old, raw-boned horses, without saddles. (Watkins 1977, 242)

In such circumstances, it seems likely, as Eric Dean has argued, that Confederate troops were, if not as elated as their Union counterparts on April 9, at least relieved when the war was over. "I am afraid that if the truth were known," one soldier wrote, "that we were not as sorry as we should have been" (Dean 1999, 94). For those soldiers, Union and Confederate, present at Appomattox in the days following the surrender, the sight of what Union general Joshua Lawrence Chamberlain described as "the dissolving-view of the Army of Northern Virginia" was both moving and bitter in equal measure. His recollection of the South's forces as "the embodiment of manhood: men whom neither toils and sufferings, nor the face of death, nor disaster, nor hopelessness could bend from their resolve" included the observation that they were "thin, worn, and famished." There was, too, anticlimax as well as relief in the war's end, as Chamberlain realized, "on the morrow, over the hillsides in the peaceful sunshine, are clouds of men on foot or horse, singly or in groups, making their earnest way . . . each for his own little home. And we are left alone, and lonesome" (Chamberlain 1994, 258, 260, 271–272).

Casting a shadow over the homecoming of both Union and Confederate troops, however, was the assassination of Abraham Lincoln—he died on April 15. This tragedy shocked the South (admittedly, it also pleased many there) almost as much as it did the North, and it made the future the more uncertain for the losing side in particular. The future, in any case, looked grim enough. Making his way home from Appomattox over ground made familiar by the many battles fought on it, Chamberlain described it as "painful to be brought into contact with the ruin, waste, and desolation that had been wrought upon proud old Virginia" (Chamberlain 1994, 288). At least he knew that his final destination would be pretty much as he had left it. Confederate soldiers could not assume the same. As Union troops were welcomed home with all the pomp and circumstance that a grateful nation could muster under such circumstances as prevailed after April 1865, their former Confederate foes made the despondent journey back to what remained of the land they had fought for. Many found only desolation. "Those that remain to see the end for which they fought—what have we left?" asked one North Carolina soldier. We "have suffered hunger, been without sufficient clothing, barefooted, lousy, and have suffered more than any one can believe, except soldiers of the Southern Confederacy. And the end of all," he sadly concluded, "is a desolated home to go to" (Leon 1913, 70).

Confederate surgeon John Wyeth, too, was shocked at the devastation he and his family encountered on their return to Guntersville, Alabama. "With the exception of half a dozen dwellings, which were spared because they sheltered the sick or wounded too feeble to be removed, the village had disappeared." The journey back had prepared Wyeth, at least in part, for what he would find once he arrived home: "As we came back on the train, nothing but lonesome-looking chimneys remained of the villages and farm-houses. They were suggestive of tombstones in a graveyard." This pattern was repeated across the state, as Wyeth soon realized:

Confederate veterans reunion, 1917. (Library of Congress)

> Bridgeport, Stevenson, Bellefonte, Scotsboro, Larkinsville, Woodville, Paint
> Rock—in fact, every town in northern Alabama to and including Decatur (ex-
> cept Huntsville, which, being used as headquarters, had been spared)—had
> been wiped out by the war policy of starvation by fire. Farm-houses, gins,
> fences, and cattle were gone. From a hilltop in the farming district a few miles
> from New Market I counted the chimneys of the houses of six different planta-
> tions which had been destroyed. About the fireplaces of some of these, small
> huts of poles had been erected for temporary shelter.

Northern Alabama, Wyeth concluded, "had paid dearly for the devotion of
her people to the cause of the South" (Wyeth 1914, 313–314).

Some former soldiers were more sanguine. On his return to New Orleans, Richard Taylor found that his "estate had been confiscated and sold,
and [he] was without a penny. The man of Uz admitted that naked he came
into the world, and naked must leave it; but to find himself naked in the
midst of it tried even his patience"(Taylor 1879, 228). The world in which
Richard Taylor found himself having to begin anew, however, was not the
world he had left to go to war for. Physical devastation, the "deplorable condition" of the land, was not the only problem that the South faced at the

The Confederacy—Sallie Brock Putnam and the Rebirth of the South

During Reconstruction, when the South was occupied by Union troops, white Southern women began what would become a lengthy and effective process of commemorating and justifying the Confederacy's existence. The many public monuments and memorials that they commissioned in honor of the Confederacy came later, when Reconstruction ended, but the personal memoirs and published diaries began to appear immediately. In 1867, Richmond, Virginia, resident Sallie Brock Putnam published one of the first of these historical memoirs, *Richmond during the War: Four Years of Personal Observations*. This diary covered the period from the "Gala Days of the War," when "cheerful adieus were waved from every window, in the flutter of snowy handkerchiefs, and bright smiling faces" to see the men off to fight, through to Richmond's evacuation in 1865. As the war took its toll, "every house was a house of mourning or a private hospital," and food shortages resulted in riots

war's end. This land, in which "widows, orphans and the aged seemed to constitute the body of the population of hopeless whites," was not a safe place but a desperate one. In the face of starvation and homelessness, animals and food "had to be vigilantly guarded" against "the scum of both armies [who] preyed on the helpless and scattered inhabitants" (Houghton and Houghton 1912, 54). That the civilian population of the South might, in 1865, have cause to fear the soldiers whom, four years previously, they had enthusiastically waved off to war was shocking but, in many ways, inevitable. In one of William Faulkner's most famous novels of the Civil War, *Absalom! Absalom!*, one of the central characters recalls how, even before the war was over, the return of the soldiers was no cause for celebration:

> It was winter soon and already soldiers were beginning to come back—the stragglers, not all of them tramps, ruffians, but men who had risked and lost everything, suffered beyond endurance and had returned now to a ruined land, not the same men who had marched away but transformed . . . we were afraid of them. (Faulkner 1990, 126)

In effect, the returning soldier dispelled many of the most cherished myths of the war itself and forced civilians to consider, in the cold light of day, the true cost of "the late unpleasantness."

Southern diarist Mary Chesnut was not prey to any illusions regarding the reality of the soldiers' lot, nor the grim responsibility they shouldered.

that transformed Putnam's understanding of the world in which she was living. In describing the impact of the war on Southern civilians, Putnam avoided any discussion of the troubling issue of slavery. Indeed, her naive view of slaves as loyal to their masters revealed that some elements of the brave new world of the postwar South would forever be alien to her. Yet, evincing more optimism than many white Southerners could muster in 1867, Putnam concluded her narrative on an upbeat note: "The energy, the enterprise, the almost universal self-abnegation, and complete devotion, with which the people of the South entered into and sustained the cause of the war prove that they are capable of still grander, and higher, and nobler enterprises." An emotionally genuine but nevertheless uncritical recollection of Confederate valor, Putnam's memoir offers an early glimpse of the ground on which the white South would indeed rise again.

"There cannot be a Christian soldier . . . Kill or be killed; that's their trade, or they are a failure" (Chesnut 1949, 332). Not everyone saw matters with such clarity. By and large, the noncombatant populations of both North and South had, as Reid Mitchell has pointed out, resolutely avoided confronting the reality—insofar as they could—of what it was that soldiers actually do: kill. Soldiers suffered, soldiers sacrificed, soldiers died; that they also killed was a discomfiting fact that fitted neither side's interpretation of the war and its meaning. To accommodate such a view of soldiers, Mitchell has argued, "would have raised questions about their integration into postwar society." He cites the example of one Union nurse who admitted to liking her "patients very much better before they are able to be dressed and walk out." Whilst she could readily respond to suffering, soldiers not in need of her care unsettled, and possibly rather unnerved her (Mitchell 1995, 146–147). In the course of the war, both sides constructed a comforting narrative that succeeded in avoiding the reality both of healthy soldiers and of conflict by portraying the war in almost romantic terms, even as they acknowledged the horrors perpetrated in war's name (Lowry 1994, 4). Confederate nurse Kate Cummings, for example, was "quite explicit that during four years of travel throughout the South, both officers and enlisted men were, without exception, perfect gentlemen." Her famous journal reported neither act nor word "would offend even the most fastidious and refined woman." Another nurse, describing the aftermath of the Battle of the

Wilderness in 1864, juxtaposed quite distressing descriptions of "the horrible confusion," death, and suffering that she witnessed with a reference to "the magnificence of the battle line, as if the two scenes of war had no connection between them (Linderman 1989, 99–100).

If the ending of the war forced many civilians into proximity with soldiers who hardly represented the beau ideal of the medieval knight, many families welcomed home men who were but shadows of their former selves. When Kate Stone's brother, Jimmy, returned home, he was "no longer a soldier but a poor discouraged boy," and it was a very "different homecoming from what we anticipated." "No feasting. No rejoicing. Only sadness and tears" (Anderson 1995, 346). Refugees from the Southern armies passed through Kate Stone's temporary dwelling in Texas, and through Mary Chesnut's, bringing home to these women, as to many across the South, the full extent of defeat and the human misery produced by the war. "Our soldiers pass daily," Chesnut recorded. "Yesterday these poor fellows were heroes, today they are only rebels, to be hung or shot at the Yankees pleasure," and there was little enough for them to come home to, she noted, only "burned towns, deserted plantations, sacked villages!" (Chesnut 1949, 525).

Even more distressing for civilians North and South was the return of prisoners from the prisoner of war camps—notorious places on both sides of which many had been unaware. These camps truly were the hidden side of the war, made visible to Union general William T. Sherman's troops as they had made their famous "March to the Sea" through Georgia and the Carolinas in the war's closing months, in the process encountering many of the Union prisoners of war at Andersonville, the Confederate prisoner of war camp in Georgia. The civilian population, however, remained relatively oblivious to the dreadful conditions in these camps, especially after 1863, when the system for the exchange of prisoners broke down; the estimated death rates for these camps was in the region of 25,000 on each side, an appalling, unnecessary and, until 1865, mainly hidden cost of the conflict. One Southern woman recalled, many years later, the return of her father, who had been a prisoner of the Union: "he had to walk all the way home from the prison camp" and "would not come into the house until he had washed and changed his clothes in one of the outhouses on the place as he was covered with vermin" (Doane, 2003, 9). Vermin were the least of returning soldiers' concerns. Northern writer Walt Whitman, who worked as a nurse during the war, was relatively inured to the sight of suffering by 1865. Yet, on viewing the return of prisoners from Andersonville, Whitman described it as a sight "worse than any sight of battle-fields, or any collec-

Confederate veteran wearing badge at Bull Run in 1911. (Library of Congress)

tion of wounded, even the bloodiest. . . . Can those be men, those little livid brown, ash-streak'd, monkey-looking dwarfs?—are they really not mummied, dwindled corpses?" For Whitman, "no more appalling sight was ever seen on this earth" (Whitman 1995, 70).

Physically, the war exerted a terrible toll, and the soldiers who limped home from the prisoner of war camps were only part of it: the sobering reality of disabled veterans was, of course, evident from the war's opening months and for the duration. Mary Chesnut recalled a Christmas celebration in 1863 during which several Confederate veterans visited, "some without arms, some without legs, and Von Borcke, who cannot speak because of the wound in this throat." A dinner companion commented, very much more in sorrow than in mirth, that they had "all kinds now, but a blind one. Poor fellows, they laugh at wounds, and yet can show many a scar" (Chesnut 1949, 341). The full extent of the physical damage done to the men of the armies and, more crucially, the full economic reality of what it would cost to support these men who could no longer, in some cases, support themselves hit North and South simultaneously in 1865, although the Union, in particular, had given the matter some attention before then.

When the war was only in its second year, Frederick Law Olmsted, secretary of the U.S. Sanitary Commission (USSC)—the largest civilian volunteer organization in the Union—perceived the need to establish some means whereby the disabled war veteran might be supported.

Olmsted's impulse arguably derived as much from the desire to avoid former soldiers being a drain on public resources as from any moral imperative, and he had clearly given the matter considerable thought. He laid out his plans for a bureaucracy of support and employment opportunities for those "soldiers of the Union army who have been seriously wounded in the performance of duty" that somewhat resembled the army itself in structure and in outlook. "The beneficiaries—or shareholders—should be under surveillance and discipline, should maintain and grow in soldierly, soldierly, prompt and correspondent habits," Olmsted proposed. "They should be uniformed and numbered, and wherever seen should be recognized and assured as trusty, orderly men, proud of their fraternity and its badges and obligations" (Olmsted 1986, 378–379). He drafted a document for the establishment of a national invalid corps, into which applicants would be accepted only if they could:

> satisfy the examiner that they have suffered severe bodily injury in defence of the Union, that they are disposed to earn their living by faithful service in whatever situation it is practicable for them to be useful, that they are not likely to disgrace and injure the corps by drunkenness, falsehood or eyeservice, but that they will regard it as their highest interest to gain for it and maintain for it a reputation for fidelity, truthfulness, trustworthiness, precision and punctuality. (Olmsted 1986, 380)

Olmsted anticipated that each applicant accepted into the corps would "be instructed, if necessary, in how it is possible for him to be useful to others in spite of the injury which he has received," and having been so instructed, be assigned to a squad or company, each with an officer in charge, and provided with accommodation, a uniform, and rations "at low rates of cost." Although it was designed to reintroduce disabled veterans back into society, Olmsted's proposal seemed more likely to keep them quite distinct from it, isolated in a world of military discipline almost evangelical in its fervour and in its expectations of the former soldiers' behavior (Olmsted 1986, 378, 380).

Above all, behind Olmsted's apparently benevolent suggestions for the care of veterans lay a profound fear of those veterans. Henry Whitney Bellows, the USSC's president, did much to acknowledge, if not actively encourage, such fear. In the "rapid disbanding of our armies," Bellows suggested, there was potential danger. The "returning soldiers, by their military service, have become more or less detached from their previous relations," he observed. He continued:

> Many of these men will be not only physically but morally disabled, and will exhibit the injurious effects of camp life in a weakened power of self-guidance and self-restraint, inducing a certain kind of indolence, and, for the time, indisposition to take hold of hard work. The possession of money in the majority of cases will increase the inducements to idleness and dissipation, as well as the exposure to imposition. (Bellows 1865)

The South had no such organization as the USSC with its fairly sweeping, if slightly chilling, ideas on how the soldier might be integrated back into society. If Southern society was at all nervous about the potential dangers posed by the returning soldier, it never expressed it in official form, although both during and after the war it had the same problems with which to contend regarding disabled veterans. Most of the veterans, however, were forced to find their own way, unencumbered—as Bellows feared Union veterans were—by too much money and its attendant moral dangers. Zachariah Cashwell, one of the central characters in Robert Hicks's Civil War novel, *The Widow of the South,* situated in the aftermath of the Battle of Franklin, Tennessee, in the last winter of the war, loses his leg—it is amputated after being broken—and contemplates the future in the aftermath of the operation. "I'd been ready to die even as surgeons sawed my leg off, and I'd been ready to die in the days after . . . . But now . . . the fuss was over, and I was going to live. I didn't know how to live, exactly, but I knew I had to figure that out now" (Hicks 2005, 174).

Hicks's fictional representation of one man's struggle to come to terms with his physical loss was paralleled in reality by thousands of Civil War soldiers who did not return home whole and whose future was equally uncertain. Amputees were only the most visible reminders of the high personal cost of the Civil War. Frequently, the invisible wounds proved the more destructive, and the more insidious for their invisibility. Joshua Chamberlain, to take just one example, sustained serious injuries in the course of the war, injuries that caused him not only physical pain but also psychological discomfort in his postwar life (Perry 1999, 313–315, 333–334). The most destructive injuries, however, frequently had no physical manifestation at all. For years after the war, many veterans suffered from what is today recognized as post-traumatic stress disorder; unable to disassociate themselves from the memories of their time in the army, possibly experiencing "survivor guilt," Civil War soldiers could not always easily

Ambrose Bierce's "A Resumed Identity"

Elusive American author Ambrose Bierce fought in some of the worst campaigns of the Western Theater, at Shiloh and at Chickamauga, but it was the Battle of Stones River (also known as the Battle of Murfreesboro) in Tennessee in the winter of 1862–1863 that inspired one of his eeriest short stories, "A Resumed Identity." Set in the war's aftermath, although that is not immediately obvious, its central character, a Union soldier, is observing a column of troops moving at dawn "with dimly gleaming rifles aslant upon their shoulders"; fearing these may be Confederates, the man takes cover. There are hints that all is not as it seems: "On every side lay cultivated fields showing no sign of war and war's ravages." A local doctor then enters the narrative. Meeting a rather upset and confused old man by the roadside, he offers help. The man tells him he has been wounded—shot—although there is

make the transition back to civilian existence. For some, as Eric Dean has shown, the "skeletons and ghosts" of the war continued to haunt their postwar lives (Dean 1999, 106). Ambrose Bierce—who fought, and was wounded in, some of the worst campaigns of the Western Theater and had a more harshly realistic view of the war than was generally acceptable during Reconstruction and beyond—addressed this subject in one of his stories, "A Resumed Identity," which dealt with the psychological displacement experienced by one Union veteran unable, at the war's end, to leave the battle behind and find his way home.

Coming to Terms with Peace

Union troops were welcomed home with bands and cheering, indeed, with two full days of unprecedented martial enthusiasm. Historian Stuart McConnell has stressed that the Grand Review of the Eastern and Western armies in Washington, D.C. in May 1865, did not just impress civilians; it provided the troops themselves with "their first opportunity to view the enormity of the organization of which they had been a part" (McConnell 1992, 3). The Grand Review of the Army of the Potomac, which took place on May 23, moved Joshua Chamberlain to an emotional reverie that Ambrose Bierce would likely have scorned as he contemplated this "farewell to comradeship so strangely dear." At the same time, Chamberlain caught a no sign of blood, and states that he is 23 years old, to the doctor's surprise. Leaving the doctor, the old man comes upon the famous Hazen Monument, set on the land known as "Hell's Half Acre" by the troops who fought there. Looking into a pool of water, the man realizes that he is not the 23-year-old soldier he believed himself to be but is in fact an old man. The shock of this realization is fatal, and the old soldier "yielded up the life that had spanned another life." Rather like Walt Whitman who, when asked in 1888 if he ever looked back to his Civil War days replied "I never left them," Bierce's Union soldier reminds us that not all the soldiers came marching home, that the war effected lasting damage on their psyches and their postwar lives, and that for many lives, indeed, there was no Reconstruction.

glimpse of the future in an event, that trivial at first sight, provided a sobering view into the postwar reality for the Civil War veteran now that the nation had no more need of soldiers as the armies disbanded and the federal government recovered much of the matériel of war, it took the opportunity to sell off army overcoats "at a cheap rate among workmen willing to buy them." This made Chamberlain furious; he saw it as "a degradation of the uniform and of the men . . . . A soldier's overcoat should stand for honor and not for poverty" (Chamberlain 1994, 327, 375–376). Poverty, however, was the lot of many of the returning troops, in the short term at least, more so in the South, for obvious reasons, but in the North, too, when society experienced the sudden return of men from the field for whom it had no immediate, obvious employment. Welcoming banners displayed at the Grand Review of the Armies in Washington on May 23 and 24, 1865, carried legends such as "The Only National Debt We Can Never Pay is the Debt We Owe to the Victorious Union Soldiers" (Dean 1999). Intended as a compliment, such a sentiment nevertheless made one veteran wonder "whether having made up their minds that they can never pay, they will not think it useless to try" (Mitchell 1989, 207).

As Union troops in Washington wondered how far the nation's gratitude would extend, those left to stabilize the peace in the South felt abandoned and remained there reluctantly. Many, as Reid Mitchell has shown, saw no reason to be in the South at all now that the war was over. "Peacekeeping did not strike the Civil War veteran as an important role"; in the words of one former soldier, "there is no stimulus for patriotism now as there was before and we feel more discontented" (Mitchell 1989, 203). African American soldiers generally had a stronger sense of what they were doing, and of the importance of the task before them—which is not to say that they, too, did not feel abandoned by a federal government that took too little account of their needs. Writing to Secretary of War Edwin Stanton from North Carolina in October 1865, one black soldier complained that "we have bin Treeated more Like Dogs then men." Reporting excessive guard duties, sometimes unrelieved for more than 48 hours, and hospitals "full of sick men" and cripples, although the regiment was reported as at full strength, he concluded that "because we are colored . . . they think that we Don't know any Better" (Berlin et al 1982, 654). Another, black soldier in common with many of his white comrades, simply wished to go home because, as he explained, his mother "has not seen my face for two years," a fairly typical request (Berlin et al 1982, 669). The shoddy treatment endured by many African American troops left in the South was highlighted by one soldier. "My family are sick and absolutely naked," wrote John Turner in July 1865. "They are also threatened with being turned into the street. Now I respectfully ask for my discharge that I may be able to attend to the wants of my family—or if I cannot obtain my discharge I earnestly petition for my pay." Supported by the military authorities, Turner received his discharge the following month, but it was small comfort given that his wife died before he made it home (Berlin et al 1982, 682–683).

It is hard to escape the conclusion that the federal government, having achieved its immediate ends in the defeat of the South, promptly forgot that Union troops remained there during the early period of Reconstruction. The issue of pay—or rather the total lack thereof—had been a sore point for the black regiments during the war; at the start of the peace it was no better. In August 1865, one commander of African American troops stationed in Texas complained that his troops had not been paid since the end of October 1864, "now nearly ten months" (Berlin et al 1982, 683–684). Wilful, if temporary, neglect by the government in whose name these soldiers served was only compounded by their treatment at the hands of returning Confederate troops. One white officer stationed in Louisiana reported "the mistreatment of Soldiers wives, and in some cases their ejectment for non-payment of rent by *returned rebels* who seem to be resuming their old positions all over the country." He acknowledged that this was against the specific orders issued by the Union authorities, orders supposedly enforced through the agents of the Freedmen's Bureau but "owing to the ignorance of many colored persons is *very* often violated." Instead, "persecution is the order of the day amongst these returned rebels against the colored race in general" and "Soldiers *in particular*" (Berlin et al 1982, 699–700, emphasis in original).

The fact was, as one Union commander pointed out to the Freedmen's Bureau, in some exasperation, "colored Soldiers families and their friends are *totally unlike* in condition to the white Soldiers families and friends," and to expect them to manage as white soldiers in the North did was to ignore the brutal reality of the South in these early months of Reconstruction. In the North, he noted, "the land is in many hands, little villages everywhere—homes and residences already provided or plenty of friends who have them," and, most importantly, "a sentiment favorable to the soldiers, their families, and cause, are scattered every where over the north and pervades the entire community." It was quite another matter in the South. Black troops helped militate against the worst violence that elements in the white South sought to inflict on their former slaves, but were themselves too often the targets of violence, whether in or out of uniform (Berlin et al 1982, 701–702). A year after the war ended, it was difficult for black veterans in the South to find work: as one agent of the Freedmen's Bureau reported from Kentucky, "many of the well disposed white people who reside at places remote from the stations where troops are posted are afraid to employ black men . . . for fear of injury to their persons or property, by the self styled regulators (Berlin et al 1982, 762).

Even in the North, the black veteran fared less well than his white counterpart. Historian Larry Logue provides figures for Rhode Island that reveal that black veterans "were four times as likely to be unemployed as white *veterans,* and five times as likely to be jobless as black *civilians*" (Logue 1966, 87). Northern black veterans, too, were often denied voting rights, whereas the Reconstruction governments in the South had, by 1867, established black male suffrage, even though this proved to be a short-term gain, swiftly and brutally removed by the Jim Crow laws instituted in the South (Shaffer 2004, 49–50).

In the early Reconstruction South, both the pressure of seeing firsthand the dire condition of the former slave population and their ill treatment at the hands of some whites, and the swift disbanding of the Union's volunteer force pushed the African American soldier out of military service relatively speedily after the war had ended. By late 1867, all black volunteer soldiers had been discharged. Many, on their return to their communities, were forcibly disarmed of the weaponry they had brought home—quite legally—from the war. Many more were, or their families were, attacked, threatened, and sometimes murdered (Shaffer 2004, 25). In vain did one

Union veteran point out, "I have defended the country in the field and most respectfully request that I be protected at home" (Berlin et al 1982, 804). Faced with the reality of the Reconstruction South, black Union veterans could have been forgiven had they failed to share the enthusiasm of one officer who, on discharging his troops at the start of 1866, assured them that "the time is coming, and is not far distant, when those who enslaved you, shall be forced to acknowledge, that to have been a colored soldier, is to be a citizen, and to have been an advocate of slavery, is but another name for traitor" (Berlin et al 1982, 785).

It was not all bad news. Historian Donald Shaffer has uncovered evidence of black veterans in the South who did well after the war, but even in such cases it was sometimes a matter of one step forward and two back. One case he cites—that of Robert Anderson, formerly a slave in Kentucky and then a soldier in the 125th United States Colored Troops—did eventually succeed in becoming a successful property owner, but in Nebraska, not in Kentucky. Another notable success story was that of Robert Smalls, a slave in Charleston, South Carolina, who had delivered a cotton steamer, the *Planter*, into Union hands in 1862, an act that garnered him both fame and a financial reward. During the war, he had supported the Union's combined operations on the South Carolina coast; after it, he became a notable public speaker and businessman and served both in the South Carolina legislature and in the U.S. Congress (Shaffer 2004, 56–57, 78–79). Smalls, like Anderson, was unusual, however. On the whole, black veterans were not widely represented in political office in the Reconstruction South, even after presidential had given way to radical Reconstruction in 1866–1867 and the Fifteenth Amendment had made the franchise for African American men the sole route back into the Union for the former Confederate states. This lack of representation signified no absence of commitment, but the tendency of black veterans to serve in their home states was limited by their number in those states—Alabama, Florida, Georgia, and Virginia—where Union recruitment had been low. Former soldiers were more strongly represented in the Reconstruction legislatures in Mississippi, North and South Carolina, and Louisiana (Shaffer 2004, 73–75). The relative success of such individuals, however, was not representative of the African American veteran's postwar experience, even if it laid the groundwork for greater—and more broadly applied—political and economic gains in the future.

It is important to distinguish between the violence against black veterans that occurred during Reconstruction and the more pervasive violence of the Jim Crow South. The racial stereotyping of the later 19th century had yet to develop; the immediate postwar South was in the grip of other—arguably more national—forces. The fact was, as Eric Dean has observed, the Civil War had 'let the genie out of the bottle,' as the violence of the war years spilled over into civilian life in the postwar era" (Dean 1999, 98). Not for nothing were Southern women sometimes apprehensive of returning soldiers, and in the North Henry Bellows's fear that the veteran represented at best, a dissolute figure and at worst, a criminal was exaggerated, certainly, but not entirely off the mark. Although John Alexander Logan, one of the founders of the Grand Army of the Republic, the Union veterans' association, declared that "[n]o outbreak, no revolution, no disaster of any magnitude has followed the segregation of these million warriors," in fact, the transition from the sword to the ploughshare was not always a straightforward one. Dean offers figures for the postwar North that reveal "two-thirds of all commitments to state prisons were men who had seen service in the army or navy," and in the South, too, crime appeared to be on the increase during the Reconstruction years (Dean 1999, 98–100; see also McConnell 1992, 20). The South, however, was met with more, and more organized, violence with the appearance of vigilante groups, "regulators," or the most famous—perhaps notorious—extralegal group, the Ku Klux Klan.

Some very famous Confederate veterans, perhaps most notably Nathan Bedford Forrest, were instrumental in the formation of the Klan in Pulaski, Tennessee, in 1866. Although its "founders asserted their ties of brotherhood as former soldiers," the Klan was hardly representative, nor inclusive of the majority of Confederate veterans (Foster 1988, 48). In implementing a brief but effective reign of terror across much of the South, such men likely did not put their identity as veterans before their identity as white Democrats. The impulse to reassert the antebellum racial order went hand in hand with the urge to establish Southern political control of the former Confederate states, and, as in all conflicts with a political dimension, infighting among even those supposedly on the same side was common. J. Banks Lyle, the Klan chief in Spartanburg County, South Carolina, was a case in point. Unable to control the increasing savagery of some Klansmen, Lyle eventually left South Carolina for Texas, possibly as much to avoid his fellow Klansmen as from any concerns he may have had to avoid federal prosecution (Poole 2004, 112). The dominance of former Confederate leaders in the Reconstruction South, in short, could not be assumed. In a world turned upside down, any authority they could claim as veterans was compromised by their extremism; was challenged by those they sought to control; and was, at times, wholly ineffectual. When Klan violence peaked during the state elections in North Carolina in 1870, it was sufficiently severe that the militia were called out in two counties, Caswell and Alamance. This response was the start of a committed federal suppression of a vigilante force that had spiraled out of control. The Force Act of 1870, followed by a second act in 1871 and the Enforcement (or Ku Klux Klan) Act of that year, were accompanied by a wave of arrests of Klansmen across the South. Together, they effectively outlawed the Klan in its 19th-century incarnation.

While much of the Confederate veteran vigilante activity in the Reconstruction South had a racial dimension, it was not exclusively aimed at restricting the rights of black Union veterans or former slaves. Other groups, too, were the focus of Southern wrath, most notably those white Southerners who had fought for the Union. The fact that white Southerners *had* fought for the Union was discomfiting at the time, and somewhat downplayed since, but it was a fact, and such men, for obvious reasons, were not likely to reach an easy truce with their former Confederate neighbors. It seemed to one Southerner, at least, that the war would be "carried on indefinitely between private citizens" long after its official termination. (Current 1994, 195) With Reconstruction came the opportunity, for some, to settle old scores. Union general Lewis Merrill, for one, complained that "loyal" Southerners in the vicinity of Chattanooga "constantly mislead officers in regard to the character of citizens with whom they are brought into contact by allowing some private wrong or quarrel to influence their statements in regard to them." (Current 1994, 199–200) Armed bands of former Confederates wreaked havoc in Alabama and Florida, and Unionist Southerners clashed with their former foes in Tennessee and Virginia. As President Andrew Johnson handed out pardons like sweets to ex-Confederates, both black and white Unionists in the South found life increasingly intolerable, and sometimes life threatening (Current 1994, 208; Freehling 2002).

Both black and white Union veterans in the South were very much caught between two still warring worlds. On the one hand they could apply—as veterans in the North could—for veterans' benefits, but these were of little value when neither their homes nor their persons were safe from the attentions of groups such as the Klan. Albion Tourgée observed how Union men were "ostracized and proscribed socially" in the South to such an extent that Union veterans were "compelled to discard the blue they have worn with honor, to protect themselves from insult and violence" (quoted in Current 1994, 204). They could also join the Southern branches of the GAR, and through those both assert their identity as veterans and work toward political ends in support of the Republican Party. In the violence and chaos of the Reconstruction South, that was not always, as

Tourgée had realized, the best course of action, since the slightest sugges-
tion that any man had served in the Confederate forces, however tem-
porarily, on a compulsory basis or as a matter of expedient, was a bar to
membership in this overtly patriotic Union organization.

At the same time, not every Unionist veteran in the South endured a
life of misery during Reconstruction, as not every Confederate veteran, by
any means, sought to terrorize his neighbors, black or white. Some of those
who might have felt inclined to do so were restrained by the very palpable
presence of Union troops, some of whom took a fairly hard line as far as
restoring the peace was concerned. In Orangeburg, South Carolina, for example, the commander of the occupying forces, Alfred Hartwell, issued a
variety of proclamations for the education of the local citizenry, including
one in late May that read:

> Those capable of reason and properly informed should know that the Union is
> and shall be preserved and that slavery is dead. No expression of disloyalty will
> be allowed. (quoted in Golay 1999, 220)

Many Confederate veterans bowed to the inevitable, took the Loyalty Oath
to the reunified United States, and tried as best they could to get the crops
planted and get on with their lives. Indeed, for the majority of veterans,
north and south, the pressing need to earn a living forced them down different paths from those taken by the extremists of the Klan, not necessarily
nonviolent paths, but sufficiently restrained that they never made the
headlines. In the pursuit of a living and a better future, as they saw it, some
former Confederates even moved to the North, looking for opportunities
that the Reconstruction South could not offer. Although by no means welcomed with open arms by all, such émigrés found acceptance among their
former foes, perhaps, as historian Daniel Sutherland has suggested, because
of "the mutual respect forged, tempered, and tested in four years of combat" (Sutherland 1981, 407). This "mutual respect" was, in many ways, the
shape of things to come as far as Civil War veterans' role in the reconciliation of North and South was concerned, but not until Reconstruction itself
was a distant memory.

Conclusion

When the Civil War ended in 1865, soldiers from both sides found themselves in the awkward no man's land between war and peace, between military and civilian life. No longer soldiers—in most cases—yet hardly the

civilians they had been, their war experiences had set them apart from the societies to which they returned, and to a great extent, their status as veterans would keep them apart forever. Initially, however, as the soldiers put aside their weapons and returned to society, this status was invisible, or at least downplayed. Although commemoration of the Civil War dead, which had begun even as the war's outcome was uncertain, became formalized in the early Reconstruction period in Memorial Day, the symbolism of the living veteran was a less comforting one to contemplate, and less readily incorporated into the worlds of either the North or the South.

Memorial Day was a spontaneous development on the part of Americans north and south to commemorate the Civil War dead; grieve for the extent of the slaughter; and, as time went on, achieve some reconciliation with former foes. The first Decoration Day, when the graves of soldiers were strewn with flowers, was organized by black South Carolinians and white abolitionists. It took place in Charleston on May 1, 1865, but in 1868, the practice began to spread across Northern communities under the encouragement of John A. Logan, by then commander-in-chief of the Grand Army of the Republic. Logan urged Union veterans to preserve the memory of the war by stressing that:

> If other eyes grow dull and other hands slack, and other hearts cold in the solemn trust, ours shall keep it well as long as the light and warmth of life remain in us. Let us, then, at the time appointed, gather around their sacred remains and garland the passionless mounds above them with choicest flowers of springtime; let us raise above them the dear old flag they saved from dishonor; let us in this solemn presence renew our pledges to aid and assist those whom they have left among us as sacred charges upon the Nation's gratitude—the soldier's and sailor's widow and orphan. (Logan 1868)

Southerners kept themselves apart from the North's commemorative activities; they, too, expressed their grief by decorating the graves of the fallen; they did so at much the same time as Northerners did, and in much the same way, but there were crucial differences. For Union veterans, Memorial Day was, in its early incarnation, about coming to terms with bereavement and preserving in the national memory the very personal, individual memories of fallen comrades; it looked, in short, to the past. Former Confederates, by contrast, were gradually building a future, one in which the Civil War veteran would become a symbol of a cause lost, but by no means fully abandoned.

That future, however, was still some way off during the period of Reconstruction itself. In the North, too, although men like John Logan promoted the GAR as the body through which Union veterans would agitate for expanded war pensions for themselves, their dependents, and the dependents of those killed in the war, in fact, the veterans themselves showed little interest. Contrary to the fears of some that the nation would not seek to repay its debt to its soldiers, Union pension arrangements were, as Theda Skocpol has shown, "very generous by pre-existing historical standards in the United States and beyond." Further, "the range of potential beneficiaries also became remarkably broad," including dependent fathers and mothers and brothers and sisters of dead or disabled soldiers. Despite this generosity, the take-up rate for such benefits was remarkably low. Skocpol proposes a variety of factors at play here, including "a desire to forget the war and get on with life, an absence of financial need, unfamiliarity with the possibilities or the application procedures, and a reluctance on the part of some to take handouts from the government." By 1875, she shows, "only 6.5 percent of all veterans, or about 43 percent of the formerly wounded men" had applied for disability pensions (Skocpol 1992, 107–108). When this low uptake of pensions is combined with the declining GAR membership in the 1870s—it reached a low of 26,899 in 1876—it becomes clear that the majority of Union veterans, at least, sought to distance themselves from the war during Reconstruction (McConnell 1992, 20).

Confederate veterans relied not on the largesse of "the State," for obvious reasons, but on the generosity of individual Southern states, which varied greatly. If his inevitable exclusion from the national benefit system reinforced the Confederate veteran's identity as a defeated warrior of the "Lost Cause," tangible expressions of this identity were slow to emerge. The Lost Cause, as historian Gaines Foster has shown, did not come into full flower during Reconstruction. The efforts of the Klan, although frequently seen as instrumental in the inculcation of a lost cause mentality, in fact "did very little during the early postwar period to shape the Confederate tradition." The veterans' societies that appeared in the South, especially in Virginia, during Reconstruction suffered, as the GAR did, from a rather lukewarm response from the bulk of Confederate veterans. Only the Southern Historical Society (SHS), founded in 1869, had any lasting impact as far as perpetuating a specific Confederate tradition was concerned, and that mostly after Reconstruction had ended. After the death, in 1870, of Robert E. Lee, the Association of the Army of Northern Virginia was established in Virginia. Headed by former Confederate general Jubal A. Early, it, too, struggled to find a following beyond Virginia (Foster 1988, 48–49, 58–61).

When the gray ghosts of the Confederacy did ride again, it was to help bring Reconstruction to an end in the South. The year 1876 was America's centennial. As the North prepared to celebrate 100 years of the United States, in the South, other, less national forces were stirring. When Wade Hampton, former Confederate major general and cavalry commander, ran for the governorship of South Carolina that year, his campaign invoked the Confederacy at its best—or worst, depending on one's perspective. It did so quite deliberately. The image of the "Red Shirts," Hampton's supporters, reminded South Carolina's residents of "the times of 1861, when the boys were starting off to the army" (quoted in Poole 2004, 123). By 1876, however, the boys had long since come home, and neither Hampton's governorship nor the "Redemption" of the South as a whole had much impact on their day-to-day lives, nor made their struggle to survive in the New South any easier.

In the end, the pen proved mightier than the sword—or saber—as far as the Lost Cause and the individual veteran's role in it was concerned. Yet here, too, timing was critical. Edward Pollard's *The Lost Cause* (1866) appeared the year after the war ended but did not have the impact that its title implied. No more did works such as Alexander H. Stephens's *Constitutional View of the Late War* (1870) or Robert L. Dabney's *A Defense of Virginia* (1867). These, as their titles suggested, were more concerned with the legal implications of secession, or its prevention, and less interested—if at all—in the role of the Confederate soldier (Foster 1988, 48). The SHS's publication, the *Southern Historical Society Papers,* first appeared in 1876 but got off to a slow start. In its early years, it provided a forum for former Confederate leaders to rake over the embers of campaigns long past and had little to say about the typical Confederate soldier (Foster 1988, 59). The bulk of the publications—mostly memoirs—that would idealize the Confederate fighting man and, in time, form the bedrock of an ideology of resilience in the face of defeat came from other, frequently female, pens. They, too, could not in the main present the soldier's perspective, only the civilian's experience of the war. Until the emergence of the "Battles and Leaders" series in 1884, the Confederate veteran was, as far as the general public was concerned, silent. When he, and his Union counterpart, found a public voice, it was from the safety of the later 19th century, a time when the Lost Cause was most emphatically lost, with little danger of its rising again and the veteran himself beginning to mature into a figure less threatening to the societies of North and South than the returning soldier had been. Unlike the Civil War dead, age did weary the Civil War veteran, and it was that aging, perhaps, that finally permitted him back into a world that, as long as he retained the potential to return to the arts of war, remained wary, indeed afraid, of him.

References and Further Reading

Anderson, John Q., ed. 1995. *Brokenburn: The Journal of Kate Stone, 1861–1868*. Introduction by Drew Gilpin Faust. Baton Rouge: Louisiana State University Press.

Bellows, Henry Whitney, 1865, *Sanitary Commission Report. No. 90*. New York: U.S. Sanitary Commission.

Berlin, Ira, Thavolia Glymph, Steven F. Miller, Joseph P. Reidy, Leslie S. Rowland, and Julie Saville, eds. 1982. *Freedom: A Documentary History of Emancipation, 1861–1867*, Series 2, *The Black Military Experience*. New York: Cambridge University Press.

Bierce, Ambrose, 2000 [1892]. "A Resumed Identity," in *Tales of Soldiers and Civilians and Other Stories*. Reprint London: Penguin Books, 143–148.

Chamberlain, Joshua Lawrence. 1994 [1915]. *The Passing of the Armies: The Last Campaign of the Armies*. Reprint. Gettysburg, PA: Stan Clark Military Books.

Chesnut, Mary Boykin. 1949 [1905]. *A Diary from Dixie*. Reprint. New York: Appleton and Co.

Current, Richard Nelson. 1994. *Lincoln's Loyalists: Union Soldiers from the Confederacy*. New York: Oxford University Press.

Dean, Eric T. 1999. *Shook Over Hell: Post-Traumatic Stress, Vietnam, and the Civil War*. Cambridge, MA: Harvard University Press.

Doane, L. E. 2003. A Young Girl Meets Her Soldier Father." (Online information; retrieved 5/1/08.) http://memory.loc.gov/learn/features/timeline/civilwar/soldiers/doane.html.

Faulkner, William. 1990 [1936]. *Absalom, Absalom!* Revised ed. New York: Vintage.

Foster, Gaines M. 1988. *Ghosts of the Confederacy: Defeat, the Lost Cause, and the Emergence of the New South*. New York: Oxford University Press.

Freehling, William W. 2002. *The South vs. The South: How Anti-Confederate Southerners Shaped the Course of the Civil War*. New York: Oxford University Press.

Golay, Michael. 1999. *A Ruined Land: The End of the Civil War*. New York: John Wiley and Sons.

Hicks, Robert. 2005. *The Widow of the South*. London: Bantam.

Houghton, W. R., and M. B. Houghton. 1912. *Two Boys in the Civil War and After*. (Online publication; retrieved 5/1/08.) http://docsouth.unc.edu/fpn/houghton/houghton.html.

Leon, Louis. 1913. *Diary of a Tar Heel Confederate Soldier.* (Online publication; retrieved 5/1/08.) http://docsouth.unc.edu/fpn/leon/menu.html.

Linderman, Gerald F. 1989. *Embattled Courage: The Experience of Combat in the American Civil War.* New York: Macmillan.

Logan, John Alexander. 1868. General Orders No. 11, May 5. (Online information; retrieved 5/1/08.) http://www.usmemorialday.org/order11 .html.

Logue, Larry. 1966. *To Appomattox and Beyond: The Civil War Soldier in War and Peace.* Chicago: Ivan R. Dee.

Lowry, Thomas P. 1994. *The Story the Soldiers Wouldn't Tell: Sex in the Civil War.* Mechanicsburg, PA: Stackpole.

McConnell, Stuart. 1992. *Glorious Contentment: The Grand Army of the Republic, 1865–1900.* Chapel Hill: University of North Carolina Press.

Mitchell, Reid. 1989. *Civil War Soldiers: Their Expectations and Their Experiences.* New York: Touchstone.

Mitchell, Reid. 1995. *The Vacant Chair: The Northern Soldier Leaves Home.* New York: Oxford University Press.

Olmsted, Frederick Law. 1986. *The Papers of Frederick Law Olmsted,* vol. IV, *Defending the Union: The Civil War and the U.S. Sanitary Commission, 1861– 1863,* ed. Jane Turner Censer. Baltimore: Johns Hopkins University Press.

Perry, Mark. 1999. *Conceived in Liberty: Joshua Lawrence Chamberlain, William Oates, and the American Civil War.* London: Penguin.

Poole, W. Scott. 2004. *Never Surrender: Confederate Memory and Conservatism in the South Carolina Upcountry.* Athens: University of Georgia Press.

Posner, Richard A., ed. 1992. *The Essential Holmes: Selections from the Letters, Speeches, Judicial Opinions, and Other Writings of Oliver Wendell Holmes, Jr.* Chicago: University of Chicago Press.

Shaffer, Donald R. 2004. *After the Glory: The Struggles of Black Civil War Veterans.* Lawrence: University Press of Kansas.

Sickles, Daniel E. 1891. "Further Recollections of Gettysburg." *North American Review,* March.

Skocpol, Theda. 1992. *Protecting Soldiers and Mothers: The Political Origins of Social Policy in the United States.* Cambridge, MA: Belknap Press.

Sutherland, Daniel E. 1981. "Former Confederates in the Post–Civil War North: An Unexplored Aspect of Reconstruction History." *Journal of Southern History* 47 (3): 393–410.

Taylor, Richard. 1879. *Destruction and Reconstruction: Personal Experiences of the Late War*. (Online publication; retrieved 5/1/08.) http://docsouth.unc .edu/fpn/taylor/menu.html.

Tourgée, Albion W. 1887. "The Renaissance of Nationalism." *North American Review*, January.

Watkins, Sam R. 1977 [1882]. *Co. Aytch*. Reprint. New York: Touchstone.

Whitman, Walt. 1995 [1883]. *Specimen Days and Collect*. Reprint. New York: Dover.

Wyeth, John A. 1914. *With Sabre and Scalpel; the Autobiography of a Soldier and Surgeon*. (Online publication; retrieved 5/1/08.) http://docsouth .unc.edu/fpn/wyeth/menu.html.

Primary Documents

Richard Taylor Discusses the Impact of the South's Military Collapse

The son of former U.S. President Zachary Taylor, Richard Taylor was a sugar planter and slaveholder in Louisiana when the Civil War began. He joined the Confederate Army in 1861 as colonel of a Louisiana regiment and in the course of the war rose to the rank of lieutenant general. The following document is taken from Taylor's memoirs, published shortly before his death in 1879. In this extract, Taylor discusses the poverty and suffering endured in the South in the decade after Appomattox. He also highlights social conflicts in other parts of the nation and suggests that the Civil War had a detrimental impact on the entire United States, not least due to the radical politics of the Republican government.

The military collapse of the South was sudden and unexpected to the world without . . . but the world can not properly estimate the fortitude of the Southern people unless it understands and takes account of the difficulties under which they labored. Yet, great as were their sufferings during the war, they were as nothing compared to those inflicted upon them after its close.

Extinction of slavery was expected by all and regretted by none, although loss of slaves destroyed the value of land. Existing since the earliest colonization of the Southern states, the institution was interwoven with the thoughts, habits, and daily lives of both races, and both suffered by the sudden disruption of the accustomed tie. Bank stocks, bonds, all personal property, all accumulated wealth, had disappeared. Thousands of houses, farm-buildings, work-animals, flocks and herds, had been wantonly burned, killed, or carried off.

The land was filled with widows and orphans crying for aid, which the universal destitution prevented them from receiving. Humanitarians shuddered with horror and wept with grief for the imaginary woes of Africans; but their hearts were as adamant to people of their own race and blood. These had committed the unpardonable sin, had wickedly rebelled against the Lord's anointed, the majority. Blockaded during the war, and without journals to guide opinion and correct error, or, we were unceasingly slandered by our enemies, who held possession of every avenue to the world's ear.

Famine and pestilence have ever followed war, as if our Mother Earth resented the defilement of her fair bosom by blood, and generated fatal diseases to punish humanity for its crimes. But there fell upon the South a calamity surpassing any recorded in the annals or traditions of man. . . . The leaders of the radical masses of the North have indicted such countless and cruel wrongs on the Southern people as to forbid any hope of disposition or ability to forgive their victims; and the land will have no rest until the last of these persecutors has passed into oblivion.

During all these years the conduct of the Southern people has been admirable. Submitting to the inevitable, they have shown fortitude and dignity, and rarely has one been found base enough to take wages of shame from the oppressor and maligner of his brethren. Accepting the harshest conditions and faithfully observing them, they have struggled in all honorable ways, and for what? For their slaves? Regret for their loss has neither been felt nor expressed. But they have striven for that which brought our forefathers to Runnymede, the privilege of exercising some influence in their own government. Yet we fought for nothing but slavery, says the world, and the late Vice-President of the Confederacy, Mr. Alexander Stephens, reëchoes the cry, declaring that it was the corner-stone of his Government. . . .

Since the tocsin sounded we have gone from bad to worse. During the past summer [1877] laborers, striking for increased wages or to resist diminution thereof, seized and held for many days the railway lines between East and West, stopping all traffic. Aided by mobs, they took possession of great towns and destroyed vast property. At Pittsburgh, in Pennsylvania, State troops attempting to restore order were attacked and driven off. Police and State authorities in most cases proved impotent, and the arm of Federal power was invoked to stay the evil.

Thousands of the people are without employment, which they seek in vain; and from our cities issue heart-rending appeals in behalf of the suffering poor. From the Atlantic as far to the west as the young State of Nebraska, there has fallen upon the land a calamity like that afflicting Germany after the Thirty Years' War. Hordes of idle, vicious tramps penetrate rural districts in all directions, rendering property and even life unsafe; and no remedy for this new disease has been discovered. Let us remember that these things are occurring in a country of millions upon millions of acres of vacant lands, to be had almost for the asking, and where, even in the parts first colonized, density of population bears but a small relation to that of western Europe. Yet we daily assure ourselves and the world that we have the best government under the canopy of heaven, and the happiest land, hope and refuge of humanity.

Purified by fire and sword, the South has escaped many of these evils; but her enemies have sown the seeds of a pestilence more deadly than that rising from Pontine marshes. Now that Federal bayonets have been turned from her bosom, this poison, the influence of three fourths of a million of negro voters, will speedily ascend and sap her vigor and intelligence. Greed of office, curse of democracies, will impel demagogues to grovel deeper and deeper in the mire in pursuit of ignorant votes. Her odd breed of statesmen has largely passed away during and since the civil war, and the few survivors are naturally distrusted, as responsible for past errors. Numbers of her gentry fell in battle, and the men now on the stage were youths at the outbreak of strife, which arrested their education. This last is also measurably true of the North. Throughout the land the experience of the active portion of the present generation only comprises conditions of discord and violence. The story of the six centuries of sturdy effort by which our English forefathers wrought out their liberties is unknown, certainly unappreciated. Even the struggles of our grandfathers are forgotten, and the names of Washington, Adams, Hamilton, Jay, Marshall, Madison, and Story awaken no fresher memories in our minds, no deeper emotions in our hearts, than do those of Solon, Leonidas, and Pericles. But respect for the memories and deeds of our ancestors is security for the present, seed-corn for the future; and, in the language of Burke, "Those will not look forward to their posterity who never look backward to their ancestors."

Source: Taylor, Richard (CSA). 1879. Destruction and Reconstruction: Personal Experiences of the Late War. New York: D. Appleton and Co., 230, 235–236, 238, 268–270.

Freedmen on the Plantations

With the abolition of slavery and the passage of the Thirteenth Amendment in 1865, Southern labor relations entered a new and uncertain era. Landowners were forced to negotiate contracts with freedmen and freedwomen who embraced their independent status and strived to determine for themselves both who they worked for and on what terms they worked.

The extract below was printed in the *New Orleans Daily Picayune* in January 1866 and concerns reports on freedmen's behavior on nearby plantations during the recent Christmas holidays. The discussion develops into a scathing attack on the conduct and attitude of black plantation workers and exposes many of the engrained prejudices of the Southern white population during the Reconstruction era, prejudices that were a legacy of racial stereotypes constructed during slavery. The article adopts a proslavery stance, arguing that freedmen and freedwomen were "much better off" before emancipation and that only white Southerners were capable of both controlling African Americans and providing for their welfare.

Gentlemen recently from the plantations report that the freedmen during the most recent holidays generally demeaned themselves in an orderly and peaceful manner. With the exception of a too free indulgence in whiskey, upon which no legal or police restraints are now imposed, the holidays on the plantations passed off quietly and peacefully. The same authorities, however, report very unfavorably as to the condition of these unfortunate victims of experimental legislation and political intermeddling. Though on all the plantations they have been promptly and fully paid at as high a rate of wages as are allowed to agricultural laborers in Europe, and have had the most liberal allowance of rations, and many of them have cultivated small patches, it was exceedingly rare to find a single one who at the end of the year had a dollar left.

It is represented to us by just and impartial observers that their condition was never so poor, so desolate, so ragged, and uncomfortable in every way. Their appearance exhibits a painful degeneration of the race. Their minds are constantly disturbed by the changes, and rumors of changes in their condition, in their legal status, and in their social prospects. Wiser and more experienced people might be well perplexed by the same causes. In the hope of getting a higher rate of wages than are offered to them, or of having plantations of their own, they decline to make any permanent contracts, but work on from day to day in a careless, thoughtless, slovenly manner. No laboring class in the world could prosper or improve in this condition, and no capitalist will invest or continue his capital in a business dependent on such uncertain and unreliable labor. The freedman in this unsettled condition has no home; he has no motive to improve his situation; he lays by nothing, surrounds himself with no comforts, forms and cherishes no domestic ties or social friendships; he becomes the reckless and careless child of change and accident; eternally disquieted in his mind and habits. Under these influences no wonder he becomes the victim of the two most powerful foes he has ever encountered, which are now making fearful havoc in this physical and moral nature. They are "religion" and whiskey. . . . It is an idea of religion which . . . is more generally regarded as an apology for, an expiation of, and even a cover and shield for vice, dishonesty, and immorality. Any degree of these, it is almost universally believed by them, can be atoned for by a certain amount of shouting, or of singing, or in listening to the senseless rigmaroles which are bellowed out to them by their preachers. Of late, these preachers have become more numerous, and have obtained an influence which enables them to fleece the poor freedmen of all their little savings. This is done under various pretexts—to build meeting houses, to have proper funeral ceremonies over their dead relatives, long since consigned to the grave, or to secure them religious services on their own burial, or to raise funds for some of the various societies which have been organized—or rather which are about to be organized—for the promotion of the political rights of freedmen. These societies are not to trouble themselves about the social condition of the freedmen. It is their political elevation that is alone thought of. . . .

That other great bane of the freedmen, which has obtained such a terrible domination over them, is the appetite for alcoholic drink—always a strong appetite with people of a partial or low degree of moral and intellectual development and without social restraints. Under the old system, the authority of the master and the stringent police provisions then in force, held this appetite and habit of the negroes under control. The difficulty of then obtaining spirits, was one of the causes of their rapid increase, in comparison with working classes of other countries, where the habit of drinking strong liquors is so largely indulged. . . .

The great source of the errors of those who have assumed the control of the legislation and regulation of the freedmen, is the lack of practical knowledge of, and appreciation of their condition, and the attempt to substitute therefor abstract theories and closet ideologies. These errors, too, are prompted by an unworthy, unjust and unfounded suspicion that the chief danger to the freedman, to guard against which these regulations seem to be altogether directed, is from the oppression and unjust designs of the planter and employer—a danger which, if there was the slightest foundation for the suspicion, could always be promptly arrested by law; and at the same time making no provision against far greater perils to the freedman, from his own passions and weaknesses, suddenly emancipated from all restraint, and exposed to temptations and influences more debasing, corrupting and fatal, and inflicting a far worse servitude, than the old slave system.

Source: New Orleans Daily Picayune, *January 5, 1866.*

"Domestic Relations of the Freedmen"

Under slavery, African American family life was fragile. Though strong bonds of kinship and community were formed by slaves across the South, ties between husbands and wives, parents and children could be broken at any time and were always subservient to slaveholders' whims and economic interests. Emancipation brought with it opportunities for African Americans to reunite and rebuild their families, but this outcome was rarely a straightforward process, as illustrated in the article below, which is taken from the May 1866 edition of the journal of the National Freedman's Relief Association.

The domestic relations of the freedmen, if indeed they can be said to have any, are, to use one of their own expressions, "the most twisted-up affairs conceivable." This, however, is one of the legitimate fruits of slavery, and it will take many generations of freedom to bring them out of their present condition of chaos. What most surprises one in this connection is, that families having no legal bond hang together as well as they do.

"My husband and I have lived together fifteen years," says the mother of a large family of children, "and we wants to be married over again now."

"I have lived with my husband twenty-one years," says another. "He has always been good to me, and my ways have pleased him, and so we are both satisfied." "She is my fifth wife," says an old man, of the present incumbent of his bed and board, "and I believe I could live with her anywhere."

"They kept my husband away from me [for] three years," says Judy, "and tried to make me marry another man, but I wouldn't do it. They couldn't make me love anybody but Sam; of course they couldn't, and I wouldn't marry anybody else. But if my master found him on his grounds, he'd whip him; and if his master knew of his being away from home, he'd whip him; and then they sold him away, and I couldn't hear where he was."

Yet among many remarkable instances of family devotion and constancy, we must not be surprised to find occasional exceptions.

"Do you think," I asked of a sick woman, "that your husband will ever return to take care of you and his little children?" "Do' know, missus, men is so kind o' queer like, 'pears like dar's no 'pending on 'em any how."

"My husband done lef' me for good," said another. "'Pears like men isn't studyin' 'bout one woman now'days, dey's studyin' 'bout two or three." These uncharitable remarks were doubtless aimed only at persons of their own color, and intended to have no wider application.

"Why in the world," I asked of a sensible woman, who was calling her boy "Jeff Davis," across the way, "Did you give that name to your child?" "I didn't want to call him so, missus, but ole master named him, and I couldn't help it; I wanted to call him Thomas."

Still greater is the uncertainty as to age. "I am seventeen or seventy," says a young woman; and a middle-aged man asks for something for his old mother, "thirty years old." The dates from which they reckon are, Christmas, Planting time, Fourth of July, and Corn time; and the un-lucky waif who does not make his advent at one of these epochs, must date from that nearest. From the mixed character of his domestic rela-tions has perhaps arisen the charge that the negro is wanting in domestic affection.

That there should be some grounds for such accusation does not appear strange, when we consider that to the slave an increase of children is only an increase of gain to the pocket of his owner. The child born under bondage belongs neither to father nor mother, but to master. The parents can not even select a name for it, and are sure of possessing it only during the first month. After that their only parental privilege is to labor at odd moments for its maintenance; and at any day it may be separated from them forever by sale, or division of estate. This, they say, is so much worse than death, "because when your child dies, you know where it is; but when he is sold away, you never know what may happen to him. . . ."

That the negro is incapable of the truest and most devoted affection, and that his heart, in absence is afflicted with the same longing for kindred as the heart which throbs under a white skin, is attested by abundant proof. Witness the anxiety of mothers peering into every strange face, to see if they can discern some trace of the long-lost child, their agonized ex-pressions, when attempting to relate the horrible tale of separation, old men begging to have letters written to the place where their boys were last heard from, children undertaking long and tiresome journeys because they can not repress the yearning to see once more the face of the old father or mother if peradventure they be yet alive. . . .

The kindness of the colored people toward orphans, and homeless children is remarkable, and in this respect their humanity often puts to shame that of the whites. Perhaps the sad experience of their race in the rending of domestic ties, and the sorrows of orphanage may account for the tenderness with which they regard these unfortunates, and the readiness with which they place them among their own children, and divide with them their scanty morsel.

Poplar Springs, VA, April 9, 1866

Source: The National Freedman. A Monthly Journal Devoted to the Promotion of Freedom, Industry, Education, and Christian Morality in the South, *May 1866, 143–145.*

Jonathan Trowbridge on Black Life and Labor in Chattanooga, 1866

As African Americans negotiated the transition from slavery to freedom, they had to find new ways to provide food, clothing, and shelter for themselves and their families. Though no longer bound by slavery, freedpeople still had only limited choice over the work they undertook. Tens of thousands headed to cities in search of employment and poor relief, but many were soon forced to return to the countryside as a result of Freedmen's Bureau policies that were primarily concerned with stabilizing labor relations and minimizing the disruption that abolition brought to agricultural production.

In this document, Jonathan Trowbridge comments on the struggles of African Americans to find work in and around Chattanooga in the aftermath of the Civil War. He provides evidence of the strength of the black community in the city and indicates the degree to which African Americans lived and functioned independently of white influence. Trowbridge was a noted Northern writer who spent four months touring eight states across the postwar South. In reports on his travels, Trowbridge focused on the destruction that the war had caused to Southern lands and property, as well as postwar social and economic conditions.

Notwithstanding there were three thousand negroes in and around Chattanooga, Captain Lucas, of the Freedmen's Bureau, informed me that he was issuing no rations to them. All were finding some work to do, and supporting themselves. To those who applied for aid he gave certificates, requesting the Commissary to sell them rations at Government rates. He was helping them to make contracts, and sending them away to plantations at the rate of fifty or one hundred a week. "These people," said he, "have been terribly slandered and abused. They are willing to go anywhere, if they are sure of work and kind treatment. Northern men have no difficulty in hiring them, but they have no confidence in their old masters." It was mostly to Northern men, leasing plantations in the Mississippi Valley, that the freedmen were hiring themselves. The usual rate of wages was not less than twelve nor more than sixteen dollars a month, for full hands.

The principle negro settlement was at Contraband, a village of huts on the north side of the river. Its affairs were administered by a colored president and council chosen from among the citizens. These were generally persons of dignity and shrewd sense. They constituted a court for the trial of minor offences, under the supervision of the Bureau. Their decisions, Captain Lucas informed me, were nearly always wise and just. "I have to interfere, sometimes, however, to mitigate the severity of the sentences." These men showed no prejudice in favor of their own color, but meted out a rugged and austere justice to all.

One afternoon I crossed the river to pay a visit to this little village. The huts, built by the negroes themselves, were of a similar character to those I had seen at Hampton, but they lacked the big wood-piles and stacks of corn, and the general air of thrift. Excepting the ravages of the small-pox, the community was in a good state of health. . . .

I entered several of these houses. . . . I found a middle-aged woman patching clothes for her little boy, who was at play before the open door . . . I asked the woman how her people were getting along.

"Some are makin' it right schacklin'," she replied, "there's so many of us here. A heap is workin', and a heap is lazin' around." Her husband was employed whenever he could get a job. "Sometimes he talks like he'd hire out, then like he'd sooner take land—any way to git into work. All have to support themselves somehow."

Source: Trowbridge, J. T. 1866. The South: A Tour of Its Battle-Fields and Ruined Cities. *Hartford, CT: L. Stebbins, 251–253.*

"Juhl" on Black Protest and Economic Conditions in South Carolina

Between 1865 and 1871, Julius J. Fleming recorded his thoughts on social, political, and economic aspects of Reconstruction in more than two hundred letters published in the *Charleston Courier* under the pen name "Juhl." Born in Charleston in 1823, Fleming served as a minister and school principal prior to the war and subsequently qualified as a lawyer. At the time his first letters appeared in the *Courier*, he was a magistrate in Sumter, a town of some two thousand people in the heart of the South Carolina Low Country.

In this extract from a letter published in November 1866, Fleming records freedpeople's organized protests against exploitative labor conditions. Depicting the leaders of the protest in a positive light, Fleming is sympathetic to African Americans' economic plight but is opposed to black political activity.

A very large assemblage of the colored people met here today at the Freedmen's Tabernacle located in the southern suburbs. The exercises were opened with singing and prayer, after which a number of addresses were delivered setting forth the absolute inadequacy of one-third of the crop as a just remuneration for the labor of the year. The speakers dwelt upon the present condition of the freedmen without land, without homes, and without resources, and in many cases unsupplied with shoes and clothing with the winter close at hand. They expressed the conviction that the only safe conditions on which they could make engagements for the future would be for the land and labor to divide the field products share and share alike. The speakers were intelligent freedmen, and all belonged to this state and district, and the immense audience not only behaved with utmost decorum, but appeared unanimous and deeply in earnest.

A local magistrate [probably Fleming himself], who was present by special invitation, being called on for his counsel embraced the opportunity of impressing upon their minds the real causes of their present destitution. The contracts of the present year were an experiment—adopted and approved by the military and the bureau—and were unequal in their operation and productive, in some cases, of great injustice, hardships, and dissatisfaction. The seasons, too, had been so remarkably unpropitious that planters and employers were alike involved in a common disappointment and common suffering. The system of a pro rate of the crop was liable to very grave objections, while stated wages would ensure to every man, in proportion to his skill, character, and capacity, a certain compensation easily defined and ascertained. On this plan, whenever an employer and employee concluded to part company during the year, it would be easy for the former to ascertain his dues to the latter and to pay the same either in money or by note maturing at the end of the year. The entire crop would then belong to the planter, and all disputes about its division be entirely avoided. . . .

It is worthy of note that during the four hours of this gathering of freedmen not a word was said about political rights, Negro suffrage, or Negro equality. The first and last note of the occasion was on the same chord, a fair and remunerative return for the services of the laborer and the ways and means of saving the destitute multitude from starvation and death.

This meeting is but one of many which have been held in various parts of the country for a like purpose. There is not doubt that the movement is a general one, and when the character, numbers, and position of the freedmen are considered, the matter assumes an importance which may claim the attention of the state.

Your correspondent has carefully watched the animus of this movement and has been unable to detect in it anything like defiance or disre-
spect towards the superior race . . . .

Source: Moore, John Hammond, ed. 1974. The Juhl Letters to the Charleston
Courier: A View of the South, 1865–1871. *Athens: University of Georgia Press,
134–137.*

Letter from Georgeanne Cook to Freedmen's Teacher Lucy Chase, 1866

Freedom was cherished by all African Americans, but for many, the struggle to
survive from day-to-day persisted long after slavery had been abolished. In this
brief letter written on behalf of Jane Bright to a former teacher, Georgeanne Cook
records the deprivation of black life in Norfolk, Virginia.

Miss Chase, Teacher, Norfolk City
Norfolk City Dec 27th 1866

This woman are a poor creature with 5 children and are much in need of
clothen and desire the help of the mission She ware once the slave of mc-
toush and has never reseav eney thing from the govenment i had to stop
my children from School be cause thay had not clothing to go to School her
name are Jane Bright Sign by

GEORGEANNE COOK

Source: American Antiquarian Society. 2006. (Online document; retrieved 5/2/08.)
http://mac110.assumption.edu/aas/Manuscripts/Students/cook.html

Extracts from Letters Written by Margaret Newbold Thorpe, a Northern Teacher in Virginia, 1866

Inspired by diverse motives of religion, philanthropy, and, in some cases, self-interest, hundreds of Northern women headed into the Southern states in the early
years of Reconstruction to work as teachers in schools for the freedmen and
freedwomen. As a teacher in Virginia, Margaret Thorpe experienced the former
slaves' enthusiasm and commitment to learning, but, as she documents in the following extracts from her letters, she also witnessed the great financial hardships
that both blacks and whites faced during Reconstruction.

Fort MaGruder, 4 Mo. 28th, 1866

Respected Friend—By the enclosed report thee will see the school of which we have charge is still large as it was last month—158 being the entire number attending day school, and 210 the entire number in day and night schools together. Recently the usual attendance has diminished owing to pressing spring work. Ours is not a village, or a camp school, the children come from several surrounding plantations—some of them a distance of three miles. Quite a number of our night scholars come that distance and attend regularly. . . .

November 1866

We have more scholars than last year, and our Sunday School is very large, both old and young have an intense desire to read the Bible, and are so pleased even when they can tell what the small words are. . . .

We are very busy now, much more so than last winter, then the Government issued rations, and now that is stopped.

You know the beautiful choice song "In 1863 Abe Lincoln set the nigger free!" That was three years ago only, and now they must be self-supporting. Only think of these people here, renting the poor ground and eking out a living somehow, of course we help a great deal for our Northern friends generously answer our appeals for money. While we had the Freedmen's Bureau all cases of suffering were reported to the officer stationed here and he would give relief, but now we have all this to attend to, and at times my heart aches as if it would burst to do so little to help these heroic patient workers. The people are greatly in need of shoes; we have purchased some and have given away all of our own that we can possibly spare; we have written home for two dozens to be sent to us as soon as possible. Government has established hospitals for the poorest of the people but the one at York[t]own is such a cold miserable inefficiently served and inefficiently supplied that it does not seem much of a change for the better for the sick to be taken there.

The country seems bankrupt, the white people seldom pay the negroes whom they employ. I often believe that they really have no money with which to pay their debts. Everyone is poor and the suffering is heartbreaking. We are trying to induce some of these young men and women to go North. Government will pay for their transport. . . .

The best of the colored men and women are anxious not to [be] beggars, but to earn enough to pay for what they want, so we sold the goods to them for a mere nominal amount, ten cents a yard for goo[d] strong cloth for men's clothes; with this money we purchased garden seeds, medicine and other inexpensive necessities. In this way we encourage a feeling of self-respect and independence; of course the number of those who buy is much smaller than the number of those to whom we give. It is nothing short of heroic to live and work as some of these people are doing, the land is so terribly poor and the white people have so little money, and at the stores everything is about double the price charged for the same in the North. . . .

Source: Morton, Richard L., ed. 1956. "Life in Virginia by a 'Yankee Teacher,' Margaret Newbold Thorpe." Virginia Magazine of History and Biography 64: 181–182, 190–191, 193.

Letter from Rosa Buchanan Lunday to President Andrew Johnson

The abolition of slavery affected white Southerners in many different ways. For those like Rosa Buchanan Lunday, who had made their livelihood from hiring slaves, the financial implications were grave. Conditioned by racist notions of white supremacy to believe that only African Americans were suited to hard agricultural labor and that poverty was an especially heavy burden for whites to bear, Rosa Lunday here details the sufferings she and her family endured during the Civil War and its immediate aftermath in a letter to President Andrew Johnson.

Wadesboro' N.C.
Sept. 15th/65

To His Excellency Andrew Johnston [sic], Sir—

Your Excellency is of course aware of the unhappy condition to which the issue of the late Rebellion had seduced the people of these Southern States, but it has occurred to me that perhaps those in authority over us,—whose clemency we have already experienced, may not fully understand and appreciate—the deplorable I may say truly appalling—situation of one class of our population; I refer to those of us whose entire property consisted in negroes—, and without the usual accompaniment of lands—Providence has cast my lot among this unfortunate class—Having derived my entire income from the *hire* of negroes—I am today in a more helpless situation than were any of the slaves, under the old order of things—for they were, and are, free from the terrible anxieties about the ways & means of living, to which our minds are prey—The habits of hard labor to which most of *them* have been accustomed render them comparatively independent— Since producers and others are compelled to have their labor and give them its price. It will be said, that the same field is open to all; but the *real* sufferers from the emancipation of slaves have not even the cheering prospect of well paid labor before them—Since they are not fitted—by nature or habit, for any kind of hard work—A superior education—is no security against want—for there is among our people a great reluctance to giving employment to teachers—: the learning of books seems to be considered a superfluity that can easily be dispensed with—One of the saddest results of this feeling of poverty, is the intense selfishness of one toward another, in this land—This feature is becoming more & more perceptible— The repairing of ruined fortunes is becoming a general mania—To contend with such a state of feeling is most hopeless—

My own case is particularly deplorable—I am the widow of a young physician—and have an invalid mother, (who was brought up in affluent circumstances) and a little daughter, both quite dependent on my exertions—From ease and comfort we are suddenly reduced to extreme poverty, and without any prospects of mitigating its evils—, which are more keenly felt by those who have never been familiar with our privations—If suffering only fell upon those who aided or encouraged the rebellion it might be looked upon as a just retribution, but rather the contrary is the case—

Having been destitute of male relatives since the year '59 I cannot charge the war with having brought to us any heavier troubles, than have already been mentioned—but we did sustain a very severe loss, at the hands of Gen. Kilpatrick's raiders, in last March—They entered my private chamber, and robbed me of a large amount of valuables, which to me possessed from association a far higher value than their mere equivalent in money, being mostly old family relics etc. Members of the order of Free Masons were in many cases respected & left unmolested—but these robbers choose to ignore the fact of which they had proofs in the course of their plundering—My husband belonged to the order—I do not know that there is, or ever will be any society in the whole United States for the relief of sufferers from the war, neither do I know that any public measures will be adopted, with the same object—but I have ventured to give the facts of the case, out of a multitude of similar ones—; though it is true that in the circle of my acquaintance, I know of no other one, that is so utterly desolate— . . .

Very Respectfully
CARE JAS. THREADGILL
Wadesboro N.C.

Source: McPherson, Elizabeth Gregory, ed. 1950. "Letters from North Carolina to Andrew Johnson." North Carolina Historical Review, *27, 480–481.*

"Another Social Difficulty—A Colored Man Ejected from Railway Cars"

Following the passage of the Civil Rights Act of 1866 and the onset of radical Reconstruction, African Americans across the United States instigated protests against the practice of segregation on public transport. In 1867, streetcars were boycotted in a number of major cities, and legal proceedings were started against railroad companies that discriminated against nonwhite passengers. In this article from the *New York Tribune*, a publication that endorsed the radical platform, a reporter in Richmond, Virginia, describes the experiences of Alfred Howe on his train journey from New York to Wilmington, North Carolina, and his efforts to seek redress for his treatment by the railroad company.

From our special correspondent, Richmond, Va., Sept. 7, 1867.

Another case of equality, similar to that of the Canadian colored man, who was denied his rights by a steamship company, has occurred in Virginia. In this, however, there can be no plea of foreign nationality urged. On Thursday last, a colored man named Alfred Howe purchased in New-York from the agent of a railway company a first-class ticket, through from that city to Wilmington, N.C. He proceeded on his passage smoothly and quietly, traveling as did other passengers until he arrived at Fredericksburg on the Richmond, Fredericksburg and Potomac Railroad, when the conductor attempted to eject him from the cars, because he insisted on occupying the seat to which he was entitled, having paid for it. To avoid a difficulty, however, Howe, with the kindest consideration, took a seat in the car allotted by the Company to colored people, in which, under protest, he rode to within 12 miles of this city, when the conductor again presented himself, demanding his ticket. This Howe refused to surrender, stating it was his intention to resort to legal remedies against the Company, and as an evidence of his claim upon them, he wished to preserve the ticket. The conductor, astonished at such a monstrous presumption on the part of a "nigger," again reiterated his demand, which was responded to by a determined though respectful refusal from Howe. Force was then used by the conductor and after a struggle, in which Howe manfully resisted, he was ejected from the cars, about 1 1/2 o'clock in the morning, 12 miles from Richmond, where he was obliged to walk, arriving here early in the day. When the office of the Freedmen's Bureau was opened, Howe presented himself to Gen. O. Brown, commissioner for this District, and related his case. The General, after mature consideration, found it was one over which the Bureau had no control, and referred Howe to United States commissioner Chahoon, who also could afford no relief. The latter, however, willing to serve the injured man as much as possible, gave him the necessary legal advice, and, acting under this, Howe is about to institute an action for damages against the railroad company, in Judge Underwood's Court, where, no doubt, he will receive justice.

Source: New York Tribune, *September 10, 1867, p. 1, col. 4.*

Testimony of Charlotte Fowler before the Joint Select Committee to Inquire into the Condition of Affairs in the Late Insurrectionary States

In the early 1870s, the Ku Klux Klan was responsible for hundreds of assaults and murders across many parts of the former Confederate states. In response, Congress enacted several pieces of legislation, known as the Enforcement Acts, and established a joint congressional committee to investigate Klan activities. The committee collected several volumes of testimony from all manner of people affected by and involved in Klan violence. In the extract included here, Charlotte Fowler, a black woman from Spartanburg, South Carolina, describes how her husband was murdered by the Klan in 1871 and speculates on why he was targeted. Just months after this interview was conducted, President Ulysses S. Grant used the powers of the Enforcement Acts to declare martial law and suspend the right of habeas corpus in Spartanburg and eight other counties in South Carolina. Klan activity would decline in the area thereafter, but racially motivated violence remained a feature of South Carolina politics and played a critical role in the restoration of Democratic Party rule in the state in 1876.

Spartanburgh [sic], South Carolina, July 6, 1871
Charlotte Fowler (colored) sworn and examined.

By the Chairman:
Question: Where do you live?
Answer: On Mr. Moore's premises.
Question: Do you know in what township?
Answer: No, sir; my son does.
Question: Is it in this county?
Answer: No, sir; I did live in Spartanburgh County with my husband, before the old man was killed; but now I live with my son.
Question: How long ago is it since your husband was killed?
Answer: It was the 1st of May.
Question: What was his name?

Answer: Wallace Fowler.

Question: Tell how he was killed.

Answer: The night he was killed—I was taken sick on Wednesday morning, and I laid on my bed Wednesday and Thursday. I didn't eat a mouthful; I couldn't do it, I was so sick; so he went out working on his farm . . . . He kept coming backward and forward to the house to see how I got and what he could do for me . . . . When he came home he cooked something for me to eat, and said: "Old woman, if you don't eat something you will die." . . . He got up and pulled off his clothes and got in bed . . . . I was only by myself now, for the children were all abed. Then I got up and went into the room to my bed. I reckon I did not lay in bed a half an hour before I heard somebody by the door; it was not one person, but two— ram! Ram! Ram! At the door. Immediately I was going to call him to open the door; but he heard it as quick as lightning, and he said to them: "Gentlemen, do not break the door down; I will open the door;" and just as he said that they said: "God damn you, I have got you now." . . . and just then I heard the report of a pistol, and they shot him down . . . .

Question: What else?

Answer: I didn't know that anybody had anything against the old man; everybody liked him but one man, and that was Mr. Thompson. Somewhere along summer before last he [Fowler] had planted some watermelons in his patch; and he kept losing his watermelons, and one day he said he would go and lay, and see who took them; and sure enough he caught two little white boys; one was Mr. Thompson's boy and the other was Mr. Millwood's boy . . . they had cut up a whole lot of the melons . . . . Then Mr. Thompson fetched on so about the watermelons.

Question: How long was that before the old man was killed?

Answer: The watermelons were took this summer a year ago . . . .

Question: Do you mean by this that Thompson had anything to do with the killing of the old man?

Answer: I'm going to tell you my opinion about it. I didn't see Mr. Thompson's face, for he had a mask on; but he was built so. He lives close to us, and I saw him every day and Sunday.

Question: Did these men have masks on?

Answer: Only the one that shot him.

Question: What kind of mask?

Answer: It was all around the eyes. It was black; and the other part was white and red; and he had horns on his head . . . .

Question: Do you mean to say that you believe his being killed was caused by the quarrel about the watermelons?

Answer: I can tell you my belief. There is a parcel of men who were on the plantation working Mr. Jones's land, and my old man was one of them that tended Mr. Jones's land. Mr. Jones had had a whole parcel of poor white folks on the land and he turned them off, and put all these blacks on the premises that they had from Mr. Jones, and I don't know what it could be, but for that and the watermelons. That was the cause why my old man is dead, and I am left alone. (Weeping.) . . .

By Mr. Stevenson:

Question: What other work did he [Fowler] do?

Answer: Nothing but farming. Every time Mr. Jones wanted anything from this town, he sent him and another old gentleman that lived there. They killed him, and they whipped another nearly to death; and they shot another in the head, but the ball was so much spent that it did not kill him, and the doctor got the ball out.

Question: Was that the same night?

Answer: Yes, sir. . . . That gentleman intended to clean them out off of the plantation. . . .

By Mr. Stevenson:

Question: What are these men called that go about masked in that way?

Answer: I don't know; they call them Ku-Klux.

Question: How long have they been going about in that neighborhood?

Answer: I don't know how long; they have been going a long time, but they never pestered the plantation until that night. . . .

Question: Did your old man belong to any party?

Answer: Yes, sir.

Question: What party?

Answer: The radicals. . . .

Question: Was he a pretty strong radical?

Answer: Yes, sir; a pretty strong radical. . . .

Question: Did he talk to the other colored people about it?

Answer: No, sir; he never said nothing much. . . . He never traveled anywhere to visit people only when they had a meeting. . . .

Question: Did he make speeches at those meetings?

Answer: No, sir.

By the Chairman:

Question: Are the colored people afraid of these people that go masked?

Answer: Yes, sir; they are as 'fraid as death of them. There is now a whole procession of people that have left their houses and are lying out. You see the old man was so old, and he did no harm to anybody; he didn't believe anybody would trouble him.

By Mr. Stevenson:

Question: Did he vote at the last election?

Answer: Yes, sir.

Source: Affairs in the Late Insurrectionary States. 42nd Cong., 2nd Sess. 3. South Carolina 1. *1872. Washington, D.C.: Government Printing Office, 386–392.*

Freedmen's Bureau Agents Report from Demopolis, Alabama

The letters and reports of Freedmen's Bureau agents who were stationed in the South provide one of the richest sources available for studying Reconstruction. The excerpts presented here are taken from monthly reports submitted by the Bureau office in Demopolis, Alabama, which oversaw Bureau operations across five counties in the western part of the state. They demonstrate the range of the Bureau's responsibilities, the challenges that agents faced in their attempts to protect the freedmen, and how quickly and extensively local conditions changed in the years after the Civil War.

C. W. Pierce to Col Kinsman, Sub Asst. Commissioner, Montgomery, Ala[bama]. General Report for the month of May 1867.

Demopolis, June 11, 1867.

I. GENERAL SUMMARY OF THE WORK OF THIS OFFICE

The business of this Office this year differs in many respects from that of last year, as there were then several cases, almost daily, of assault and outrages by whites upon freedmen, while this year the work of the Office consists in general supervision of the interests of the Freedmen, namely: settling last years and inspecting, correcting & approving this years contracts, explaining their rights and duties under the same, hearing their complaints of outrages and wrongs & rectifying the same, settling difficulties between freedmen, answering letters of inquiries from planters & others, supervising the issue of rations to the destitute; the hospital & asylum, establishing schools, looking after the administration of justice under the Civil Law when freedmen are interested etc etc. . . .

III. FEELING BETWEEN THE RACES

The feeling between the Races is improving although there is still much suspicion on the part of the Blacks and prejudice on the part of the Whites.

A. S. Bennett to Brevet Maj. George Shorkley.
General Report for the month of March 1868

Demopolis, March 31, 1868

Nothing unusual has transpired in this vicinity, but in some parts of the Dist[rict] aggravated disturbances have occurred. In Green County the agent J. A. Yordy has deemed it advisable to leave his post in consequence of violence towards others and threats against himself the facts of which are about as follows.

On Saturday March 14th Rev. G.B.F. Hill a quiet unobtrusive gentleman who has been engaged in teaching [and] superintending schools for freedmen in the county was assaulted and severely beaten by prominent citizens and notified to leave the county within a certain time. He did so and upon representation to Headquarters a detachment of U.S. troops were sent to Eutaw and made arrests of several that were engaged in the assault upon Mr Hill. Mr Yordy was advised by friends to leave the place for a time as there is not sufficient influence among the well disposed citizens to restrain the lawless portion of the community and violence towards him was feared. He is here now and does not propose to return unless troops are sent there to protect him.

C. W. Pierce to Brevet Maj. George Shorkley.
General Report for the month of June 1868

Demopolis, June 30, 1868

The businesses of the office have materially increased during the month, and the quite of may has been superceded by frequent complaints by Freedmen of assaults, being turned off upon trivial excuses. There is evidently an increasing disposition to harass and oppress the colored people for the purposes of gain and from political motives; the severe labor in the crops is over and pretexts are evidently sought upon which to get rid of the laborers. In some localities the fear among the freedmen has approximated to terrorism, several parties have been placed under bonds and the freedmen reassured that they will be protected in their civil and political rights. Similar reports are received from the agents at Eutaw and Greensboro.

Source: Records of the Assistant Commissioner for the State of Alabama, 1865–1870, Bureau of Refugees, Freedmen, and Abandoned Lands. Demopolis, Alabama. *No date. Washington, D.C.: National Archives.*

Interview with African American Rev. Frank T. Boone, Little Rock, Arkansas, c. 1936–1938

Freedpeople faced various challenges as a result of their emancipation. Many were legacies of the slave system, while others developed as a result of the process of Reconstruction. Many years afterward, the formerly enslaved and later generations of African Americans were interviewed about their experiences during slavery, the Civil War, freedom, and Reconstruction by the Works Progress Administration Slave Narrative Project (WPA). Established in the 1930s as part of the New Deal initiative during the Great Depression, the WPA project collated more than 200,000 interviews with African Americans in 17 of the former slaveholding states. These interviews have been regarded with caution by some historians, who argue that they are unreliable as a true testimony of enslaved life. However, others have stressed the unreliability of any source material and argue that, as long as historians are aware of the narratives' problematic nature, they should be used to explore the ways that African Americans recollected various aspects of their lives during slavery and freedom.

In this extract of an interview with black freedman Rev. Frank T. Boone, conducted by Samuel S. Taylor, Boone recollects his memories of the Reconstruction era in Virginia, where his family had lived, and later in South Carolina, where he moved in 1880. His account recalls various aspects of the Reconstruction era, in particular the hopes and expectations of the formerly enslaved at the end of the Civil War and the potential of freedmen and freedwomen if they were provided with practical support, such as access to land. Boone also recounts the political activity of freedmen in South Carolina, where he stood for local office during Reconstruction.

In an earlier part of the interview Boone states that he was "born free" in Nansemond County, Virginia. His mother had previously been a slave to a Quaker family who had freed her at the age of 21, while his father had "always been free." In addition, Boone recollects that his grandmother on his father's side had owned slaves, but he admits that he had not realized the people concerned had been enslaved until after the war was over.

I hear my mother and uncle talk about what the slaves expected. I knew they was expecting to get something. They weren't supposed to be turned out like wild animals like they were. I think it was forty acres and a mule. I am not sure but I know they expected something to be settled on them. If any of them got anything in Virginia, I don't know anything about it. They might have been some slaves that did get something—just like they was here in Arkansas.

Old man Wilfong, when he freed Andy Wilfong in Bradley County, Arkansas, gave Andy plenty. He did get forty acres of land. That is right down here out from Warren. Wilfgong owned that land and a heap more when he died. . . . They were others who expected to get something, but I don't know any others that got it. Land was cheap then. Andy bought land at twenty-five and fifty cents an acre, and sold the timber off it at the rate of one thousand dollars for each forty acres. He bought hundreds of acres. . . . He had seven boys and two girls and he gave them all forty acres a piece when they married. Then he sold the timber off of four forties. Whenever a boy or girl was married he'd given him a house. He'd tell him to go out and pick himself out a place.

He sold one hundred and sixty acres of timber off for four thousand dollars, but if he had kept it for two years longer, he would have got ten thousand dollars for it. The Bradley Labour Company went in there and cut the timber all through.

Wilfongs master's name was Andrew Wilfong, same as Andy's. His master came from Georgia, but he was living in Arkansas when freedom came. Later on Andy brought the farm his master was living on when freedom came. His master was then dead.

When I first went to South Carolina, them niggers was bad. They organized. They used to have an association known as the Union Laborers, I think. The organization was like the fraternal order. I don't know's they ever had any trouble but they were always in readiness to protect themselves if any conflict arose. It was a secret order carried on just like any other fraternal order. They had distress calls. Every member has an old horn which he blew in times of trouble. I think that some kind of organization or something like it was active when I came here. The Eagles (a big family of white people in Lonoke County) had a fight with members of it once and some of the Eagles were killed a year or two before I came to this state.

I lived in a little town by the name of Mcgray. The town I was in, they had never had more than fifteen or twenty Republican votes polled. But I polled between two hundred and three hundred votes. I was one of the regular speakers. The tickets were in my care too. You see, they had tickets in them days and not the long ballots. They didn't have long ballots like they have now. The tickets were sent to me and I took care of them until the election. In the campaign I was regularly employed through the Republican Campaign Committee Managers.

Source: Works Progress Administration Slave Narrative Project, Arkansas Narratives, *vol. 2, pt. 1, Federal Writer's Project. Washington, D.C.: Manuscript Division, Library of Congress.*

Eleventh Annual Report of the Commission of Home Missions to Colored People, Protestant Episcopal Church, A.D. 1875–1876. St. Mark's Church, Wilmington, North Carolina, Rev. C. O. Brady

By the mid-1870s, hopes of a radical reconstruction of Southern society had faded amidst a welter of violence, economic depression, political corruption, and growing Northern apathy toward the fate of the freedpeople. Yet the work of black education and community building persisted, with churches and missionary societies retaining a prominent role in working with African Americans as government involvement declined. As this report on a church in North Carolina documents, however, even the most philanthropic white missionaries often held racist views and perceived their work as part of a long-standing Christian mission to "civilize" people of African descent.

I am happy to be enabled to report progress in the work in which, by the providence of God, I am permitted to be engaged. There has been a steady increase in the number of communicants. We report for the Ecclesiastical Year, ending March 31, 1876, one hundred and fifty-one communicants, with an average attendance of about one hundred. . . . The Parish school is visited by your Missionary every morning, and its exercises opened with the reading of the Holy Scriptures and Prayer; on Fridays, the children are instructed in the Catechism and singing. The average attendance at the Church Services is quite large; at the Sunday-school, 120; at the Week-day or Parish school, 120. Thus the Services are regularly conducted every week during ten months of the year, and it is gratifying to observe a marked progress in the Parish, especially among the children; the latter are better dressed—I mean more neat and cleanly—better behaved, and more correct in deportment generally; while the congregation of St. Mark's will compare favorably with any in the county as regards respectability. The Parish also is gradually exerting an influence on the community of Colored people generally, especially among those who are becoming educated—the rising generation. . . .

Since my last annual report, the congregation of St. Mark's have shown great energy in their endeavors to complete the wood finish, and coloring, oiling, etc., of the interior of their church. By their efforts they have succeeded in oiling a portion of the woodwork and in kalsomining the walls a pale blue, which produces quite a cheerful and appropriate effect.

The year past has been one of extreme hardness, and the people have found it difficult in many instance to get along, their efforts having been greatly crippled, yet we have got through the year comparatively free from debt. We hope to begin our work this Fall with renewed vigor, and to press it on towards the great end, *i.e.,* the ingathering of the many precious redeemed souls among the Anglo-African race in America. . . .

St. Mark's Parish, as you know, is in union with the Diocesan Convention, and is yearly represented by the Minister in charge and delegates. And I am extremely gratified to bear testimony of the hearty and cordial reception of the delegates who represent Colored Parishes by the Bishops of the Diocese as well as by the Clerical and Lay delegates. All goes on in harmony and in Christian sympathy with the weaker brethren, and it is quite apparent that we are growing more and more in favor each year of our existence with the community, and especially Churchmen and the Clergy. . . .

Conclusion

The past eleven years have shown conclusively, again and again, what can be accomplished by earnest, faithful work in behalf of the Colored people of the South. There is only one real solution of the whole African question. Human legislation has attempted it, but in many important particulars it has failed. No section of our country has as yet apprehended the true condition and destiny of the Colored man, or been successful in his general elevation. It is not in the mere counsels of men that this is to be accomplished. All plans fail, and treasure be expended in vain, until we seek his true elevation as an Immortal being, through the medium, of the Gospel of Grace. The only true civilizer is Christian teacher; and the only elevation worthy of the name, must be based on an intelligent Christianity.

Respectfully submitted, by order of the Executive Committee:

CHAS. H. HALL *Chairman.*

C.C. TIFFANY, *Corresponding Secretary.*

WELLINGTON E. WEBB, *Secretary Exec. Committee.*

40 Bible House, New York, Oct. 1, 1876

Source: African American Perspectives: Pamphlets from the Daniel A. P. Murray Collection, 1818–1907. *(Online document; retrieved 5/2/08.) http://memory.loc.gov/ cgi-bin/query/r?ammem/murray:@field(DOCID+@lit(lcrbmrpt2215div9)).*

"Postwar Notes"

After the Civil War, Southern whites looked back on the antebellum years fondly and constructed idealized memories of race relations under slavery. Echoing the paternalistic and racist assumptions of the proslavery advocates of the mid-19th century, they argued that African Americans had been content and loyal slaves but were unprepared and unfit for freedom. These sentiments were shared by Sarah Conley Clayton, a white woman who had been a teenager in Atlanta during the Civil War. In this extract from her memoirs, written in the early 1900s, Clayton attacks President Abraham Lincoln for signing the Emancipation Proclamation and contends that the years after abolition witnessed a decline in black living standards and increased immorality and crime.

The great cry with L [Abraham Lincoln] was the Union, yet a reading of his second inaugural address will show what he was for. He may have been a great and good man, but to the Southern people there is one blot not easily forgotten, and that was the signing of the Emancipation proclamation at the time he did. Its emancipation of slaves was not general, but for the belligerent [Confederate] States, and the belief was, it was done then under the impression that the slaves in their great eagerness for freedom, as was the supposition of the North, would rise in insurrection and wipe us off the face of the earth, and that while they were thus busily engaged our men would of course rush to the rescue and leave them [the federal armies] to have things their way. And, lo and behold! The negroes still took the utmost care of us.

Now whether he [Abraham Lincoln] was urged into this [signing the Emancipation Proclamation] or did it voluntarily is not yet clear to me. (It was far worse than the robbery of us.)

In speaking of the negro there was one fortunate quality given him that made the unkind treatment many had to bear very much easier for him than it would have been possible for the white man, that was his childlike disposition, very soon forgetting his sorrows or inquiries, this was the black man; a mixture of blood brought desire for freedom, the more the greater and harder for him to bear his troubles [illegible words] while the greatest number were, by far, better off, the children, the old, the sick, it is far better to have them free; there was great responsibility attached to owning them. But if the Northerner thinks he has ended their suffering instead of changing it, all he has to do is to come down and investigate for himself; let him see something of the treatment of the old and the poor children, the way husbands and wives beat each other, and the way the sick have to suffer; the chain gang, the penitentiary. And as to morality, they say we fail to teach them. If there has been any improvement nobody has found it out, their own preachers fail on that and other crimes. And I should like to know what is thought of his [the negro's] criminal tendency these days. He was saved temptation to that in slavery, for in rare cases did it amount to more than lying and stealing, with his inborn immorality.

Source: Sarah "Sallie" Conley Clayton. 1999. Requiem for a Lost City: A Memoir of Civil War Atlanta and the Old South, *ed. Robert Scott Davis. Macon, GA: Mercer University Press, 170–171.*

Address Delivered before the South Carolina Historical Society on Their Twenty-First Anniversary, May 19, 1876, by William J. Rivers

Founded in 1855, the South Carolina Historical Society met for the first time after the Civil War in May 1876 at the Hibernian Hall in Charleston. Chosen to deliver the Society's Anniversary Address was William J. Rivers, a professor of ancient languages and president of Washington College, who had been a leading advocate of secession and had delivered the last Anniversary Address in 1861, just weeks after the firing on Fort Sumter. In his 1876 speech, Rivers drew on a white supremacist, state's rights interpretation of South Carolina's political history to defend the actions and ideals of the white South, critique the role of Northerners in slavery and Reconstruction, and attack African American political influence in the state. The speech was made at a time of growing political violence in South Carolina that would eventually lead to the election of Wade Hampton as governor and the end of Republican Party rule.

. . . what can I choose on this occasion but to speak, feebly as it may be, of that which continually occupies our thoughts—the condition of the State, the misapprehension of others regarding our policy in the past, and regarding our attitude at the present moment? . . .

Inasmuch as there is by others a continued reiteration of the subject of emancipation, we must reluctantly say a word about it; premising that no disposition, not even a thought, is ever entertained among us to reverse, if we had the power to do so, this issue of the late war. The benefits to ourselves of the termination of slavery will ultimately be acknowledged by every one at the South. It may even have been brought about, in the course of time, by our own voluntary act. But the suddeness [sic] and irritation of the hostile mode of its accomplishment by the North must, we are inclined to believe, be condemned in history as unwise and unphilanthropical. If it were wrong for us to hold slaves, it was a wrong encouraged by the legislation of the British Parliament. And the negroes brought hither, came to us in large numbers in the ships of New England, herself a slave-holder and, next to England, our principle slave dealer. It was computed from our custom house records, that during the four years preceding 1808, there were brought to this port 39,075 slaves. Of these, 21,027 were imported by foreigners, chiefly British; 14,605 by natives of Northern States; and only 3443 by citizens of slave-holding States. The money paid for the large portion introduced by our Northern brethren remains, I suppose, to this day in their coffers at home. If slavery were wrong, they must share the opprobrium with us, if they will share nothing else. . . .

A republican form of government which is guaranteed to us by our original compact, has come to mean, under the new development, one dependent on nothing else than a numerical majority, with suffrage, by every man without regard to race, color, previous condition of servitude, property, or education. And so cheap and indiscriminate has become this right of citizenship that even women are claiming participation in it. . . .

. . . the war-worn men who have survived are now, with unabated love for the State and reverence for its old chivalric spirit, patiently and hopefully waiting for a returning sense of justice in their Northern fellow-citizens, and the coming of a permanent reconciliation based upon a generous appreciation of their motives in the past, and of their honor and probity and manly courage. And they are saying to those whom they met in the field, and to the wily politicians who have misled them, lift high between heaven and earth the scales of justice, and let the world look on to decide between us, for in the confidence which truth inspires, we fear not the verdict of its righteous judgment! . . .

The right of self-government is our heir-loom the heir-loom of the Anglo-Saxon race in this country, and of no other race. Actuated by friendliness and a spirit of equal justice to all around us, and to every honest stranger who arrives, yet we would be untrue to ourselves as South Carolinians if we looked not forward to our mastery here, to a time when the State, awakening from her helplessness in which she has lain confounded and paralyzed by the unexpected superposition over her of her former servile population, will exhibit her indwelling power by an harmonious re-establishment of her government on its old basis of justice and honor, notwithstanding her present apparent impotence amidst baffling, incongruous, and inimical interventions. . . .

And we, the descendents of that people, shall not witness our inheritance of principles laboriously acquired through hundreds of years, transferred instantaneously and permanently to another race, who have in themselves no guidance of training or experience, and nothing of the vital force which sustains our political growth. . . .

But let us hold fast and cherish all that has been in conformity with these principles, and with our exaltation as a race, and with our heritage as freemen. For God has not abandoned us. He still rules the nations of the earth by providences which we may not fully comprehend; but they give us assurance that He will uphold us and strengthen us if we trust in Him; and will send forth in the fullness of time His righteous vengeance against falsehood, and fraud, and wickedness in high places, and against all who wilfully pervert truth and justice, and betray the rights and freedom of their people.

Source: "Address Delivered before the South Carolina Historical Society on Their Twenty-First Anniversary, May 19, 1876, by William J. Rivers." 1876. Charleston, SC: The New and Courier Job Presses, 14–15, 16–17, 18, 21, 22, 28.

Oliver Wendell Holmes Memorial Day Address at Keene, New Hampshire, 1884

The Civil War had engendered a great deal of misery, heartache, and loss on all individuals who lived through it, whether on the Confederate or Union side. For many, the world was turned upside down during the war, and when it finally ended in 1865, deep emotional and mental scars remained alongside the physical and tangible wounds of battle. Among the pressing and grave concerns that faced both individuals and the nation in the decades after Appomattox was the process of reconciliation between the triumphant Union and the defeated Confederacy. How were Americans to forgive and forget the conflicts of war? White Americans had long held the notion of "the union" as a sacred symbol of their revolutionary political ideals, and it was enshrined in the nation's motto, "E Pluribus Unum" (Out of many, one). The secession of many Southern states from the Union in 1861 fractured this image of a coherent whole, and the process of reconciliation at war's end was a long and painful one.

In the extract that follows, Oliver Wendell Holmes, a Union veteran, law professor, and jurist, delivers a Memorial Day speech in which he advocates a spirit of reconciliation between North and South based on the valor and sacrifices of all Civil War veterans. Such sentiments were widely held in the Northern states and were indicative of the public's greater concern with cementing reunion than with revolutionizing Southern race relations.

Not long ago I heard a young man ask why people still kept up Memorial Day, and it set me thinking of the answer. Not the answer that you and

I should give to each other—not the expression of those feelings that, so long as you and I live, will make this day sacred to memories of love and grief and heroic youth—but an answer which should command the assent of those who do not share our memories, and in which we of the North and our brethren of the South could join in perfect accord.

So far as this last is concerned, to be sure, there is no trouble. The soldiers who were doing their best to kill one another felt less of personal hostility, I am very certain, than some who were not imperilled by their mutual endeavors. I have heard more than one of those who had been gallant and distinguished officers on the Confederate side say that they had no such feeling. I know that I and those whom I knew best had not. We believed that it was most desirable that the North should win; we believed in the principle that the Union is indissoluble; we, or many of us at least, also believed that the conflict was inevitable, and that slavery had lasted long enough. But we equally believed that those who stood against us held just as sacred convictions that were the opposite of ours, and we respected them as every man with a heart must respect those who give all for their belief. The experience of battle soon taught its lesson even to those who came into the field more bitterly disposed. You could not stand up day after day in those indecisive contests where overwhelming victory was impossible because neither side would run as they ought when beaten, without getting at last something of the same brotherhood for the enemy that the north pole of a magnet has for the south—each working in an opposite sense to the other, but each unable to get along without the other. As it was then, it is now. The soldiers of the war need no explanations; they can join in commemorating a soldier's death with feelings not different in kind, whether he fell toward them or by their side. . . .

Comrades, some of the associations of this day are not only triumphant, but joyful. Not all of those with whom we once stood shoulder to shoulder—not all of those whom we once loved and revered—are gone. On this day we still meet our companions in the freezing winter bivouacs and in those dreadful summer marches where every faculty of the soul seemed to depart one after another, leaving only a dumb animal power to set the teeth and to persist—a blind belief that somewhere and at last there was rest and water. On this day, at least, we still meet and rejoice in the closest tie which is possible between men—a tie which suffering has made indissoluble for better, or worse.

When we meet thus, when we do honor to the dead in terms that must sometimes embrace the living, we do not deceive ourselves. We attribute no special merit to a man for having served when all were serving. We know that, if the armies of our war did anything worth remembering, the credit belongs not mainly to the individuals who did it, but to average human nature. We also know very well that we cannot live in associations with the past alone, and we admit that, if we would be worthy of the past, we must find new fields for action or thought, and make for ourselves new careers.

But, nevertheless, the generation that carried on the war has been set apart by its experience. Through our great good fortune, in our youth our hearts were touched with fire. It was given to us to learn at the outset that life is a profound and passionate thing. . . . Year after year the comrades of the dead follow, with public honor, procession and commemorative flags and funeral march—honor and grief from us who stand almost alone, and have seen the best and noblest of our generation pass away.

Source: Oliver Wendell Holmes. 1992 [1884]. "An Address Delivered on Memorial Day, May 30, 1884, at Keene, N.H., before John Sedgwick Post No. 4, Grand Army of the Republic." In Richard A. Posner, ed. 1992. The Essential Holmes: Selections from the Letters, Speeches, Judicial Opinions, and Other Writings of Oliver Wendell Holmes, Jr. *Chicago: University of Chicago Press, 80, 86–87.*

Reference

***The Birth of a Nation* (1915)**   Notorious silent movie based on Thomas Dixon's novel *The Clansman* and directed by D. W. Griffith. *The Birth of a Nation* helped to entrench in the public mind a view of Reconstruction as a disastrous period in U.S. history during which the Ku Klux Klan saved the nation from African American ignorance and Republican Party corruption.

Black Codes   Passed in the former Confederate states in 1865 and 1866, Black Codes were an attempt by Southern whites to replicate those legislative measures that had controlled the lives and labor of African Americans during slavery. The first codes, passed in Mississippi and South Carolina, were the most repressive and overtly racist in their regulation of black civil and legal rights. Among their key provisions, the codes prohibited black men and women from voting, serving on juries, testifying against white people, and drinking and carrying weapons. In addition, the codes severely restricted black occupational opportunities, empowered white "masters" to determine the working hours and conditions of their black "servants," and provided that black youths could be forcibly apprenticed until the age of 21. All African Americans were also required to carry a form of indentification or risk arrest. Following Northern and Republican Party opposition to these first Black Codes, other states introduced codes that avoided explicit mention of race but in practice still functioned with the aim of controlling all aspects of black life, including marriage, property ownership, and geographical and occupational mobility.

Most of the provisions of the Black Codes were eventually repealed through the actions of the army and the Freedmen's Bureau and by the passage of the Civil Rights Act of 1866. However, the codes remained significant as a symbolic statement of the white South's intent to limit African

American freedom. The Black Codes additionally served to convince many in the North that continued federal intervention in the former Confederate states was necessary to protect the fundamental rights of freedmen and freedwomen.

Bruce, Blanche K. **(1841–1898)**   Born a slave in Virginia in 1841, Blanche K. Bruce was one of the first African Americans to be elected to government. He served as senator for the state of Mississippi from 1875 to 1881 and subsequently held a number of other governmental posts, including registrar of the treasury.

Bureau of Refugees, Freedmen and Abandoned Lands   More commonly known as the Freedmen's Bureau, the Bureau of Refugees, Freedmen and Abandoned Lands was a government agency created in March 1865. Under the command of General Oliver Howard, hundreds of bureau agents were stationed across the Southern states and in the District of Columbia to provide health care, welfare, and poor relief; negotiate labor contracts and resolve disputes between African Americans and white employers; and oversee the administration of the criminal justice system. In conjunction with Northern benevolent associations, the bureau also established more than three thousand schools for freedpeople. The larger mission of the Freedmen's Bureau was to win white Southerners over to a vision of freedom for the African American community based on a shared sense of equality.

The Freedmen's Bureau was originally intended to operate for only 12 months, but the Freedmen's Bureau Act (1866) extended the life of the Bureau for two more years. At its peak, the bureau maintained 900 agents in the South, but in 1868, with the Military Reconstruction Acts in force and many freedmen able to vote, Congress deemed most of the bureau's activities no longer essential. From the beginning of 1869, most bureau agents were withdrawn from the South and the bureau's remit was restricted to deal only with education and black veterans' affairs until 1872 when it was finally disbanded. While the Freedmen's Bureau provided valuable aid for millions of former slaves, its work was hampered by a lack of resources, insufficient powers, doubts about its constitutionality, and agents' paternalistic and often disparaging attitudes toward the freedpeople, their culture, and society. *See also* Freedmen's Bureau Bill.

Cardozo, Francis L. **(1837–1903)**   Born in Charleston, South Carolina, to a successful Jewish businessman and his free black wife, Cardozo is most famous during the Reconstruction period for his role in the education of freedpeople, primarily in his native city. In 1866, he was instrumental in establishing the Avery Normal School, which trained African American teachers. Cardozo was elected to South Carolina's Constitutional Convention in 1868, becoming the first African American to hold an official post in the state.

carpetbagger   Derogatory term used to describe Northerners in the South during Reconstruction. It was most often applied to politicians, businessmen, and Republican Party supporters.

Chesnut, Mary Boykin Miller (1823–1886)   Mary Chesnut is most famous for writing a diary about her experiences during the Civil War and her observations on how the conflict affected the home front and Southern society. She started the diary in February 1861 and made entries until August 1865. Chesnut reflected upon the effects of emancipation, the introduction of colored troops into the Union army, the effects of surrendering to the Union, and the first few months after the Confederacy's defeat.

Civil Rights Act (1866)   Extended citizenship to all persons born or naturalized in the United States and established legal procedures for enforcing equal civil rights for all citizens regardless of race or previous enslavement. President Andrew Johnson vetoed this legislation, but Congress overrode the veto and it became law in April 1866.

Civil Rights Act (1875)   Enacted by the outgoing Republican Congress, the Civil Rights Act outlawed racial segregation in all public accommodations regulated by law, such as theaters and railroads. The act also prohibited the disqualification from jury service of former slaves and citizens of any race or color and set fines of between $500 and $5,000 for individuals who violated these provisions. In 1883, the U.S. Supreme Court ruled the Civil Rights Act unconstitutional. *See also* Civil Rights Cases.

Civil Rights Cases (1883)   A U.S. Supreme Court ruling concerning five appealed cases in which African Americans claimed to have been denied equal treatment in contravention of the Civil Rights Act of 1875. In a split opinion, the Court determined that the act was unconstitutional on the grounds that the Fourteenth Amendment (from which the act derived its power) did not apply to incidents of private discrimination by individuals.

Colfax Massacre   In April 1873, the Louisiana-based White League, a paramilitary group intent on securing white rule in Louisiana, opened fire on a courthouse in Grant Parish that had been occupied by approximately four hundred African Americans, including state militiamen and Republican legislator William Ward, in an attempt to secure Republican Party rule in the area. More than one hundred African Americans and three members of the White League were killed. Some 40 of the African American dead had been summarily assassinated in a nearby cotton field after being taken as prisoners when the courthouse was initially attacked.

Compromise of 1877 By 1876, the Republican state governments elected during Reconstruction had lost power in all Southern states except Florida, Louisiana, and South Carolina. When the Republican candidate, Rutherford Hayes, stood against Democrat Samuel Tilden for president in 1876, the outcome of the closely fought contest was determined by events in these three states, in each of which both parties claimed victory. Following months of dispute, a compromise was struck in early 1877. According to the compromise, Hayes became president and the Democrats assumed control of the three contested Southern states. Hayes also agreed to withdraw all remaining federal troops from the South, signaling the end of extensive and systematic federal efforts at Reconstruction. *See* Hayes, Rutherford B.

congressional (radical) Reconstruction This term refers to the period beginning in mid-1866 when Republicans in Congress began to take control of Reconstruction, rejecting the policies of President Johnson in favor of a more radical restructuring of Southern society and the nation. Since before the end of the Civil War, congressional Republicans had criticized the Reconstruction policies of both Abraham Lincoln and Andrew Johnson as too lenient. When Congress reconvened in December 1865, it consequently refused to recognize the governments reconstructed in the former Confederate states under Johnson's policies and appointed a 15-man committee to investigate the credentials of those states' newly elected senators and representatives. In 1866 and 1867, Congress passed a series of Reconstruction acts over President Johnson's veto that aimed to extend to African Americans in the South equal civil rights, voting rights, and protection of the laws. Other radical proposals included the redistribution of land to the freedpeople, but this controversial policy was never acted on. As early as 1868, radical influence was compromised by election defeats and by the mid–1870s a new generation of Republican politicians, responding to the interests of northern business and manufacturing interests, had shifted the Party decisively from the radical agenda.

convict leasing System of criminal punishment established in all Southern states except Virginia in the decades after the Civil War. Convicts were hired out to work for private companies at occupations including railroad building and mining. Ostensibly, convict leasing was designed to save states the costs involved in holding convicts in penitentiaries. However, the system also served the economic interests of the white elite and was consistent with white supremacist racial ideology. An overwhelming majority of convicts were African Americans who provided a large pool of cheap and servile labor and worked and lived in conditions akin in some respects to slavery. By the 1870s, convict leasing provided a valuable source of revenue to Southern state governments, but over the next decade opposition to the system grew in response to reports of inhumane conditions and horrendously high death rates among convicts. In 1890, Mississippi became the first state to pass legislation to abolish convict leasing, replacing it with a form of state-controlled labor, although in practice this transition did not occur until the early-20th century when, as in other southern states, change resulted from political and economic considerations rather than humanitarian concerns.

copperhead   Derogatory term for a Northerner who sympathized with the South during the Civil War and Reconstruction.

Davis Bend   A Mississippi plantation owned during the antebellum period by Confederate President Jefferson Davis and his brother, Joseph, Davis Bend was run under Union military governance during the latter years of the Civil War. General Ulysses S. Grant instructed officials to lease its lands to the freedmen and freedwomen in 1863, and by 1864 the entire tract of land was claimed for the exclusive use of the freedpeople, who paid only for tools, mules, and food. Davis Bend was thus an experiment in black freedom, and by 1865, it had proved remarkably successful. Working as a collective community with an independent system of government, Davis Bend proved the ability of freedpeople to embrace the possibilities of freedom. In 1866, Joseph Davis sold the plantation to his former slave, Benjamin Montgomery, and for the next two decades, the plantation was run along cooperative lines.

Douglass, Frederick (1818–1895)   Born a slave in Talbot County, Maryland, Frederick Douglass escaped from slavery in 1838 and became the leading black voice in campaigns for the abolition of slavery and civil rights for all, most particularly African Americans and women. He published numerous books, pamphlets, and newspapers, including a narrative of his life in slavery and the antislavery periodical the *North Star*. He also helped to organize the first women's rights convention at Seneca Falls, New York, in 1848.

During Reconstruction, Douglass served as president of the Freedman's Savings Bank and later as consul-general to the Republic of Haiti from 1889 to 1891. In 1892, the Haitian government appointed Douglass as its representative at the Chicago World's Fair. He died at his home of a heart attack in February 1895.

Dunn, Oscar J. (1820?–1871)   Born into slavery in Louisiana, Oscar J. Dunn made several attempts to escape and eventually bought his own freedom. Dunn rose to political prominence during Reconstruction as the first African American lieutenant-governor of Louisiana, a post he held from 1868 to 1870. Previous to this, he had also served as state senator during 1868. Dunn died of pneumonia in 1871.

Elliott, Robert Brown (1842–1884)   Claiming to have been born in England and educated at Eton College, Elliott was an influential African American voice in politics and public life after the Civil War. Elliott served as a Republican in the South Carolina State House of Representatives from 1868 to 1870 and was elected to the U.S. Congress in 1870. After two terms, he returned to the state House of Representatives in 1874 and moved to New Orleans in 1881, establishing a successful law firm before his death in August 1884.

Emancipation Proclamation   Issued by Abraham Lincoln on January 1, 1863, in practice, the Emancipation Proclamation freed few people. It applied only to those slaves residing in territory in rebellion against the federal government and therefore did not bring about the immediate freedom of slaves in border South states such as Maryland and Kentucky, which remained loyal to the Union, or in areas further south that had already fallen under Union control. Despite these limitations, the Emancipation Proclamation marked an important shift in the war aims of the United States, for it confirmed to Americans—and the world—that the civil war was now being fought not only to preserve the Union but also to end slavery. The proclamation also gave presidential approval to the enlistment of African American soldiers in Union forces, which Congress had sanctioned in the Militia Act of 1862.

Enforcement Acts   Between May 1870 and June 1872, Congress passed four acts intended to ensure that federal Reconstruction law was enforced across the Southern states. In particular, the Enforcement Acts aimed to counter the rising tide of violence against African Americans in the South and prevent Southern white Democrats from restricting the civil rights that African Americans were afforded by the Fourteenth and Fifteenth Amendments. The First Enforcement Act (May 1870) made federal crimes out of any actions, such as the bribing or intimidation of voters and election officials, that obstructed, or involved conspiracy to obstruct, the conduct of elections and the efforts of individuals to vote or exercise other constitutional rights. The conspiracy sections of the act strengthened federal authority against white terrorist organizations such as the Ku Klux Klan. Punishments for violating the Enforcement Act included fines of up to $5,000 and a maximum of 10 years imprisonment. Further acts established special deputy marshals to oversee elections in large cities, provided for federal supervision of voting in congressional elections, criminalized conspiracies to restrict civil rights, and made special provisions for overseeing elections in rural districts. *See also* Ku Klux Klan Act.

exodusters   In the late 1870s, following the restoration of white supremacist governments in the former Confederate states and the disappointments of Reconstruction, many African Americans left the South and headed west in the hope of establishing themselves and their families as homesteaders in Kansas. As a consequence, the African American population of Kansas, which stood at 16,250 in 1870, more than doubled by 1880 to just over 43,000. Westward migration of the African American population to Kansas and subsequent relocation to states such as Colorado and Nebraska continued throughout the 1880s and 1890s, as thousands sought to rebuild their lives on the frontier. *See also* Homestead Act (1862).

Field Order Number 15   As Union armies swept through Georgia in late 1864 and 1865, they faced the problem of the formerly enslaved becoming displaced refugees. In response, Gen. William T. Sherman issued a series of special field orders, the most notable of which was Number 15, announced in Savannah, Georgia, on January 16, 1865. Under the terms of the order, each freed family was granted 40 acres of land on the Sea Islands, which stretched along the eastern seaboard from Charleston to Florida. Although the land was awarded only for one year, news spread quickly amongst emancipated African Americans and quickly led to the hope that the government would provide "40 acres and a mule" to every newly emancipated head of household. These hopes were never realized, and in September 1865, President Johnson ordered that even the land granted to freedmen by Field Order Number 15 be returned to its former owners.

Fifteenth Amendment   Passed by the Republican-controlled Congress on February 26, 1869 and ratified one year later, the Fifteenth Amendment to the U.S. Constitution extended voting rights to African American men in

Northern and border South states who had not been enfranchized by earlier Reconstruction legislation. The amendment was motivated not only by egalitarian principles but also by the Republican Party's determination to ensure that African Americans, who would mostly vote Republican, could cast their ballots. As Democrats regained control of Southern state governments, they took steps to limit black suffrage, seemingly in contravention of the Fifteenth Amendment. However, few such constitutional violations were ever prosecuted.

Forten, Charlotte (1837–1914) African American schoolteacher born in Philadelphia in 1837. In 1862, Forten traveled south to St. Helena Island, South Carolina, where she taught formerly enslaved men and women at the Penn School. She remained on the island for two years before ill health forced her to return to the North.

Fourteenth Amendment Ratified on July 9, 1868, the Fourteenth Amendment defined the rights of U.S. citizens and prohibited states from limiting those rights without legal due process. Additionally, the amendment limited the representation in Congress of states that violated any group's civil rights and prohibited people who had supported the Confederacy from holding public office. Although readily ratified in the Northern states, the amendment was initially rejected by all former Confederate states except Tennessee. In response, Congress made ratification a condition of Southern states' readmission to the Union. In landmark rulings issued in the Slaughter-House Cases of 1873 and the Civil Rights Cases of 1883, the U.S. Supreme Court severely limited the scope of the Fourteenth Amendment and left the federal government powerless to prosecute individuals, as opposed to states, for violating its provisions. *See also* Slaughter-House Cases; Civil Rights Cases.

Freedman's Savings Bank Incorporated by Congress on March 3, 1865, the Freedman's Savings and Trust Company provided banking facilities and encouraged saving among former slaves. The Panic of 1873 forced the bank into insolvency, and it closed the following year, causing thousands of investors to lose their deposits.

Freedmen's Bureau Bill (1866) When the Freedmen's Bureau was first created in March 1865, its authority was set to expire one year after the conclusion of the Civil War. With the passage of the Freedmen's Bureau Bill in July 1866, the Bureau's life was extended until 1868. Additionally, the Bureau was granted expanded judicial powers to decide whether African Americans were being deprived of their rights as citizens and to punish offenders, even calling upon the army if necessary. President Johnson held these measures to be in violation of the Constitution on the grounds that they subjected white Southerners to arbitrary questioning by bureaucrats without any legal protection or a jury trial. Johnson vetoed the bill when it first passed Congress in February 1866, but he was powerless to act when the bill was passed a second time with support from more than two-thirds of both houses of Congress. *See also* Bureau of Refugees, Freedmen, and Abandoned Lands.

Freedmen's conventions In the years immediately after the Civil War, statewide conventions of freedmen were held in almost all of the former Confederate states. In cities including Raleigh, North Carolina; Little Rock, Arkansas; Nashville; Augusta, Georgia; New Orleans, Lousiana; and Charleston, South Carolina, delegates who mostly had been chosen by mass meetings or at church services in local communities gathered to discuss their common interests, problems, and aspirations. The conventions served as evidence of the rapid evolution of African American politics and marked the emergence of a new class of black political leaders who would play leading roles at the state and national level during the years of radical Reconstruction.

Gideon's Band A group composed mainly of women reformers, teachers, and missionaries from the Northern states who went to the South Carolina Sea Islands to work with the freedpeople.

Grand Army of the Republic An organization composed of former Union soldiers founded by Benjamin F. Stephenson in 1866. In 1868, the Grand Army called for a memorial day to commemorate Union soldiers who had died in the Civil War. This day was originally christened "Decoration Day" and was held on May 30 each year. After World War I, the event was rechristened "Memorial Day" and designated as a day of remembrance for all men and women who had been killed in active service for the United States. Memorial Day is now held every year on the last Monday in May. At its peak in 1890, membership of the Grand Army totaled 490,000.

Grant, Ulysses S. (1822–1885) Eighteenth president of the United States. The greatest Union war hero, Grant became president of the United States after defeating his Democratic rival, Horatio Seymour, in the election of 1868. His nomination as the Republican candidate for the White House came shortly after the impeachment trial of President Andrew Johnson. During his first of two terms as president, Grant oversaw a period of radical

Reconstruction in which a number of African Americans were elected to government and positions of power at the federal and local levels. However, Grant was increasingly vilified in both the North and South, and his second term was scarred by corruption scandals and economic depression that contributed to the end of Reconstruction.

Greeley, Horace (1811–1872)   Editor of the *New York Tribune,* Greeley was nominated for president in 1872 by a group of Liberal Republicans who had defected from Ulysses S. Grant's administration because of its corruption. Greeley won the support of many Democrats during a campaign in which he stressed states' rights and self-determination. Despite his vision of sectional reconciliation, he failed to defeat Grant, the incumbent president.

Hampton Institute   Established in Virginia in 1868, Hampton Institute was an agricultural college and school for freedpeople that promoted industrial training and practical manual pursuits.

Hampton, Wade (1818–1902)   Born in Charleston, South Carolina, Wade Hampton was a wealthy planter who served in the U.S. Senate from 1858 until South Carolina seceded from the Union in 1861. After fighting in many of the major battles of the Civil War, Hampton became a leading opponent of radical Reconstruction, although he largely abstained from involvement in state politics until 1876, when he ran for governor of South Carolina. Benefiting from the support of the Red Shirts' campaign of violence against black voters, Hampton was declared the winner of the disputed election by the South Carolina Supreme Court in the wake of the compromise of 1877. Hampton served as governor until 1879 and subsequently represented South Carolina in the U.S. Senate until 1891. *See also* Hayes, Rutherford B.; Red Shirts.

Hayes, Rutherford B. (1822–1893)   Born in Delaware, Ohio, Rutherford B. Hayes graduated from Harvard and practiced law in Cincinnati before the Civil War. Having been wounded several times in battle, Hayes stood successfully as a Republican Party candidate for Congress in 1864 and served as governor of Ohio for a total of five years between 1868 and 1877. In March 1877, Hayes was inaugurated president of the United States in the aftermath of the disputed election of the previous November. *See* Compromise of 1877.

Homestead Act (1862)   Federal legislation enacted in 1862, the Homestead Act provided 160 acres of undeveloped land in the American West to any family head or individual person provided he or she was at least 21 years of age and lived on and improved the land over a period of at least five years. Land speculators frequently violated these provisions, and a majority of settlers did not complete the process of establishing a homestead. Nevertheless, the act was of extreme significance to African Americans after the demise of Reconstruction in 1877, as they seized the opportunity to leave the South and migrate to regions such as Kansas and Colorado. *See also* exodusters.

Howard, Oliver (1830–1909)   A general who fought for the Union in the Civil War, Howard was appointed commissioner of the Freedmen's Bureau in May 1865. He was also instrumental in the founding of Howard University, where he served as president from 1869 to 1874.

Howard University   Planned by the First Congressional Society of Washington, D.C., and chartered by an act of Congress in 1867, Howard University provided for the racial uplift and education of freedpersons. With early financial support from the Freedmen's Bureau, Howard trained students from all racial backgrounds, but primarily African Americans, in subjects including the liberal arts, theology, teaching, and medicine.

Hyman, John A. (1840–1891)   Born into slavery in Warren County, North Carolina, John Adams Hyman was elected to the North Carolina State Senate in 1868 and served for six years before winning a seat in the U.S. Congress in March 1875. After a single two-year term in national politics, Hyman returned to North Carolina, where he held a number of state offices in the late 1870s. He died in Washington, D.C., in 1891.

Johnson, Andrew (1808–1875)   Seventeenth president of the United States. Born in Raleigh, North Carolina, Andrew Johnson worked as a tailor in Greenville, Tennessee, before entering public life and eventually winning election as governor of Tennessee in 1853 and as a U.S. senator in 1857. Though an advocate of slavery, Johnson was a critic of the Southern planter elite, opposed secession, and supported the Union throughout the Civil War. Appointed military governor of Tennessee by President Abraham Lincoln in 1862, Johnson was nominated Lincoln's vice-presidential running mate in 1864 in order to shore up support for the president among white Southern Unionists.

Following Lincoln's assassination, Johnson was sworn in as president of the United States on April 15, 1865. Though his policies for Reconstruction did not diverge greatly from those pursued by Lincoln during the war years, Johnson's presidency was marked by clashes over the direction of Reconstruction with Republicans in Congress, who demanded a more radical restructuring of Southern society. After two years of conflict in which the president repeatedly obstructed congressional legislation, in March 1868, Johnson was impeached by the House of Representatives for violating the Tenure of Office Act, a law that Congress had passed to ensure that Johnson could not remove members of his own cabinet without first gaining congressional approval. Johnson survived his impeachment trial before the Senate by a single vote, but his political influence was destroyed. After seven years out of public office, in March 1875, Johnson was once again elected by the people of Tennessee to the U.S. Senate. He died four months later. *See also* presidential Reconstruction; Stanton, Edwin; Tenure of Office Act.

Joint Committee on Reconstruction   Established by Congress in December 1865, the Committee comprised six senators and nine representatives who were charged with investigating conditions in the ex-Confederate states and making recommendations on Reconstruction policy. After hearing testimony from hundreds of witnesses, the committee issued a report in April 1866 condemning the new governments established in the South after the Civil War and concluding that most white Southerners remained antagonistic toward the U.S. government. The committee recommended that no ex-Confederate state be permitted to participate in the federal government until it guaranteed the civil rights of all citizens and excluded prominent Confederate sympathizers from holding office.

Ku Klux Klan   Formed in 1866 in Pulaski, Tennessee, the Ku Klux Klan was a secret society that developed into a powerful paramilitary force that aimed to undermine black economic and political advancement and restore white supremacist rule to the South. From the late 1860s to the early 1870s, members of the Klan, who included many ex-Confederate soldiers, perpetrated brutal acts of violence against African Americans and their white, Republican allies. The Klan did not have a centralized structure or chain of command, but it nonetheless spread to local communities across the South, notably in parts of Alabama, Georgia, South Carolina, Tennessee, and Virginia.

Ku Klux Klan Act   Passed by Congress on April 20, 1871, the Ku Klux Klan Act (also known as the Third Enforcement Act) empowered the federal government to punish individuals who conspired or acted to deprive citizens of equal rights and protection of the laws. It also permitted the president to suspend the writ of habeas corpus in counties experiencing organized violence and to use the military against anti–civil rights groups and individuals. Persons indicted under the act were subject to prosecution in U.S. district or circuit courts and liable to punishments of up to six years imprisonment or a fine of no more than $5,000. In October 1871, President Ulysses S. Grant used the Ku Klux Klan Act to impose martial law and suspend the writ of habeas corpus in nine counties in South Carolina where Klan violence was so extensive that it was deemed to constitute a rebellion against the United States. Hundreds of Klansmen were arrested and tried in federal courts on charges of conspiring to deprive African Americans of their civil rights. In total, 831 men were indicted, but only 27 were convicted, in addition to 71 who pleaded guilty. Five other defendants were acquitted and all other charges were dropped. In the summer of 1873, the last of the convicts remaining in prison was released by presidential pardon. *See also* Enforcement Acts; Ku Klux Klan.

Lee, Robert E. (1807–1870) Born in Virginia and a graduate of West Point, Lee was appointed commander of the Army of Northern Virginia in June 1862 and general-in-chief of the Confederacy in January 1865. On April 9, 1865, Lee's surrender to Ulysses S. Grant at Appomattox Courthouse marked the end of the Civil War. In the following years, Lee supported President Andrew Johnson's program for Reconstruction and opposed plans for full civil equality for freedpeople. In the decades after his death in 1870, Lee attained iconic status in the former Confederate states as the greatest Southern war hero and a symbolic touchstone for the Lost Cause ideology. When a statue of Lee was unveiled on Richmond, Virginia's Monument Avenue in 1890, more than 100,000 people attended the dedication ceremony.

Lincoln, Abraham (1809–1865) Sixteenth president of the United States. Born in Kentucky, Lincoln settled with his family in Illinois in 1830 and, over the next decade, passed the bar exam, established a thriving law practice, and became active in Whig Party politics. He served in the state legislature from 1834 to 1841 and in the U.S. Congress from 1847 to 1849. In the early 1850s, the collapse of the Whigs led Lincoln to assume a leading role in the newly formed Republican Party. He stood as the party's vice-presidential candidate in 1856 and, despite failing in his bid to win a seat in the U.S. Senate in 1858, was elected president in 1860.

Days after Lincoln's election, South Carolina seceded from the Union, and within weeks of his inauguration, the Civil War had begun. Though a long-time opponent of slavery, Lincoln had the initial war aim of preserving the Union, but following several disastrous military campaigns in 1862, and under pressure from abolitionists within his own party, on January 1, 1863, he issued the Emancipation Proclamation, freeing the 4 million

African Americans who remained enslaved in lands under Confederate rule and redefining the war as a battle to end slavery.

Lincoln never developed a detailed plan for Reconstruction, but in his Amnesty Proclamation of December 1863, he set out terms under which the process of readmitting the Confederate states to the Union could begin. Known as the "Ten Percent Plan," Lincoln's proposal offered amnesty to any of the seceded states that were willing to take an oath to support the Constitution of the United States and the emancipation of the enslaved. He declared that when 10 percent of the voters who had been registered in a state in 1860 had taken such an oath, that state could begin the process of reconstruction. This amnesty offer was initially tested in Louisiana, where Michael Hahn was inaugurated governor in March 1864. Arkansas soon followed suit.

On April 14, 1865, Abraham Lincoln was assassinated at Ford's Theatre in Washington, D.C., by John Wilkes Booth, a pro-Confederate actor. *See also* Emancipation Proclamation; presidential Reconstruction; Wade-Davis Bill.

Lynch, John R. (1847–1939) Born a slave in Louisiana, John R. Lynch was freed during the Civil War and settled in Natchez, Mississippi. In 1869, he became a justice of the peace and later the same year was elected to the Mississippi House of Representatives, becoming the first African American speaker of the House in 1872. Lynch also served two terms in the U.S. Congress from 1872 to 1876. In 1913, Lynch published a book, *The Facts of Reconstruction,* in which he critiqued the then prevalent view of Reconstruction in which the freedmen and freedwomen were portrayed in an unfavorable light and the racist views of former slaveholders were endorsed to the detriment of the formerly enslaved. Lynch died in Chicago at the age of 92.

Military Reconstruction Acts The 39th Congress passed four military reconstruction acts between March 1867 and March 1868 in response to increased racial violence in the South, the refusal of most Southern states to ratify the Fourteenth Amendment, and President Andrew Johnson's veto of the Civil Rights and Freedmen's Bureau acts of 1866. Under the terms of the first Military Reconstruction Act, passed on March 2, 1867, the 10 Southern states that had not been readmitted to the Union were organized into five military districts, each under the command of a U.S. general with troops at his disposal. The commanding generals were required to arrange for new elections to be held in each state and to oversee the registration of African American voters and ensure their protection at the polls.

The second, third, and fourth military reconstruction acts strengthened the authority of the military generals over state officials and set further rules for voter registration, the assembly of state conventions, and the drawing up and ratification of new constitutions.

Nash, Charles E. (1844–1913) Born in Louisiana, Charles Nash acquired a trade as a bricklayer in antebellum New Orleans. During the Civil War, he fought in the 82nd Regiment of Company A., United States Volunteers and lost part of his right leg in one of the final battles of the war. In 1874, he was elected to the U.S. House of Representatives. After failing in his bid for reelection, Nash returned to bricklaying. He died in 1913.

Nast, Thomas (1840–1902) Cartoonist and long-time proponent of equal rights for African Americans, Thomas Nast published numerous satirical illustrations depicting the people and politics of Reconstruction in journals such as *Harper's Weekly.*

New Orleans Riot Rioting broke out in New Orleans in July 1866 when a white mob that included Confederate veterans and municipal police officers attacked black and white Republicans who had reconvened the Constitutional Convention of 1864 with the aim of extending the suffrage to black male voters. By the time federal troops eventually arrived to help quell the violence, 37 men were dead, including 34 African Americans and 3 whites who supported the radical cause.

Olmsted, Frederick Law (1822–1903) Frederick Law Olmsted was a landscape architect who designed many well-known city parks around the United States. During the Civil War, he served as executive secretary on the U.S. Sanitary Committee (USSC), which cared for Union soldiers who had fallen sick as a result of the conflict. Olmsted was also one of the primary founders of the Union League Club of New York, the stated aim of which was to cultivate support for the Union and whose activities included raising funds for the USSC. New York's Union League Club was a precursor of the Union Leagues that developed during Reconstruction and served an important role in politicizing the freedmen. Olmsted died in 1903 in Belmont, Massachusetts.

Panic of 1873 On September 18, 1873, the Philadelphia investment bank Jay Cooke and Company went bankrupt after several of the railroad firms in which it had invested defaulted on their loan repayments. As one of the major banking firms in the nation, the collapse of the Cooke Company prompted an economic panic as share prices collapsed and the New York

Stock Exchange was forced to close its doors for 10 days. What followed was at the time the most severe economic depression in U.S. history. Lasting for six years, the depression brought about the bankruptcy of 18,000 businesses, caused a massive slowdown in railroad building, and saw unemployment reach a peak of 14 percent. As the depression persisted, Democrats made major political gains in the 1874 midterm elections and, with Northerners increasingly preoccupied with their own economic concerns, interest in the fate of African Americans in the South declined.

Penn School, St. Helena Island   In 1862, abolitionists from Pennsylvania sent Laura M. Towne, a Northern schoolteacher, and her friend, Ellen Murray, to organize and run a school on St. Helena Island, which had been occupied by Union troops in 1861. The school offered a curriculum of arithmetic, reading, and writing, as well as geography and classical languages. After 1870, the school also trained teachers. Laura Towne remained on the Sea Islands for nearly 40 years, continuing to run the school until her death in 1901. *See also* Port Royal Experiment.

Pinchback, Pinkney B. S. (1837–1921)   Born to a slave mother and her former master, Pinkney Benton Stewart Pinchback was a black politician in Louisiana in the early 1870s. A leading campaigner for political and civil rights among the free black communities of Louisiana during the Reconstruction era, in December 1872, he became the first African American in any state in the Union to hold the position of governor when he succeeded the suspended governor of Louisiana Henry C. Warmouth, who was facing impeachment proceedings. Pinchback spent only a few weeks in office before, in January 1873, he was replaced by William Kellogg, who was belatedly declared the winner of disputed elections held the previous fall. Pinchback subsequently won a seat in the U.S. House of Representatives but was forced from office by a racially motivated campaign that charged him with election fraud. Later in life, Pinchback studied law and graduated from Straight University, a predominantly African American institution in New Orleans, at the age of 50.

Port Royal Experiment   Taking place on the South Carolina Sea Island of St. Helena in 1862, the Port Royal Experiment was intended to prepare the formerly enslaved for full civil equality in post–Civil War society. Union forces took St. Helena by force, causing the island's slaveholders to take flight and leave behind 10,000 slaves. The biggest thrust of this initiative was education, and the establishment of the Penn School on the island, administered by Laura M. Towne, was its greatest achievement. Other elements of the experiment included yearly contracts for the freedpeople drawn up under the supervision of the army. However, this contract labor system kept most of the formerly enslaved landless and poor. *See also* Penn School, St. Helena Island.

presidential Reconstruction   From the end of the Civil War until mid-1866, the course of federal Reconstruction was set by President Andrew Johnson. Johnson laid out his Reconstruction policies in May 1865. With the exception of prominent Confederate officials and elite Southerners who owned taxable property valued at more than $20,000, Johnson granted pardons to all Confederates who would swear an oath of loyalty to the Union and accept the abolition of slavery. Additionally, in order to facilitate the restoration of the rebel states to the Union, Johnson called conventions at which the constitutions of the Southern states would be amended to recognize the abolition of slavery. However, no provisions were made in any of the former Confederate states for the formerly enslaved either to vote or hold office. By 1866, Johnson's policies were at odds with the demands of Republicans in Congress for a more radical reconstruction of Southern politics and society. Over the following two years, Johnson repeatedly vetoed legislation passed by Congress, including the Civil Rights Act of 1866 and the Freedmen's Bureau Bill. In 1867, Johnson further antagonized Congress by issuing a proclamation providing amnesty for all but 300 of the most prominent Confederates. By this time, however, Johnson's position vis-à-vis Congress had been fundamentally weakened. In the midterm elections of 1866, radical Republicans won sufficient seats in Congress to override the presidential veto and were able to force through their very different Reconstruction agenda despite the president's continued opposition. *See also* congressional (radical) Reconstruction; Johnson, Andrew; Lincoln, Abraham.

radical Reconstruction   *See* congressional (radical) Reconstruction.

Rainey, Joseph Hayne (1832–1887)   Rainey was the second African American to win a seat in Congress and the first to serve in the U.S. House of Representatives. Born into slavery in South Carolina in 1832, Rainey grew up a free man after his father, a successful barber, purchased the family's liberty. During the Civil War, Rainey and his wife managed to escape the Confederate draft by moving to Bermuda, where Rainey established himself as a barber and his wife worked as a dressmaker. Following the end of the Civil War, Rainey returned to South Carolina and was elected to the state Senate in 1870 and to Congress later the same year. He was reelected four times, serving until 1879 and becoming the longest-serving African American congressman until the 1950s.

Readjuster Party   Political party in Virginia named for its central policy of introducing legislation to "readjust" the state debt downward. In 1879, the Readjusters won control of the Virginia General Assembly. Although supported mainly by lower-class whites, the Readjusters also actively sought African American votes. Once in power, they appointed substantial numbers of African Americans to public office, increased support for black schools and the mentally ill, abolished the poll tax, and ended the use of the whipping post as a form of criminal punishment.

Red Shirts   Supporters of Wade Hampton's gubernatorial campaign in South Carolina in 1876, the Red Shirts were a paramilitary force that used violence to suppress Republican Party meetings and contributed to the restoration of Democratic Party rule in the state.

Redeemer governments   Name given to the Democratic Party governments that were elected in all of the former Confederate states between 1869 and 1876. "Redemption" came first to the Upper South, with Republican governors losing power in Tennessee and Virginia in 1869 and 1870. On assuming office, Democratic governments worked to undermine black political and civil rights in contravention of congressional Reconstruction legislation. In the following years, states in the Deep South also fell under Democrat control, although the supremacy of Redeemer governments in Florida, Louisiana, and South Carolina was not secured until the compromise of 1877, when Rutherford B. Hayes agreed to withdraw all remaining federal troops from the South in order to secure the presidency of the United States.

Revels, Hiram (1822–1901)   The first African American to serve in the U.S. Senate, Hiram Revels was born free in North Carolina in 1822 and educated at Knox College in Illinois. He became a preacher for the African Methodist Episcopal church, serving as a chaplain through the Civil War. During Reconstruction, Revels's primary concern was with the education of the formerly enslaved. He was elected to the state Senate in 1869 and, after retiring from Congress, became president of Alcorn University, an institution established for African Americans during Reconstruction.

Roanoke Island   Captured by Union forces in February 1862, Roanoke Island was subsequently settled by thousands of runaway and freed slaves who arrived as refugees from the North Carolina mainland. During 1862, these contrabands formed a new community, complete with a school, churches, and family homes before, in the spring of 1863, the Union army began to exercise increased control over the island. With the support of Northern missionaries, Union officials established a colony of freedpeople at Roanoke, envisaging it as a haven for the wives and children of African American men enlisted in the Union ranks.

scalawag   Derogatory term used to describe Southern whites who supported the Republican Party during Reconstruction.

Seward, William H. (1801–1872)   William Henry Seward was born in New York in 1801. He studied and practiced law before winning election to the New York Senate in 1831, serving as governor of New York from 1838 to 1842, and as a Whig senator in the U.S. Congress from 1849. With the collapse of the Whigs in the early 1850s, Seward joined the newly formed Republican Party and unsuccessfully sought the party's presidential nomination in both 1856 and 1860. Following Abraham Lincoln's election as president, Seward was appointed secretary of state. He survived an attempt on his life on the same night that Lincoln was assassinated and remained in the office until 1869. Although a leading advocate of the abolition of slavery during the antebellum era, Seward became more conservative during the 1860s and, after the Civil War, was one of Andrew Johnson's most prominent supporters and an opponent of the radical Republicans who controlled Congress.

Sharecropping   Labor system that became widespread across the Southern states during Reconstruction whereby poor agricultural workers farmed plots of land as tenants in return for paying a share of the crop to the landowner once the harvest had been gathered. In theory, this system provided a means for impoverished Southerners to control their own lives as it freed them from the direct supervision of white employers, did not require the payment of rent upfront, satisfied their desire for land, and potentially facilitated upward social mobility if the crops produced were sufficiently profitable. However, this ideal of economic autonomy was rarely realized. While sharecropping had traditionally allowed for tenants to pay a specific amount to work the land for a given time while retaining control over their lives, labor, and produce, as African Americans became a majority of sharecroppers during Reconstruction, many found themselves in an unbreakable cycle of debt, victims of unscrupulous white corruption, and subject to new labor laws that made sharecropping an effective form of racial and labor control. Employers were given complete authority over production processes and produce on their land, and by law, tenants and workers could be arrested if they attempted to sell any of the produce themselves.

In order to prevent economic independence, legislation was also developed to prevent tenants from grazing, hunting, fishing, and trespassing on "private" lands.

Slaughter-House Cases (1873) Block of cases appealed to the U.S. Supreme Court by New Orleans butchers who claimed that their constitutional rights were violated by a monopoly on the slaughterhouse business established by the state of Louisiana. The Court ruled that the Fourteenth Amendment protected only the rights of national citizenship and not state citizenship and that the monopoly was consequently constitutional. As a result of this decision, state legislation that restricted African American civil rights, such as segregation laws, was deemed consistent with the Constitution.

Smalls, Robert (1839–1915) Born into slavery in Beaufort, South Carolina, in 1839, Robert Smalls escaped to freedom with his family during the Civil War by taking charge of the Confederate steamboat *The Planter*. He surrendered to the Union blockades and turned *The Planter* over to the U.S. Navy. During Reconstruction, Smalls waged no fewer than five successful election campaigns for state office. He served in the South Carolina State House of Representatives between 1865 and 1870 and in the state Senate from 1871 to 1874.

Southern Homestead Act (1866) Passed by Congress on June 21, 1866, the Southern Homestead Act aimed to increase the number of independent yeoman farmers in the South and reduce rates of sharecropping and tenancy, especially among African Americans. Under the terms of the legislation, 46 million acres of public land were made available in Alabama, Arkansas, Florida, Louisiana, and Mississippi. Any individual was permitted to claim up to 160 acres of land, which they were required to improve and occupy for at least five years in order to acquire full ownership. In practice, administration of the Homestead Act proved complex and flawed and was hindered by corruption and violent resistance from Southern whites. Other problems that undermined the act included the poor quality of much of the land, disputes over ownership, and the poverty of most claimants. Although the Southern Homestead Act enabled substantial numbers of African Americans to acquire land, by the time it was repealed in 1876, a majority of settlers had abandoned their homesteads.

Special Order Number 15 Issued in March 1864 by John Eaton, the superintendent of Contrabands in the Department of Tennessee and

Arkansas, Special Order 15 was a military edict that instructed Union army clergy to "solemnise the rite of marriage among freedmen."

Stanton, Edwin (1814–1869) Secretary of War in the Andrew Johnson administration, Stanton is most famous for the role he inadvertently played in the impeachment of the president in 1868. When Stanton opposed Johnson's decision to veto the First Reconstruction Act, the president attempted to force him from office. Stanton refused to leave, and his actions were supported by Congress. Republicans charged that Johnson was in violation of the Tenure of Office Act (1867), and they subsequently initiated proceedings for his impeachment. *See also* Tenure of Office Act; Johnson, Andrew.

Stevens, Thaddeus (1792–1868) Born and educated in New England, Thaddeus Stevens was one of the most famous radical Republicans during Reconstruction. As an advocate of free public education and the rights of African Americans in Pennsylvania, he won public acclaim. However, his proposal that Confederate land should be divided up between the formerly enslaved and Northern settlers failed to pass Congress.

Sumner, Charles (1811–1874) Radical Republican Charles Sumner was the Senate's leading voice in opposing slavery. During the 1850s, Sumner made a number of antislavery speeches, one of which resulted in him being beaten with a cane by fellow congressman Preston Brooks of South Carolina. Sumner was left unconscious, and he took three years to regain his health and return to the Senate. Thereafter, he played a prominent part in the politics of the Civil War and Reconstruction. He took a leading role in President Andrew Johnson's impeachment trial and was extremely critical of both Abraham Lincoln and Ulysses S. Grant for not doing more to advance black civil rights. Consequently, Sumner supported Horace Greeley in the 1872 presidential election contest against President Grant.

Ten Percent Plan *See* Lincoln, Abraham; presidential Reconstruction.

Tenure of Office Act Passed by Congress on March 2, 1867, the Tenure of Office Act required that the Senate approve the removal of any federal official whose appointment was also subject to Senate confirmation. *See also* Stanton, Edwin; Johnson, Andrew.

"The swing around the circle" tour President Andrew Johnson undertook a disastrous tour of Northern states in August 1866 in an attempt to garner support for his policies in the upcoming midterm elections. Faced with heckling crowds, Johnson launched stinging attacks on his political opponents that were perceived as shameful and inappropriate and caused many Northerners to lose sympathy with their president.

Thirteenth Amendment Passed by Congress on January 31, 1865, and ratified on December 6 of the same year, the Thirteenth Amendment to the Constitution abolished slavery and involuntary servitude in the United States, except as a punishment for crime imposed by judicial due process. The amendment also granted Congress the power to enact legislation to enforce abolition.

Tilden, Samuel (1814–1886) A native of New York State, Tilden studied law and established a successful legal practice in the late antebellum era. He became increasingly active in Democratic Party politics after the Civil War and served in the State Assembly and as governor of New York before standing, ultimately unsuccessfully, as the Democratic nominee for president in the controversial election of 1876. *See also* Hayes, Rutherford B.

Tourgée, Albion Winegar (1838–1905) Born in Ohio and educated at the University of Rochester, Albion Tourgée fought for the Union during the early years of the Civil War. In 1864, Tourgée was admitted to the bar, and the following year he moved to Greensboro, North Carolina, where he settled with his new wife, Emma L. Kilborne. During Reconstruction, Tourgée worked as a lawyer and civil rights activist, taking on many African American clients. As one of the most prominent white advocates of black equality, Tourgée was derided as a carpetbagger when he first joined the Republican Party in 1867, and he suffered further harassment when he was appointed as a state superior court judge in 1868. After losing his seat on the bench in 1874, Tourgée began writing novels. His most famous work was *A Fools Errand by One of the Fools* (1881), which was based upon his superior court experiences. After returning to the North in 1879, Tourgée died in Bordeaux, France, where he was serving as consul, in 1905.

Turner, Benjamin S. (1825–1894) Benjamin Sterling Turner was born into slavery in Halifax County, North Carolina, and raised from an early age in Alabama. Despite laws prohibiting the teaching of the enslaved, Turner obtained an education and, after the Civil War, became a successful businessman. During Reconstruction, Turner stood as a Republican candidate for Congress and, in 1870, became the first African American elected to the U.S. House of Representatives from the state of Alabama.

Union League Founded in Philadelphia in 1862 to bolster support for the Union, during Reconstruction, Union Leagues (also known as Loyal

Leagues) were established and funded by radical Republicans across the South with the aim of politicizing newly enfranchised freedmen. Local Union League chapters provided a forum through which formerly enslaved men could voice their collective political interests and protest against the remaining vestiges of the slave system.

Wade-Davis Bill   Legislation proposed in July 1864 by Republican Sen. Benjamin F. Wade and Rep. Henry Winter Davis as a more radical alternative to Abraham Lincoln's Ten Percent Plan. The Wade-Davis Bill provided that a state might begin reconstruction only when 50 percent or more of the voters had pledged loyalty to the Constitution, slavery had been abolished, and the Confederate debt repudiated. The bill also disbarred Confederate military and civilian officers from participation in the process of reunion. Lincoln refused to sign the bill despite pressure from within his own party. *See* Lincoln, Abraham.

Bibliography

Abbott, Richard H. 1991. *Cotton and Capital: Boston Businessmen and Antislavery Reform, 1854–1868.* Amherst: University of Massachusetts Press.

Abbott, Richard H. 2004. *For Free Press and Equal Rights: Republican Newspapers in the Reconstruction South.* Athens: University of Georgia Press.

Abel, Annie Heloise. 1915. *The American Indian as Slaveholder and Secessionist.* Cleveland, OH: Arthur H. Clark.

Abel, Annie Heloise. 1919. *The American Indian as Participant in the Civil War.* Cleveland, OH: Arthur H. Clark.

Abel, Annie Heloise. 1925. *The American Indian under Reconstruction.* Cleveland, OH: Arthur H. Clark.

Alexander, Adele Logan. 1991. *Ambiguous Lives: Free Women of Color in Rural Georgia, 1789–1879.* Fayetteville: University of Arkansas Press.

Anderson, John Q., ed. 1995. *Brokenburn: The Journal of Kate Stone, 1861–1868.* Baton Rouge: Louisiana State University Press.

Andrews, Sidney. 2004. *The South since the War: As Shown by Fourteen Weeks of Travel and Observation in Georgia and the Carolinas,* ed. Heather Cox Richardson. Baton Rouge: Louisiana State University Press.

Ash, Stephen V. 1988. *Middle Tennessee Society Transformed, 1860–1870: War and Peace in the Upper South.* Baton Rouge: Louisiana State University Press.

Ash, Stephen V. 2002. *A Year in the South: 1865: The True Story of Four Ordinary People Who Lived through the Most Tumultuous Twelve Months in American History.* New York: Palgrave Macmillan.

Ayers, Edward L. 1984. *Vengeance and Justice: Crime and Punishment in Nineteenth-Century America.* New York: Oxford University Press.

Ayers, Edward L. 1993. *The Promise of the New South: Life after Reconstruction.* New York: Oxford University Press.

Ayers, Edward L. 1995. *Southern Crossing: A History of the American South, 1877–1906.* New York: Oxford University Press.

Ayers, Edward L. 2003. *In the Presence of Mine Enemies: War in the Heart of America, 1859–1863.* New York: W. W. Norton.

Baggett, James A. 2004. *The Scalawags: Southern Dissenters in the Civil War and Reconstruction.* Baton Rouge: Louisiana State University Press.

Bailey, M. Thomas. 1972. *Reconstruction in Indian Territory: A Story of Avarice, Discrimination, and Opportunism.* New York: Kennikat Press.

Baker, Bruce E. 2007. *What Reconstruction Meant: Historical Memory in the American South.* Charlottesville: University of Virginia Press.

Bardaglio, Peter W. 1995. *Reconstructing the Household: Families, Sex, and the Law in the Nineteenth-Century South.* Chapel Hill: University Press of North Carolina.

Barney, William L. 1990. *Battleground for the Union: The Era of the Civil War and Reconstruction, 1848–1877.* Englewood Cliffs, NJ: Prentice Hall.

Benedict, Michael L. 1986. *The Fruits of Victory: Alternatives in Restoring the Union.* London: University of America Press.

Berlin, Ira, Thavolia Glymph, Steven F. Miller, Joseph P. Reidy, Leslie S. Rowland, and Julie Saville, eds. 1982–1993. *Freedom: A Documentary History of Emancipation, 1861–1867.* 4 vols. Cambridge: Cambridge University Press.

Berlin, Ira, and Leslie S. Rowland. 1996. *Families and Freedom: A Documentary History of African American Kinship in the Civil War Era.* New York: New Press.

Berwanger, Eugene H. 1981. *The West and Reconstruction.* Urbana: University of Illinois Press.

Blair, William. 2003. *Cities of the Dead: Contesting the Memory of the Civil War in the South, 1865–1914.* Chapel Hill: University of North Carolina Press.

Blassingame, John. 1973. "Before the Ghetto: The Making of the Black Community in Savannah, Georgia, 1865–1880." *Journal of Social History* 6 (4): 463–488.

Blassingame, John. 1976. *Black New Orleans, 1860–1880.* Chicago: University of Chicago Press.

Bleser, Carol., ed. 1990. *In Joy and in Sorrow: Women, Family, and Marriage in the Victorian South.* New York: Oxford University Press.

Blight, David W. 1989. *Frederick Douglass' Civil War: Keeping Faith in Jubilee.* Baton Rouge: Louisiana State University Press.

Blight, David W. 2002. *Race and Reunion: The Civil War in American Memory.* Cambridge, MA: Harvard University Press.

Bolt, Christine. 1987. *American Indian Policy and American Reform: Case Studies of the Campaign to Assimilate the Indians.* London: Allen and Unwin.

Brown, Elsa Barkley. 1989. "Womanist Consciousness: Maggie Lena Walker and the Independent Order of Saint Luke." *Signs* 14:610–633.

Brown, Thomas J. 2006. *Reconstructions: New Perspectives on the Postbellum United States.* New York: Oxford University Press.

Bryant, Jonathan M. 1996. *How Curious a Land: Conflict and Change in Greene County, Georgia, 1850–1885.* Chapel Hill: University of North Carolina Press.

Burr, Virginia Ingraham, ed. 1990. *The Secret Eye: The Journal of Ella Gertrude Clanton Thomas, 1848–1889.* Chapel Hill: University of North Carolina Press.

Burr, Virginia Ingraham. 1991. "A Woman Made to Suffer and Be Strong: Ella Gertrude Clanton Thomas, 1834–1907." In *In Joy and In Sorrow: Women, Family, and Marriage in the Victorian South, 1830–1900,* ed. Carol Bleser. New York: Oxford University Press.

Burton, Geoffrey. 1995. *Indian Territory and the United States, 1866–1906.* Norman: University of Oklahoma Press.

Burton, Orville Vernon. 1985. *In My Father's House Are Many Mansions: Family and Community in Edgefield, South Carolina.* Chapel Hill: University of North Carolina Press.

Burton, Orville Vernon, and Robert C. McMath, Jr., eds. 1982. *Toward a New South? Studies in Post–Civil War Southern Communities.* Westport, CT: Greenwood Press.

Butchart, Ronald E. 1980. *Northern Schools, Southern Blacks, and Reconstruction: Freedmen's Education, 1862–1875.* Westport, CT: Greenwood Press.

Butchart, Ronald E., and Amy F. Rolleri. 2003. "Reconsidering the 'Soldiers of Light and Love': Color, Gender, Authority, and Other Problems in the History of Teaching the Freedpeople." *The Freedmen's Teachers Project.* (Online

article; retrieved 5/5/08.) http://www.coe.uga.edu/ftp/docs/Reconsider
Soldiers.pdf

Bynum, Victoria. 1992. "Reshaping the Bonds of Womanhood: Divorce in
Reconstruction North Carolina." In *Divided Houses: Gender and the Civil War,*
ed. Catherine Clinton and Nina Silber. New York: Oxford University Press.

Bynum, Victoria E. 2001. *The Free State of Jones: Mississippi's Longest Civil War.*
Chapel Hill: University of North Carolina Press.

Camejo, Peter. 1976. *Racism, Revolution, Reaction, 1861–1877: The Rise and Fall
of Radical Reconstruction.* New York: Monad Press.

Campbell, Randolph B. 1997. *Grass-Roots Reconstruction in Texas, 1865–1880.*
Baton Rouge: Louisiana State University Press.

Candeloro, Dominic. 1975. "Louis Post as a Carpetbagger in South Carolina: Reconstruction as a Forerunner of the Progressive Movement." *American Journal of Economics and Sociology* 34:423–432.

Carpenter, John A. 1962. "Atrocities in the Reconstruction Period." *Journal
of Negro History* 47 (4): 234–247.

Carter, Dan T. 1985. *When the War Was Over: The Failure of Self-Reconstruction
in the South, 1865–1867.* Baton Rouge: Louisiana State University Press.

Cashin, Joan. 1992. " 'Since the War Broke Out': The Marriage of Kate and
William McLure." In *Divided Houses: Gender and the Civil War,* ed. Catherine
Clinton and Nina Silber. New York: Oxford University Press.

Castel, Albert. 1979. *The Presidency of Andrew Johnson.* Lawrence: University
Press of Kansas.

Cawardine, Richard J. 2003. *Lincoln.* London: Pearson Education.

Censer, Jane T. 2003. *The Reconstruction of White Southern Womanhood, 1865–
1895.* Baton Rouge: Louisiana State University Press.

Chadwick, John White, ed. 1969 [1899]. *A Life for Liberty: Anti-Slavery and
Other Letters of Sallie Holley.* Reprint. New York: Negro Universities Press.

Chamberlain, Joshua Lawrence. 1994 [1915]. *The Passing of the Armies: The Last
Campaign of the Armies.* Reprint. Gettysburg, PA: Stan Clark Military Books.

Chesnut, Mary Boykin. 1949 [1905]. *A Diary from Dixie.* Reprint. New York:
Appleton.

Cimbala, Paul A. 1989. "The Freedmen's Bureau, the Freedmen, and Sherman's Grant in Reconstruction Georgia, 1865–1867." *Journal of Southern
History* 55:597–632.

Cimbala, Paul A. 1997. *Under the Guardianship of the Nation: The Freedmen's Bureau and the Reconstruction of Georgia, 1865–1870.* Athens: University of Georgia Press.

Cimbala, Paul A. 2005. *The Freedmen's Bureau: Reconstructing the American South after the Civil War.* Malabar, FL: Krieger.

Cimbala, Paul A., and Randall M. Miller, eds. 1999. *The Freedmen's Bureau and Reconstruction: Reconsiderations.* New York: Fordham University Press.

Clark-Davis, Elizabeth. 1987. " 'This Work Had a End': African American Domestic Workers in Washington D.C., 1910–1940." In *"To Toil the Livelong Day": America's Women at Work, 1790–1980,* ed. Carol Groneman and Mary Beth Norton. Ithaca, NY: Cornell University Press.

Click, Patricia. 2001. *Time Full of Trial: The Roanoke Island Freedmen's Colony, 1862–1867.* Chapel Hill: University of North Carolina Press.

Clinton, Catherine. 1995. *Tara Revisited: Women, War, and the Plantation Legend.* New York: Abbeville Press.

Clinton, Catherine. 1999. *The Other Civil War: American Women in the Nineteenth Century.* New York: Hill and Wang.

Cohen, William. 1991. *At Freedom's Edge: Black Mobility and the Southern Quest for Racial Control, 1861–1915.* Baton Rouge: Louisiana State University Press.

Cook, Robert. 2003. *Civil War America: Making a Nation, 1848–1877.* London: Longman.

Cox, LaWanda. 1994. *Lincoln and Black Freedom, a Study in Presidential Leadership.* Columbia: University of South Carolina Press.

Cullen, Jim. 1992. " 'I's a Man Now': Gender and African American Men." In *Divided Houses: Gender and the Civil War,* ed. Catherine Clinton and Nina Silber. New York: Oxford University Press.

Culpepper, Marilyn Mayer. 2002. *All Things Altered: Women in the Wake of Civil War and Reconstruction.* Jefferson, NC: McFarland.

Culpepper, Marilyn Mayer. 2004. *Women of the Civil War South: Personal Accounts from Diaries, Letters, and Postwar Reminiscences.* Jefferson, NC: McFarland.

Current, Richard N. 1994. *Lincoln's Loyalists: Union Soldiers from the Confederacy.* New York: Oxford University Press.

Current, Richard N. 1998. *Those Terrible Carpetbaggers: A Reinterpretation.* New York: Oxford University Press.

Dailey, Jane. 2000. *Before Jim Crow: The Politics of Race in Postemancipation Virginia*. Chapel Hill: University of North Carolina Press.

Davis, Angela. 1983. *Women, Race, and Class*. New York: Vintage Books.

Davis, Ronald L. F. 1982. *Good and Faithful Labor: From Slavery to Sharecropping in the Natchez District, 1860–1890*. Westport, CT: Greenwood Press.

Dean, Eric T. 1999. *Shook over Hell: Post-Traumatic Stress, Vietnam, and the Civil War*. Cambridge, MA: Harvard University Press.

Debo, Angie. 1970. *A History of the Indians of the United States*. Norman: University of Oklahoma Press.

Doane, L. E. 2003. "A Young Girl Meets her Soldier Father." (Online document; retrieved 5/5/08.) http://memory.loc.gov/learn/features/timeline/civilwar/soldiers/doane.html

Dossett, Kate. 2008. *Bridging Race Divides: Black Nationalism, Feminism, and Integration in the United States, 1896–1935*. Gainesville: University Press of Florida.

Doyle, Don H. 1990. *New Men, New Cities, New South: Atlanta, Nashville, Charleston, Mobile, 1860–1910*. Chapel Hill: University of North Carolina Press.

Drago, Edmund L. 1998. *Hurrah for Hampton! Black Red Shirts in South Carolina during Reconstruction*. Fayetteville: University of Arkansas Press.

Du Bois, W. E. B. 1935. *Black Reconstruction: An Essay toward a History of the Part which Black Folk Played in the Attempt to Reconstruct Democracy, 1860–1880*. New York: Harcourt Brace.

Dunning, William A. 1907. *Reconstruction: Political and Economic, 1865–1877*. New York: Harper and Bros.

Durrill, Wayne K. 1990. *War of Another Kind: A Southern Community in the Great Rebellion*. New York: Oxford University Press.

Edwards, Laura F. 1997. *Gendered Strife and Confusion: The Political Culture of Reconstruction*. Urbana: University of Illinois Press.

Edwards, Laura F. 2000. *Scarlett Doesn't Live Here Anymore: Southern Women in the Civil War Era*. Urbana: University of Illinois Press.

Edwards, Rebecca. 1997. *Angels in the Machinery: Gender in American Party Politics from the Civil War to the Progressive Era*. New York: Oxford University Press.

Ellam, Warren. 2003. "The Worst Results in Mississippi May Prove the Best for Us: Blanche Butler Ames and Reconstruction." In *Lives Full of Struggle and Triumph: Southern Women, Their Institutions and Their Communities*, ed. Bruce L. Clayton and John A. Salmond. Gainesville: University of Florida Press.

Engs, Robert F. 2004. *Freedom's First Generation: Black Hampton, Virginia, 1861–1890.* Bronx, NY: Fordham University Press.

Fain, John N., ed. 2004. *Sanctified Trial: The Diary of Eliza Rhea Anderson Fain, a Confederate Woman in East Tennessee.* Knoxville: University of Tennessee Press.

Farmer-Kaiser, Mary. 2004. " 'Are They Not in Some Sorts Vagrants?' Gender and the Efforts of the Freedmen's Bureau to Combat Vagrancy in the Reconstruction South." *Georgia Historical Quarterly* 88 (1): 25–49.

Faulkner, Carol. 2004. *Women's Radical Reconstruction: The Freedmen's Aid Movement.* Philadelphia: University of Pennsylvania Press.

Faulkner, Carol. 2005. "A Nation's Sin: White Women and U.S. Policy toward Freedpeople." In *Gender and Slave Emancipation in the Atlantic World,* ed. Pamela Scully and Diane Paton. Durham, NC: Duke University Press.

Faust, Drew Gilpin. 1992a. "Altars of Sacrifice: Confederate Women and the Narratives of War." In *Divided Houses: Gender and the Civil War,* ed. Catherine Clinton and Nina Silber. New York: Oxford University Press.

Faust, Drew Gilpin. 1992b [1894]. "Introduction." In *Macaria; Or, Altars of Sacrifice,* by Augusta Jane Evans. Baton Rouge: Louisiana State University Press.

Faust, Drew Gilpin. 1996. *Mothers of Invention: Women of the Slaveholding South in the American Civil War.* New York: Vintage.

Fields, Barbara J. 1985. *Slavery and Freedom on the Middle Ground: Maryland during the Nineteenth Century.* New Haven, CT: Yale University Press.

Finger, John R. 1984. *The Eastern Band of Cherokees, 1819–1900.* Knoxville: University of Tennessee Press.

Fitzgerald, Michael W. 1988. "Radical Republicanism and the White Yeomanry during Alabama Reconstruction, 1865–68." *Journal of Southern History* 54 (4): 565–596.

Fitzgerald, Michael W. 1998. "Republican Factionalism and Black Empowerment: The Spencer Warner Controversy and Alabama Reconstruction, 1868–1880." *Journal of Southern History* 64 (3): 473–494.

Fitzgerald, Michael W. 2000. *The Union League Movement in the Deep South: Politics and Agricultural Change during Reconstruction.* Baton Rouge: Louisiana State University Press.

Fitzgerald, Michael W. 2002. *Urban Emancipation: Popular Politics in Reconstruction Mobile, 1860–1890.* Baton Rouge: Louisiana State University Press.

Foner, Eric. 1975. "Andrew Johnson and Reconstruction: A British View." *Journal of Southern History* 41 (3): 381–390.

Foner, Eric. 1984. *Nothing But Freedom: Emancipation and Its Legacy.* Baton Rouge: Louisiana State University Press.

Foner, Eric. 1987. "Rights and the Constitution in Black Life during the Civil War and Reconstruction." *Journal of American History* 74 (3): 863–883.

Foner, Eric. 1988. *Reconstruction: America's Unfinished Revolution.* New York: Harper and Row.

Foner, Eric. 1994. "The Meaning of Freedom in the Age of Emancipation." *Journal of American History* 81 (2): 435–460.

Foner, Eric. 1996. *Freedom's Lawmakers: A Directory of Black Officeholders during Reconstruction.* Baton Rouge: Louisiana State University Press.

Foner, Eric, and Olivia Mahoney. 1995. *America's Reconstruction: People and Politics after the Civil War.* New York: HarperCollins.

Foster, Gaines M. 1987. *Ghosts of the Confederacy: Defeat, the Lost Cause, and the Emergence of the New South.* Princeton, NJ: Princeton University Press.

Frankel, Noralee. 1999. *Freedom's Women: Black Women and Families in Civil War Era Mississippi.* Bloomington: Indiana University Press.

Franklin, John Hope. 1961. *Reconstruction: After the Civil War.* Chicago: University of Chicago Press.

Freehling, William W. 2002. *The South vs. The South: How Anti-Confederate Southerners Shaped the Course of the Civil War.* New York: Oxford University Press.

Gardner, Sarah. 2004. *Blood and Irony: Southern White Women's Narratives of the Civil War, 1861–1937.* Chapel Hill: University of North Carolina Press.

Gienapp, William E. 2001. *The Civil War and Reconstruction: A Documentary Collection.* New York: W. W. Norton.

Golay, Michael. 1999. *A Ruined Land: The End of the Civil War.* New York: John Wiley and Sons.

Goldfield, David R. 1981. "The Urban South: A Regional Framework." *The American Historical Review* 86 (5): 1009–1034.

Goldin, Claudia Dale. 1976. *Urban Slavery in the Ameircan South 1820–1860: A Quantitative History.* Chicago: University of Chicago Press.

Graves, John W. 1990. *Town and Country: Race Relations in an Urban-Rural Context, Arkansas, 1865–1905.* Fayetteville: University of Arkansas Press.

Grinde, Donald A., Jr., and Quintard Taylor. 1984. "Red vs Black: Conflict and Accommodation in the Post Civil War Indian Territory, 1865–1907." *American Indian Quarterly* 8 (3): 211–229.

Gutman, Herbert. 1976. *The Black Family in Slavery and Freedom, 1750–1925.* Oxford: Blackwell.

Gutman, Herbert. 2000. "Schools for Freedom: The Post-Emancipation Origins of Afro-American Education." In *Major Problems in African American History,* vol. 2, ed. Thomas C. Holt and Elsa Barclay Brown. New York: Houghton Mifflin.

Hahn, Steven. 1983. *The Roots of Southern Populism: Yeomen Farmers and the Transformation of the Georgia Upcountry, 1850–1890.* New York: Oxford University Press.

Hahn, Steven. 2003. *A Nation under Our Feet: Black Political Struggles in the Rural South from Slavery to the Great Migration.* Cambridge, MA: Harvard University Press.

Harlan, Lewis R. 1962. "Desegregation in New Orleans Public Schools during Reconstruction." *American Historical Review* 67 (3): 663–675.

Harris, J. William. 1995. "Etiquette, Lynching, and Racial Boundaries in Southern History: A Mississippi Example." *American Historical Review* 100 (2): 387–410.

Harris, William C. 1974. "The Creed of the Carpetbaggers: The Case of Mississippi." *Journal of Southern History* 40: 199–224.

Harris, William C. 1979. *The Day of the Carpetbagger: Republican Reconstruction in Mississippi.* Baton Rouge: Louisiana State University Press.

Harris, William C. 1997. *With Charity for All: Lincoln and the Restoration of the Union.* Lexington: University of Kentucky Press.

Harris, William C. 2004. *Lincoln's Last Months.* Cambridge, MA: Harvard University Press.

Harrison, Robert. 2006. "Welfare and Employment Policies of the Freedmen's Bureau in the District of Columbia." *Journal of Southern History* 72 (1): 75–110.

Hicks, Robert. 2005. *The Widow of the South.* London: Bantam Press.

Hine, William C. 1984. "Black Organized Labor in Reconstruction Charleston." *Labor History* 25:504–517.

Hodes, Martha. 1997. *White Women, Black Men: Illicit Sex in the Nineteenth Century South*. New Haven, CT: Yale University Press.

Holland, Rupert Sargent. 1969 [1912]. *Letters and Diary of Laura M. Towne*. Reprint. New York: Negro Universities Press.

Hollandsworth, James G. 2001. *An Absolute Massacre: The New Orleans Race Riot of July 30, 1866*. Baton Rouge: Louisiana State University Press.

Holt, Sharon Ann. 1994. "Making Freedom Pay: Freedpeople Working for Themselves, North Carolina, 1865–1900." *Journal of Southern History* 60 (2): 229–262.

Holt, Sharon Ann. 2000. *Making Freedom Pay: North Carolina Freed People Working for Themselves, 1865–1900*. Athens: University of Georgia Press.

Holt, Thomas. 1979. *Black over White: Negro Political Leadership in South Carolina during Reconstruction*. Urbana: University of Illinois Press.

Hosmer, John, and Joseph Fineman. 1978. "Black Congressmen in Reconstruction Historiography." *Phylon* 39 (2): 97–107.

Hume, Richard L. 1977. "Carpetbaggers in the Reconstruction South: A Group Portrait of Outside Whites in the 'Black and Tan' Constitutional Conventions." *Journal of American History* 64:313–330.

Hunter, Tera W. 1997. *To 'Joy My Freedom: Southern Black Women's Lives and Labors after the Civil War*. Cambridge, MA: Harvard University Press.

Jaynes, Gerald David. 1986. *Branches without Roots: The Genesis of the Black Working Class in the American South, 1862–1882*. New York: Oxford University Press.

Jenkins, Wilbert L. 1998. *Seizing the New Day: African Americans in Post–Civil War Charleston*. Bloomington: Indiana University Press.

Jones, Jacqueline. 1980. *Soldiers of Light and Love: Northern Teachers and Georgia Blacks, 1865–1873*. Chapel Hill: University of North Carolina Press.

Jones, Jacqueline. 1991. "The Political Economy of Sharecropping Families: Blacks and Poor Whites in the Rural South, 1865–1915." In *In Joy and In Sorrow: Women, Family, and Marriage in the Victorian South, 1830–1900*, ed. Carol Bleser. New York: Oxford University Press.

Jones, Jacqueline. 1995. *Labor of Love, Labor of Sorrow: Black Women, Work and the Family, from Slavery to the Present*. New York: Vintage.

Jones, Jacqueline. 1998. *American Work: Four Centuries of Black and White Labor.* New York: W. W. Norton.

Josiah, Barbara P. 2004. "Providing for the Future: The World of the African American Depositors of Washington, D.C.'s Freedman's Savings Bank, 1865–1874." *Journal of African American History* 89 (1): 1–16.

Kaczorowski, Robert. 1987. "To Begin the Nation Anew: Congress, Citizenship and Civil Rights After the Civil War." *American Historical Review* 92 (1): 45–68.

Katz, William Loren. 1986. *Black Indians: A Hidden Heritage.* Baltimore, MD: Ethrac Publications.

Kelley, Robin D.G. 1996. *Race Rebels: Culture, Politics and the Black Working Class.* New York: Free Press.

Kenzer, Robert C. 1987. *Kinship and Neighborhood in a Southern Community: Orange County, North Carolina, 1849–1881.* Knoxville: University of Tennessee Press.

Kerr-Ritchie, Jeffrey R. 1999. *Freedpeople in the Tobacco South: Virginia, 1860–1900.* Chapel Hill: University of North Carolina Press.

Kimball, Gregg D. 2000. *American City, Southern Place: A Cultural History of Antebellum Richmond.* Athens: University of Georgia Press.

Kolchin, Peter. 1972. *First Freedom: The Response of Alabama's Blacks to Emancipation and Reconstruction.* Westport, CT: Greenwood Press.

La Vere, David. 2000. *Contrary Neighbors: Southern Plains and Removed Indians in Indian Territory.* Norman: University of Oklahoma Press.

Lane, Roger. 1991. *William Dorsey's Philadelphia and Ours: On the Past and Future of the Black City in America.* Cary, NC: Oxford University Press.

Lanza, Michael L. 1990. *Agrarianism and Reconstruction Politics: The Southern Homestead Act.* Baton Rouge: Louisiana State University Press.

Lebsock, Suzanne D. 1973. "Radical Reconstruction and the Property Rights of Southern Women." *Journal of Southern History* 43 (2): 195–216.

Linderman, Gerald F. 1989. *Embattled Courage: The Experience of Combat in the American Civil War.* New York: Macmillan.

Litwack, Leon. 1979. *Been in the Storm so Long: The Aftermath of Slavery.* New York: Alfred A. Knopf.

Logue, Cal M. 1979. "Racist Reporting during Reconstruction." *Journal of Black Studies* 9:335–349.

Logue, Larry. 1966. *To Appomattox and Beyond: The Civil War Soldier in War and Peace.* Chicago: Ivan R. Dee.

Lovett, Bobby L. 1981. "Some 1871 Accounts for the Little Rock, Arkansas Freedman's Savings and Trust Company." *Journal of Negro History* 66 (4): 326–328.

Lowry, Thomas P. 1994. *The Story the Soldiers Wouldn't Tell: Sex in the Civil War.* Mechanicsburg, PA: Stackpole.

Mandle, Jay R. 1978. *The Roots of Black Poverty: The Southern Plantation Economy after the Civil War.* Durham, NC: Duke University Press.

Mann, Susan A. 1989. "Slavery, Sharecropping, and Sexual Inequality." *Signs* 14 (4): 774–798.

McConnell, Stuart. 1992. *Glorious Contentment: The Grand Army of the Republic, 1865–1900.* Chapel Hill: University of North Carolina Press.

McCurry, Stephanie. 1995. *Masters of Small Worlds: Yeoman Households, Gender Relations, and the Political Culture of the Antebellum South Carolina Low Country.* New York: Oxford University Press.

McKenzie, Robert Tracy. 1994. *One South or Many? Plantation Belt and Upcountry in Civil War Era Tennessee.* New York: Cambridge University Press.

McKitrick, Eric L. 1988. *Andrew Johnson and Reconstruction.* Reprint. New York: Oxford University Press.

McMillen, Sally. 2002. *To Raise Up the South: Sunday Schools in Black and White Churches, 1865–1915.* Baton Rouge: Louisiana State University Press.

McPherson, James M. 1975. *The Abolitionist Legacy: From Reconstruction to the NAACP.* Princeton, NJ: Princeton University Press.

McPherson, James M. 1988. *Battle Cry of Freedom: The Civil War Era.* New York: Oxford University Press.

McPherson, James M., and J. Morgan Kousser, eds. 1982. *Essays in Honor of C. Vann Woodward.* New York: Oxford University Press.

Mitchell, Reid. 1989. *Civil War Soldiers: Their Expectations and Their Experiences.* New York: Touchstone.

Mitchell, Reid. 1995. *The Vacant Chair: The Northern Soldier Leaves Home.* New York: Oxford University Press.

Moneyhon, Carl H. 1994. *The Impact of the Civil War and Reconstruction on Arkansas: Persistence in the Midst of Ruin.* Baton Rouge: Louisiana State University Press.

Moneyhon, Carl H. 2004. *Texas after the Civil War: The Struggle of Reconstruction*. College Station: Texas A & M University Press.

Moore, John Hammond, ed. 1974. *The Juhl Letters to the Charleston Courier: A View of the South, 1865–1871*. Athens: University of Georgia Press.

Moreno, Paul. 1995. "Racial Classifications and Reconstruction Legislation." *Journal of Southern History* 61 (2): 271–304.

Morgan, Lynda J. 1992. *Emancipation in Virginia's Tobacco Belt, 1850–1870*. Athens: University of Georgia Press.

Morris, Robert C. 1981. *Reading, 'Riting, and Reconstruction: The Education of Freedmen in the South, 1861–1870*. Chicago: University of Chicago Press.

Myers, John B. 1971. "The Education of Alabama Freedmen during Presidential Reconstruction, 1865–67." *Journal of Negro Education* 40 (2): 163–171.

Nieman, Donald G. 1979. *To Set the Law in Motion: The Freedmen's Bureau and the Legal Rights of Blacks, 1865–1868*. Millwood, NY: KTO Press.

Nolen, Claude H. 2005. *African American Southerners in Slavery, Civil War, and Reconstruction*. Jefferson, NC: McFarland.

O'Brien, John T. 1981. "Reconstruction in Richmond: White Restoration and Black Protest, April–June 1865." *Virginia Magazine of History and Biography* 89 (3): 259–281.

Olsen, Otto H. 1965. *Carpetbagger's Crusade: The Life of Albion Winegar Tourgee*. Baltimore: Johns Hopkins University Press.

Oubre, Claude F. 1978. *Forty Acres and a Mule: The Freedmen's Bureau and Black Land Ownership*. Baton Rouge: Louisiana State University Press.

Ownby, Ted. 1990. *Subduing Satan: Religion, Recreation, and Manhood in the Rural South, 1865–1920*. Chapel Hill: University of North Carolina Press.

Painter, Nell Irvin. 1990. "Introduction: The Journal of Ella Gertrude Clanton Thomas: An Educated White Woman in the Eras of Slavery, War, and Reconstruction." In *The Secret Eye: The Journal of Ella Gertrude Clanton Thomas, 1848–1889*, ed. Virginia Ingraham Burr. Chapel Hill: University of North Carolina Press.

Pearson, Elizabeth Ware. 1969 [1906]. *Letters from Port Royal: Written at the Time of the Civil War*. Reprint. New York: Arno Press.

Pease, William, and Jane Pease. 1999. *A Family of Women: The Carolina Petigrus in Peace and War*. Chapel Hill: University of North Carolina Press.

Peiss, Kathy. 1998. *Hope in a Jar: The Making of America's Beauty Culture*. New York: Henry Holt.

Perdue, Theda. 1980. *Nations Remembered: An Oral History of the Five Civilized Tribes, 1865–1907*. Westport, CT: Greenwood Press.

Perman, Michael. 1973. *Reunion without Compromise: The South and Reconstruction 1865–1869*. New York: Cambridge University Press.

Perman, Michael. 1985. *The Road to Redemption: Southern Politics 1869–1879*. Chapel Hill: University of North Carolina Press.

Perry, Mark. 1999. *Conceived in Liberty: Joshua Lawrence Chamberlain, William Oates, and the American Civil War*. London: Penguin.

Poole, W. Scott. 2004. *Never Surrender: Confederate Memory and Conservatism in the South Carolina Upcountry*. Athens: University of Georgia Press.

Posner, Richard A., ed. 1992. *The Essential Holmes: Selections from the Letters, Speeches, Judicial Opinions, and Other Writings of Oliver Wendell Holmes, Jr.* Chicago: University of Chicago Press.

Powell, Lawrence N. 1975. "The American Land Company and Agency: John A. Andrew and the Northernization of the South." *Civil War History* 21:293–308.

Powell, Lawrence N. 1980. *New Masters: Northern Planters during the Civil War and Reconstruction*. New Haven, CT: Yale University Press.

Powell, Lawrence N. 1982. "The Politics of Livelihood: Carpetbaggers in the Deep South." In *Region, Race, and Reconstruction: Essays in Honor of C. Vann Woodward*, ed. James M. McPherson and J. Morgan Kousser. New York: Oxford University Press.

Powell, Lawrence N. 1986. *The Great Father: The United States and the American Indians*. Lincoln: University of Nebraska Press.

Quigley, David. 2004. *Second Founding: New York City, Reconstruction, and the Making of American Democracy*. New York: Hill and Wang.

Rabinowitz, Howard N. 1982. *Southern Black Leaders of the Reconstruction Era*. Urbana: University of Illinois Press.

Rabinowitz, Howard N. 1996 [1978]. *Race Relations in the Urban South, 1865–1890*. Reprint. Athens: University of Georgia Press.

Rable, George C. 1984. *But There Was No Peace: The Role of Violence in the Politics of Reconstruction*. Athens: University of Georgia Press.

Rachleff, Peter J. 1989. *Black Labor in Richmond, 1865–1890.* Urbana: University of Illinois Press.

Rankin, David C. 1974. "The Origins of Black Leadership in New Orleans during Reconstruction." *Journal of Southern History* 40 (3): 417–440.

Reese, Linda W. 2002. "Cherokee Freedwomen in Indian Territory, 1863–1890." *Western Historical Quarterly* 33 (3): 273–296.

Regosin, Elizabeth. 2002. *Freedom's Promise: Ex-Slave Families and Citizenship in the Age of Emancipation.* Charlottesville: University Press of Virginia.

Reidy, Joseph P. 1992. *From Slavery to Agrarian Capitalism in the Cotton Plantation South: Central Georgia, 1800–1880.* Chapel Hill: University of North Carolina Press.

Richardson, Heather C. 2001. *The Death of Reconstruction: Race, Labor, and Politics in the Post–Civil War North, 1865–1901.* Cambridge, MA: Harvard University Press.

Richardson, Heather C. 2007. *West from Appomattox: The Reconstruction of America after the Civil War.* New Haven, CT: Yale University Press.

Richardson, Joe M. 1979. "Francis L. Cardozo: Black Educator during Reconstruction." *Journal of Negro Education* 48 (1): 73–83.

Richardson, Joe M. 1986. *Christian Reconstruction: The American Missionary Association and Southern Blacks, 1861–1890.* Athens: University of Georgia Press.

Roark, James L. 1977. *Masters without Slaves: Southern Planters in the Civil War and Reconstruction.* New York: Norton.

Roberts, Giselle. 2003. "The New Andromeda: Sarah Morgan and the Post Civil War Domestic Ideal." In *Lives Full of Struggle and Triumph: Southern Women, Their Institutions and Their Communities,* ed. Bruce L. Clayton and John A. Salmond. Gainesville: University of Florida Press.

Rodrigue, John C. 2001. *Reconstruction in the Cane Fields: From Slavery to Free Labor in Louisiana's Sugar Parishes, 1862–1880.* Baton Rouge: Louisiana State University Press.

Rose, Willie Lee. 1964. *Rehearsal for Reconstruction: The Port Royal Experiment.* Indianapolis, IN: Bobbs-Merrill.

Rousey, Dennis C. 1985. "Yellow Fever and Black Policemen in Memphis: A Post-Reconstruction Anomaly." *Journal of Southern History* 51 (3): 357–374.

Royce, Edward. 1993. *The Origins of Southern Sharecropping*. Philadelphia: Temple University Press.

Ryan, James Gilbert. 1977. "The Memphis Riots of 1866: Terror in a Black Community during Reconstruction." *Journal of Negro History* 62 (3): 243–257.

Salvatore, Nick. *We All Got History: The Memory Books of Amos Webber*. New York: Times Books.

Saville, Julie. 1994. *The Work of Reconstruction: From Slave to Wage Laborer in South Carolina, 1860–1870*. New York: Cambridge University Press.

Schmidt, James D. 1999. *Free to Work: Labor Law, Emancipation, and Reconstruction, 1815–1880*. Athens: University of Georgia Press.

Schwalm, Leslie A. 1997. *A Hard Fight for We: Women's Transition from Slavery to Freedom in South Carolina*. Urbana: University of Illinois Press.

Schweninger, Loren. 1989. "Black Owned Businesses in the South, 1790–1880." *Business History Review* 63 (1): 22–60.

Schweninger, Loren. 1990a. "Property-Owning Free African-American Women in the South, 1800–1870." *Journal of Women's History* 1:13–44.

Schweninger, Loren. 1990b. "Prosperous Blacks in the South, 1790–1880." *American Historical Review* 95 (1): 31–56.

Scott, Anne Firor. 1970. *The Southern Lady: From Pedestal to Politics, 1830–1930*. Chicago: University of Chicago Press.

Scott, James C. 1990. *Domination and the Arts of Resistance: Hidden Transcripts*. New Haven, CT: Yale University Press.

Scott, Rebecca. 1978. "The Battle over the Child: Child Apprenticeship and the Freedmen's Bureau in North Carolina." *Prologue* 10:193–207.

Scroggs, Jack B. 1961. "Carpetbagger Constitutional Reform in the South Atlantic States, 1867–1868." *Journal of Southern History* 27:475–493.

Shaffer, Donald R. 2004. *After the Glory: The Struggles of Black Civil War Veterans*. Lawrence: University Press of Kansas.

Shank, George Kline, Jr. 1964. "Meridian: A Mississippi City at Birth, during the Civil War, and in Reconstruction." *Journal of Mississippi History* 26 (4): 275–282.

Shapiro, Herbert. 1964. "The Ku Klux Klan during Reconstruction: The South Carolina Episode." *Journal of Negro History* 49 (1): 34–55.

Shlomowitz, Ralph. 1984. " 'Bound' or 'Free'? Black Labor in Cotton and Sugarcane Farming, 1865–1880." *Journal of Southern History* 50 (4): 569–596.

Shofner, Jerrell H. 1973. "Militant Negro Laborers in Reconstruction Florida." *Journal of Southern History* 39 (3): 397–408.

Silber, Nina. 1993. *The Romance of Reunion: Northerners and the South, 1865–1900.* Chapel Hill: University of North Carolina Press.

Skocpol, Theda. 1992. *Protecting Soldiers and Mothers: The Political Origins of Social Policy in the United States.* Cambridge, MA: Belknap Press.

Small, Sandra E. 1979. "The Yankee Schoolmarm in Freedmen's Schools: An Analysis of Attitudes." *Journal of Southern History* 45:381–402.

Smallwood, James M., Barry A. Crouch, and Larry Peacock. 2003. *Murder and Mayhem: The War of Reconstruction in Texas.* College Station: Texas A & M University Press.

Smith, George Winston. 1944. "Some Northern Attitudes toward the Post–Civil War South." *Journal of Southern History* 10:253–274.

Smith, John David. 1997. *Black Voices from Reconstruction.* Gainesville: University of Florida Press.

Somers, Dale A. 1974. "Black and White in New Orleans: A Study in Urban Race Relations, 1865–1900." *Journal of Southern History* 40 (1): 19–42.

Stampp, Kenneth M. 1965. *The Era of Reconstruction, 1865–1877.* New York: Alfred A. Knopf.

Stanley, Amy Dru. 1998. *From Bondage to Contract: Wage Labor, Marriage, and the Market in the Age of Slave Emancipation.* New York: Cambridge University Press.

Sterling, Dorothy. 1994. *The Trouble They Seen: The Story of Reconstruction in the Words of African-Americans.* Cambridge, MA: Da Capo Press.

Stetson, Kennedy. 1996. *After Appomattox: How the South Won the War.* Gainesville: University of Florida Press.

Storey, Margaret M. 2004. *Loyalty and Loss: Alabama's Unionists in the Civil War and Reconstruction.* Baton Rouge: Louisiana State University Press.

Stowell, Daniel W. 1998. *Rebuilding Zion: The Religious Reconstruction of the South, 1863–1877.* New York: Oxford University Press.

Sutherland, Daniel E. 1998. "Former Confederates in the Post–Civil War North: An Unexplored Aspect of Reconstruction History." *Journal of Southern History* 47 (3): 393–410.

Sutherland, Daniel E. 1988. *The Confederate Carpetbaggers*. Baton Rouge: Louisiana State University Press.

Swann-Wright, Dianne. 2002. *A Way Out of No Way: Claiming Family and Freedom in the New South*. Charlottesville: University of Virginia Press.

Takagi, Midori. 1999. *"Rearing Wolves to Our Own Destruction": Slavery in Richmond, Virginia, 1782–1865*. Charlottesville: University of Virginia Press, 1999.

Taylor, Kay Ann. 2005. "Mary S. Peake and Charlotte L. Forsten: Black Teachers during the Civil War and Reconstruction." *Journal of Negro Education* 74 (2): 124–137.

Thompson, Elizabeth Lee. 2004. *The Reconstruction of Southern Debtors: Bankruptcy after the Civil War*. Athens: University of Georgia Press.

Thornberry, Jerry. 1974. "Northerners and the Atlanta Freedmen, 1865–69." *Prologue* 6 (4): 236–251.

Tourgée, Albion W. 1966 [1879]. *A Fool's Errand: A Novel of the South during Reconstruction*. Introduction by George M. Fredrickson. Reprint. New York: Harper and Row.

Trelease, Allen W. 1971. *White Terror: The Ku Klux Klan Conspiracy and Southern Reconstruction*. New York: Harper and Row.

Tripp, Stephen Elliot. 1997. *Yankee Town, Southern City: Race and Class Relations in Civil War Lynchburg*. New York: New York University Press.

Trowbridge, J. T. 1866. *The South: A Tour of Its Battle-Fields and Ruined Cities*. Hartford, CT: L. Stebbins.

Tunnell, Ted. 1984. *Crucible of Reconstruction: War, Rebellion, and Race in Louisiana, 1862–1877*. Baton Rouge: Louisiana State University Press.

Tunnell, Ted. 2000. *Edge of the Sword: The Ordeal of Carpetbagger Marshall H. Twitchell in the Civil War and Reconstruction*. Baton Rouge: Louisiana State University Press.

Vandal, Gilles. 1991. "Bloody Caddo": White Violence against Blacks in a Louisiana Parish, 1865–1876." *Journal of Social History* 25 (2): 373–388.

Wade, Richard C. 1964. *Slavery in the Cities, 1820–1860*. New York: Oxford University Press.

Waldrep, Christopher, and Donald G. Nieman, eds. 2001. *Local Matters: Race, Crime, and Justice in the Nineteenth-Century South*. Athens: University of Georgia Press.

Waldrip, C. B. 2002. "Sex, Social Equality, and Yankee Values: White Men's Attitudes toward Miscegenation during Mississippi's Reconstruction." *Journal of Mississippi History* 64 (2): 125–145.

Wallenstein, Peter. 2005. "Reconstruction, Segregation, and Miscegenation: Interracial Marriage and the Law in the Lower South, 1865–1900." *American Nineteenth Century History* 6 (1): 57–76.

Wang, Xi. 1997. *The Trial of Democracy: Black Suffrage and Northern Republicans, 1860–1910.* Athens: University of Georgia Press.

Warren, Henry W. 1914. *Reminiscences of a Mississippi Carpet-Bagger.* Holden, MA: [s.n.], Worcester, MA: Davis Press.

Watkins, Sam R. 1977. [1882]. *Co. Aytch.* Reprint. New York: Touchstone.

Wayne, Michael. 1983. *The Reshaping of Plantation Society: The Natchez District, 1860–1880.* Baton Rouge: Louisiana State University Press.

Weiner, Marli F. 1997. *Mistresses and Slaves: Plantation Women in South Carolina, 1830–80.* Urbana: University of Illinois Press.

West, Jerry Lee. 2002. *The Reconstruction Ku Klux Klan in York County, South Carolina, 1865–1877.* Jefferson, NC: McFarland.

Wetherington, Mark V. 2005. *Plain Folk's Fight: The Civil War and Reconstruction in Piney Woods Georgia.* Chapel Hill: University of North Carolina Press.

Whites, LeeAnn. 1977. *Social Origins of the New South: Alabama, 1860–1885.* Baton Rouge: Louisiana State University Press.

Whites, LeeAnn. 1995. *The Civil War as a Crisis in Gender: Augusta, Georgia, 1860–1890.* Athens: University of Georgia Press.

Whites, LeeAnn. 2005. *Gender Matters: Civil War, Reconstruction, and the Making of the New South.* New York: Palgrave Macmillan.

Wiener, Jonathan M. 1976. "Planter Persistence and Social Change: Alabama, 1850–1870." *Journal of Interdisciplinary History* 7 (2): 235–260.

Williams, Heather Andrea. 2002. " 'Clothing Themselves in Intelligence': The Freedpeople, Schooling, and Northern Teachers, 1861–1871." *Journal of African American History* 87:372–389.

Williams, Lou Falkner. 1993. "The South Carolina Ku Klux Klan Trials and Enforcement of Federal Rights, 1871–1872." *Civil War History* 39 (1): 47–66.

Williams, Lou Falkner. 1996. *The Great South Carolina Ku Klux Klan Trials, 1871–1872.* Athens: University of Georgia Press.

Williamson, Joel. 1965. *After Slavery: The Negro in South Carolina during Reconstruction, 1861–1877.* Chapel Hill: University of North Carolina Press.

Williamson, Joel. 1986. *A Rage for Order: Black-White Relations in the American South since Emancipation.* New York: Oxford University Press.

Willis, John C. 2000. *Forgotten Time: The Yazoo-Mississippi Delta after the Civil War.* Charlottesville: University Press of Virginia.

Woodward, C. Vann. 1951. *Origins of the New South, 1877–1913.* Baton Rouge: Louisiana State University Press.

Woodward, C. Vann. 1974. *The Strange Career of Jim Crow.* New York: Oxford University Press.

Woodward, C. Vann. 1991 [1951]. *Reunion and Reaction: The Compromise of 1877 and the End of Reconstruction.* Reprint. New York: Oxford University Press.

Wright, Gavin. 1978. *The Political Economy of the Cotton South: Households, Markets, and Wealth in the Nineteenth Century.* New York: Norton.

Wyatt-Brown, Bertram. 2001. *The Shaping of Southern Culture: Honor, Grace, and War, 1760s–1880s.* Chapel Hill: University of North Carolina Press.

Wynne, Lewis N. 1981. "The Role of Freedmen in the Post Bellum Cotton Economy of Georgia." *Phylon* 42 (4): 309–321.

Yeatman, James E. 1864. *A Report on the Condition of the Freedmen of the Mississippi, Presented to the Western Sanitary Commission, December 17th, 1863.* St. Louis. MO: Western Sanitary Commission Rooms.

Zipf, Karin L. 1999. "The Whites Shall Rule the Land or Die: Gender, Race and Class in North Carolina Reconstruction Politics." *Journal of Southern History* 65 (3): 499–534.

Zuczek, Richard. 1996. *State of Rebellion: Reconstruction in South Carolina.* Columbia: University of South Carolina Press.

Online Resources

Ayers, Edward. "Valley of the Shadow: Two Communities in the American Civil War." (Retrieved 5/5/08.) http://valley.vcdh.virginia.edu

Christine's Genealogy Websites. "Freedmen's Bureau Online." (Retrieved 5/5/08.) http://freedmensbureau.com

Click, Patricia. "The Roanoke Island Freedmen's Colony." (Retrieved 5/5/08.) http://www.roanokefreedmenscolony.com

Documenting the American South. "First-Person Narratives of the American South." (Retrieved 5/5/08.) http://docsouth.unc.edu/fpn/

HarpWeek. "Harper's Weekly Reports on Black America, 1857–1874." (Retrieved 5/5/08.) http://blackhistory.harpweek.com/

Library of Congress. "Born in Slavery: Slave Narratives from the Federal Writer's Project." (Retrieved 5/5/08.) http://memory.loc.gov/ammem/snhtml/snhome.html

Lincoln Institute. "Mr. Lincoln and Freedom." (Retrieved 5/5/08.) http://www.mrlincolnandfreedom.org/home.html

Mintz, Sidney. "America's Reconstruction: People and Politics after the Civil War." (Retrieved 5/5/08.) http://www.digitalhistory.uh.edu/reconstruction/index.html

Index

NOTE: italic page numbers indicate pictures.

973.8
Recon

Reconstruction
People and Perspectives